CONTENTS

THE PATH TO GREATNESS

MENTAL, EMOTIONAL AND SPIRITUAL

in-LIGHT-Ment

J. J. & TAMO

DISCLAIMER

The information in this book is solely for personal growth, education, and recreation. It is not a therapeutic activity such as counselling or medical advice and should not be treated as a substitute for any professional advice. In the event of any physical distress, please consult with appropriate professionals. The information and the application of any protocols in this book is the choice of each reader, who assumes full responsibility for his or her understandings, interpretations, and results. The author assumes no responsibility for the actions or choices of any reader.

ISBN 9798337529998

Author's note

In this book, you'll be diving in an ocean of thoughts from us, the authors, thoughts from other authors and random people that play an important role in bringing freedom to where it belongs, which is within our lives. If we know the names of the authors of specific passages/words, we will mention them. If we don't know, we will not. As always, remember that knowledge belongs to all. Nobody owns knowledge. Knowledge is free. When we purchase books online or in book stores we don't pay for the knowledge written in them. We pay for the time and effort that was used to put together the books' content, structure etc. If all authors kept working 9-5, there wouldn't be many if any books at all for the world. Technically, everything we need to know is already within us. Books exists because we have been disconnected from the vast knowledge that we already possess within ourselves. So, in a way reading is a must, it activates remembrance.

The most important thing in mentioning other authors (at least from our point of view) is to expose the readers (in this case "you") to other sources of knowledge and wisdom as opposed to just the thoughts of this book's authors.

We found countless of great books through them being mentioned in other people's books. If by any chance we use the word 'GOD', we mean the omnipotent creator (not an individual physical being), the unseen (although it is seen through us, plants, animals etc.), the supreme intelligence, the Source of Creation. We do not identify God as "he" or "she". We, all are Gods, little gods of course, manifestation of the true one, since we are spirits having a physical experience. If you are someone that only believes in a physical life and a Physical God somewhere up there or anywhere outside of you, then you will not grasp the idea of God being everywhere, God is in all of us, and also we are Gods. Some of the chapters are elaborations from articles we wrote in our blog. Throughout the articles of our blog, we refer to other articles from the same website [our website]. Even though we proofread this book as best as we could, it's still possible we may have missed once or twice editing out the words "blog" and "article", with the exception where those words have to be used, depending on the context of a specific subject.

Regardless of what your beliefs are, pay attention to the message of the content. If something is moral and can contribute to your life and humanity's life in a good way, then it does not matter if the message comes from us, God or a piece of brick. *THINK*.

Sometimes we write quotes without mentioning who wrote the quote. We do this because the author of the quote (assuming that person said so and not being a meme made by just anyone) has a name and last name which also other people have the same name and last name. For example, when I searched the name/last name of someone, a sport (sports are distraction a.k.a. *bread and circuses*) player came up, in another search a person that promotes division and wars came up. So, we will not indirectly promote the opposite of what we are trying to do with this book. In the grand scheme of things, who said what, it doesn't matter, the message is important.

Other book/s by **J.J. and TAMO**

Rebuild Yourself From Within
https://amzn.to/46fEyxW

Chapter 1

THE LAW OF THE MIRROR

> "To walk the path of greatness, we must first realize there is a path in the first place. To see the path, we must destroy the illusioned wall that is blocking the path. We must destroy the false ideas of who we think we are, or else we will keep going in circles. When the path appears, we can see the true depth of our existence. So far we've been living inside a pond. It is about time to dive in the deep spiritual ocean that we truly are" – **Pine G. Land**

Have you ever considered that every person you meet is reflecting a part of you back to yourself? This idea can transform our interactions and deepen our understanding of ourselves. Think about a time when you offered a helping hand to a stranger in need. Maybe you saw someone struggling to carry groceries, and you stepped in to help. In that moment, you were reflecting your own kindness and empathy. Now, recall a moment when someone's words or actions hurt you deeply. That pain could mirror your own insecurities or unresolved issues, giving you a chance to confront and heal them.

Imagine you're in a heated discussion with someone close to you. Their stubbornness frustrates you, but if you look deeper, you might find that their persistence mirrors your own determination in other aspects of life. Or think of a time when someone's joy and enthusiasm lifted your spirit. Their energy can reflect your own capacity for happiness and inspiration. Seeing others as reflections of ourselves encourages us to approach each interaction with compassion and curiosity. Instead of judging in a negative way [*there is judging right from wrong on a moral level*], we can appreciate the diverse experiences and emotions that shape each person. This mindset can lead to more meaningful and harmonious relationships.

Remember, every encounter is a chance to learn more about who we are. By observing others, we are granted insight into our own strengths, weaknesses, and potential for growth. Let's embrace these reflections and let them guide us toward becoming our best selves. We are mirrors of each other. If you think a mirrored object is the exact replica, think again. You know that in the mirror you are not exactly the same. Go in front of the mirror and lift up you right arm. In the mirror, is the right arm you are lifting up or the left one?

So, as you can see, we seem like we are mirror to each other and yet we are not. Every single one of us is unique. There are no two people that are exactly the same. Even twins are not the same. Even if they looked exactly the same, they don't think, feel the same. A coin has two sides, so do we. We have the physical and the astral/spiritual side. To see and not to see are both part of the same. The known and the unknown are part of the same.

You don't know me, you imagine me. You only see in me what you are. If you see love in me, it's because in you there is love. If you see aggression in me, it's because there is aggression in you. If you admire a quality of mine, it's because you too have that quality. If I look stupid to you, you should analyze your behaviour. If there's something about me you hate, you are hating that about you that you don't like. It's not surprising. I'm a reflection that projects your reality. Just imagine me, I'm your invention, and you will only see that in me that you recognize in yourself. If you like what you see in me, don't change it! But if you don't like it, change it up on you! I love you, because you are the mirror I chose to look at and grow. We balance each other off. May we all come to full truth and lead others to full truth.

"Every set of eyes you encounter, are your own eyes observing yourself from a different point of view" – Mateya Triglav

CAN MIRRORS BE A GATEWAY TO THE SPIRIT WORLD?

By this do I mean the mirrors each of us are? If not, then any object can be a conduit or vehicle for ephemeral energies, but a mirror is just a mirror until you put it to purpose. Don't lose your mind to fantastic thoughts. Your intention counts for more than you give yourself credit for! In African spirituality, they believe that mirrors can indeed serve as a gateway to the spirit world. Mirrors are seen as reflective surfaces that can offer glimpses into the spiritual realm. They are used in divination and communication with ancestors. When approached with respect and intention, mirrors are powerful tool for connecting with the spirit world. But whether one believes in this concept or not, it can be a matter of personal belief and cultural background.

Reminder that all technology screens are BLACK MIRRORS. Mirrors are glass, especially technological mirrors (TV, tablet, VR, cellphones etc.), they'll change your thought process if you don't think for yourself, if your intentions are not benevolent. Cellphones, TVs, tablets, computers etc, when they're turned off they are black. When they're on, the **Black Mirrors** are on, so be careful what you do within the black mirror world, use it to you advantage, meaning to use technology for benevolent reasons. For example, watch videos about gardening, read digital books about truth/love etc. Your thoughts create your reality, what you watch/do in those screen will mirror back in your life since you are an alchemist/ creator of your reality. The spirit world governs the physical world. So, you are just experiencing another reality just as you experience different realities when you engage in conversations with people that don't resonate with your perception/reality that you live on a daily basis. Mirrors are portals, whether we are talking about technological devices or actual mirrors you have on the walls of your house. They are portals to other realities/dimensions.

All realities/dimensions exist within your mind. In Victorian era, when someone died, they always covered all mirrors in the whole house and it was meant seriously. Perhaps they knew something we don't know? Perhaps that's how entities from other dimensions (spiritual/astral world) enter our world, through the mirrors. Personally, I almost never look at myself in the mirror, definitely not at night, especially when I'm drowsy before going to sleep, or when/ if I wake up in the middle of the night to go to the bathroom. Do you know why? Because when you are drowsy, the brain is in Alpha state/brainwave, which means that the veil between the spiritual world and the physical world is the thinnest, which means that is an opportunity for an entity to slip into you (your subconsciousness).

From a young age I and others I know have noticed that people looked slightly different in the mirror than the way we see them in front of us. The mirror always made them look slightly less attractive (visually). And I mean when you look in the mirror without having put anything on your face such as make up, hair gel/spray, and deodorants. All these mess up with your brain waves/sense of self attractiveness, lipsticks or any other man-made poison/illusion that men or women put on their faces and other places in their bodies. Just a quick analyzation of the word "make-up" should tell you that anything you are putting on your face is covering the real thing, you have been deceived to deny your natural state of beauty for a fake one.

The only true mirrors are lakes, oceans, sees, rivers because they are 100% natural, there is no evil intention behind the creation of natural waters. We are waters, we grew for 9 months (actually 10 months, having in mind that originally every month had same equal **28 days**, 40 weeks=**1 month** has 4 weeks, so 10 months) in the mother's womb. Everything is a two-way relationship. If you are a confused person, a person that lies, keeps grudge on people, unhappy with yourself, even if you look at yourself as a reflection on the surface of the lake, you will see who you think you are and not who you truly are. To see who you truly are, delete the one you think you are.

> "You cannot bring the same old you in front of the mirror and expect the mirror to suddenly show you a different "you". In the same way, you cannot expect the world to suddenly change for the better if you still haven't changed at all. So don't try to change the reflection in the mirror, make an effort to change yourself first and the reflection will follow." – **Mateya Triglav**

WE ARE PAVING THE ROAD TO GREATNESS

We are acting as gatekeepers, allowing in certain energies with great care, for we have a plan of intention to alter a distant future by altering a very distant past. We are simultaneously located in all of these places, playing our part. We have agreed to be a stimulator and energy facilitator for us in many of the different realities where we are located. Versions of us are also located in some of the eleven other libraries throughout this universe, and we are operating as systems busters there as well. Remember, as a member of the Family of Light you carry the vibration and intent of change wherever you go—altering the system you find yourself in. Feel this out, and be open to an infusion of knowing how vast you are, and how grand the plan is.

Many members of the Family of Light will become library cards or tour guides to those who will match you frequency for frequency, and love for love. You will bring about a merging through love that will create a new ownership and direction of this place that you call Earth. Remember that Prime Creator is in all things, so part of the true purpose of the Living Library of Earth [**Akashic Records**] is to blend and merge consciousness so that you may experience and access the magnificent knowledge that is stored here. The key here is to love and value yourself and Earth.

When a world such as ours is in the process of spiritual evolution, there is an opportunity for any and all who have ever been involved with the library to make a cosmic leap. Therefore, many beings come from far and wide to participate, bringing their own agendas and creating plans within plans. There is much healing to take place, for many species who we would consider to be dark or negative are also drawn to our Earth at this time.

They are here to wake us up and stimulate us with their own "badness" to remind us of something. Remember, this is a world of polarities, and shadow defines light. These energies are here not to be bombed, killed, or destroyed, even though governments may tell us that these visitors are evil. They are here to heal, to infuse themselves with the vibrations of light and love, and to come into a higher state of being in their own species because they have forgotten what those on Earth have forgotten—that ***we are all one***.

Those in fear will attract the unclear and unhealed portions of themselves as exterior beings. Misuse of life and power draws its mirror experience. You will come to understand that you are what you are afraid of. Fear is created in your mind, what you fear, will mirror back into your life. Fear doesn't just mean fear of a monster, or fear of heights or any other fear in the physical world. Fear of what might happen tomorrow or next month or after 5 years is worse than fear of something that you can physically see. Illusion/delusion is very powerful.

We make up stories in our mind about nonsense, fear of what could or might happen, meanwhile the present moments disappear since we occupy our mind with supposed things that may never happen. Live in the moment, enjoy the present blissful existence. It's fine to prepare yourself for a future outcome but do bot be attached to future potentials that have not happened yet. You can use the future potentials through imagination, but use it to your advantage. Imagine positive outcomes so that you cause the universal law of manifestation to rearrange the circumstances on satisfying your demands (imagination). The universe is your servant, it exists to bring you anything that you desire. Use it to your advantage, to create a life of bliss and freedom for you, those around you and the world (collectively when many people manifest benevolence from benevolent intentions).

As Rimias K. Neo points out in the book, *Gain Wisdom Through Practiced Knowledge*:

"The artificial mirror is a liar. If you look into the mirror and think you are handsome or beautiful, then you are looking in the wrong place. You cannot exist in two different places at the same time. You exist only in your mind/heart. This depends on your perception of the reality you live in. Do you live in the body or in the mind?".

Chapter 2

DIMENSIONS – THEORY OR FACT?

Our current existence is a sophisticated simulation, designed to mirror Heaven or Gaia. This simulation serves as a testing ground for souls, a realm where the purity and readiness of each soul are evaluated for their potential to ascend to a higher state of consciousness. This means that ***what we experience as life, is a controlled environment crafted to challenge and refine our spiritual essence.*** This chapter is a theory and/or a fact depending on if you have achieved self realization yet or not, depending on if you have realized that death is no different than when you graduate in school from the first grade to the second. Let's suppose that it is true (the bolded statement above), that it is controlled. You may say that we do not have a free will. Creation/life does not exist just for us human spirits/being, it exist for animals, birds, insects etc. Can animals build a building, or can they speak words like us? Well, with the exception of parrots and/or some other species of animals/birds being able to speak, in limited form, but that's not the point here.

The point is that animals do not worry about things that we people do or have to do in our daily life. Animals do what they're supposed to do, automatically. Only humans are severely handicapped through their false thinking process. You have people that say that we don't have free will and yet these very same people are not even doing basic operations or thinkings that is required of them by common sense. Then there are other people who know a thing or two, they make fun of others that know less than them. The creation has everything for us to be free, it's people that deny themselves the freedom to be free.

There are natural rules that rule creation, they are rules that never change.

Only man-made rules are changed by human themselves to fit their agendas and local morality. So, this life is not controlled by some bogeyman, call it devil if you wish. But even if it was true that there is an entity Devil, even Devil has to follow the rules of creation. What many don't understand is that people have lost their ability to create, they lost the knowledge that we are Gods and Goddesses, and because of this the so-called Devil or evil beings are using people's ignorance to create their own paradise and people's hell.

The so-called controllers always tell us what they are doing, but people don't pay attention, people have been too distracted with sports, politics, materialism, chasing wealth and riches for them to continue struggling because people don't know that wealth is within. When you think for yourself, you make healthy choices. Healthy choices create circumstances that are in your favour. If you ever felt in a victim mentality, that's because you are not putting the effort to change what made you a victim in the first place. In this theory, everyone currently living has already experienced physical death. Death, as we understand it, is merely an illusion.

Our current state transcends physical death; this life is another stage in our ongoing spiritual journey. The true purpose of this journey is to prepare us for a 5D frequency of existence, which is the true existence outside of the simulation. The simulation's primary role is to act as a quarantine zone between the physical (3D) realm and the non-physical spiritual realm (5D). This separation is crucial as it allows pure souls to prove their ability to peacefully coexist with the inhabitants of the true heavenly realm, an eternal utopia. By navigating the challenges of this simulation, souls demonstrate their readiness to enter the 5D realm.

This simulated Earth functions as a form of purgatory. While the real utopia exists elsewhere [higher dimensions/realities], we are here to rehabilitate and heal, gradually returning to our true nature. This true nature involves controlling an avatar body, which comes with a veil of forgetfulness about our real identities. This forgetfulness is necessary for the soul's growth and rehabilitation process.

Our true essence is that of a higher self, which is essentially plugged into this simulation. This situation can be seen as a life sentence for actions taken in the 5D realm or as a transitional phase after dying in the 3D realm. The simulation serves to rehabilitate us, ensuring we do not bring any negative traits into the 5D Earth. Some souls may have volunteered to return to assist with this crucial transition. Thus, this simulation acts as a gatekeeper to the true Earth, often referred to as Heaven.

The concept of the higher self aligns with the idea that our actual selves are plugged into this matrix-like simulation. It allows us to assimilate to our true loving nature. The goal is to enable peaceful coexistence in the real Garden of Eden, which is Gaia or the 5D Earth. In the 5D realm, communication is entirely telepathic, allowing direct transmission to and from God. In our current simulated existence, to achieve this level of communication, one must transcend 3rd and 4th density of consciousness and reach a 5D frequency. This transcendence demonstrates to God that the soul is ready to return home upon the "death" of the avatar body. However, it is essential to remember that all of this is part of the simulation.

If a soul fails the mission of reintegration within this simulation, it will reincarnate until it succeeds. This cycle of reincarnation ensures that only those who are fully prepared and purified can enter the true 5D realm, maintaining its state of eternal peace and harmony.

In summary, our current existence is a meticulously crafted simulation designed to test and purify souls. Death is an illusion, and life here is a stage in our spiritual journey towards the true 5D Heaven. The simulation serves as a quarantine, ensuring that only those ready for peaceful coexistence in the true utopia make it through. This purgatorial simulated Earth allows for rehabilitation, healing, and rediscovery of our higher selves. Successful navigation through this simulation, achieving a 5D frequency of consciousness, ensures direct communication with God/Source and readiness for the true natural existence on Gaia/Heaven. Failure to transcend and purify leads to reincarnation, repeating the cycle until the soul achieves the necessary purity and readiness for coexistence together on Gaia (5D-7D).

DIMENSIONAL GRADUATION:

Let's make something clear, your soul and your physical body is the same thing. Meaning that they are both sides of the same coin. They are not separate from each other. A body cannot exist without a soul (this is something that the dark magicians/controllers of this realm attempt to accomplish through A.I immortality synthetic/fake biologic robots/entities. We use the phrase "your soul or your spirit" because we cannot see the spirit. You can actually see it when you properly meditate but I'm speaking in general which most people cannot see their higher self. We live in a duality world that's why we see and think in duality.

Our soul's journey involves graduating through various dimensions and densities, each stage representing a higher state of consciousness and spiritual evolution. Here is a brief description of the dimensions. Usually, people are sceptical and that's a good thing instead of being a gullible person. Truth is felt. Sometimes it just clicks, you have a remembrance all of a sudden and some other times, in the case of reading books or talking in person to anyone, their words trigger remembrance in you.

1D to 3D:
In the first stage, thought is manifested into creation. This includes the material world and the initial stages of physical existence, where the soul experiences the physical realm and begins its journey of self-discovery and learning. Everything in existence has consciousness.

Animals may not rationalize like us but it doesn't make them any lesser than us. As a matter of fact, for many reasons animals are better than us. I don't need to explain, we can clearly see in our society with how people try to manipulate each other for personal gain, people are envy of each other, hurt and kill each other. Many people create families that are not based on love but from lust (having made decision from a carnal pleasure/lower mind mentality).

3D to 5D:
Our current existence falls within this range, a simulation designed to test and prepare souls for higher dimensions. This stage acts as a quarantine between the physical (3D) and the non-physical spiritual realm (5D). Do not be confused by thinking that 5D is somewhere else. 5D is where you are right now. 5D reality or dimension is not a physical place, it is a state of mind. That's all there is in creation, the MIND (All That is, the Supreme Creation or the ONE). We are simply miniatures of the GREATE ONE, or simply reflections of the GREAT ONE, or made in the image (on an energetic/frequency level) of the GREAT ONE. The simulation allows pure souls to prove their ability to peacefully coexist with those in the true heavenly realm, where

eternal utopia exists. Until people realize that within are found all the answers, we cannot live a utopian life, at least not on a collective level.

5D to 7D:
This stage represents our true nature outside of the simulation, where we fully embody our higher selves. Here, we rediscover our true essence, control our avatar bodies, and shed the veil of forgetfulness. Souls at this stage are fully aware of their higher nature and operate in a realm of unconditional love and harmony. This and any other level above is only non-physical, even though you can still have a body in the 3D physical world but operating on 5D, 7D and up. Do not be concerned at all with 7D and up. I'm writing a bit about the higher dimensions just for curiosity, to excite a bit your brain. Just as a teacher of the 8th grade should not overwhelm a 5th grader with 8th grade knowledge.

7D to 9D:
At this level, souls transcend the higher self. This stage involves integrating the lessons and wisdom acquired in previous dimensions, further refining the soul and preparing it for even higher states of existence. Souls here are on the brink of complete unity with the divine. Again, the higher you go (not as in travelling physically with your body) the closer you are to the Divine Intelligence or the Great ONE. I will try to not use at all or as least as possible the word "GOD" because that word has been bastardized. Allah, God, Yahweh are simply beings/deities that play gods. That was fine to a certain point that humanity needed guidance. But now, we are at a point where we can become "Gods" like them, meaning we can become the best version we could ever be. And to achieve this we must throw away old beliefs and embrace inner knowingness. You cannot develop inner knowingness with a beLIEf mindset.

9D to 11D:
This stage is preparation for transcending into union with the prime creator. Souls in this dimension undergo the final stages of purification and enlightenment, aligning themselves completely with the divine will and preparing for ultimate union with the creator. Prime Creator (actually Creation) is us from our most perfect knowledgeable state of existence. Some questions are better left alone such as "What's the name of the Creator, or how does the Creator looks like, or who created everything?". Asking questions

is great because that's how we learn by questioning ourselves and outside reality (even though the external reality is a projection from our own consciousness). But when we are still in kindergarten what good will it do if we ask high school questions? It will only cause us confusion, arguing with one another as I personally see it all the time in real life and/or on social media.

11D to Prime Creator:
In the highest dimensions, souls experience both objective and subjective union with the creator. They graduate 11D/12D and become one with the prime creator, embodying the essence of the divine and completing their journey of ascension. In my humble opinion, if we reach 11D then we would probably be bored, we should be happy that we are where we are because we are constantly learning. A lot of people think (as do I to a certain point) that this reality on Earth is a prison. Well, it can be a prison if you think so. But when you shift mindset from blaming others to being responsible for your own action, then the prison becomes a school. I'm using the word 'school' to describe learning true knowledge. I am not taking about the hijacked left-brained mainstream school system that only teaches children on how to become obedient, materialistic in a hive mind "*working for corporations*" mentality.

Don't become too overwhelmed with the dimensions subject. Try to not let your mind analyze too much to the point that you develop psychotic tendencies. Whichever subject you study/research, make sure to remind yourself that life is simply a play. Enjoy the moment, be in the moment most of the time with occasional peak at the so called past and the supposed future.

Everything that you experience is a fact for your reality. In the grand scheme of things, no matter what you do, you are walking the path. If what you do, is of a negative intention or unintentional (from not knowing yourself point of view), then you are going backwards on the same path. Yes, we say or think that everyone is on their own path, but in reality there is only one true path. All other paths are simply illusions to cause us to correct course, or a better way to look at it is to continue the momentum as opposed to be distracted left and right.

Unless you practice knowledge, any information remains a theory. The sky is not blue to everyone. There are people that see inverted colors, they see the green and blue and vice versa. Some others are color blind. So, who are we to say what is a fact for others? Whatever you think, always remember to bring yourself in the moment. It is perfectly fine to be curious and excite your mind but don't lose yourself in the process.

Chapter 3

THREE DIFFERENT VIEWPOINTS OF CONSCIOUSNESS

"Everything is consciousness. People assign beliefs/meanings to anything in their lives based on their current level of consciousness at any given time. Religion, spirituality, and consciousness are distinct concepts that intersect in profound ways, each offering unique perspectives and benefits to individuals seeking meaning and fulfillment in life."

Religion [organized religion] - Spirituality - Consciousness

Religion: Religion refers to a structured system of beliefs, practices, rituals, and moral codes centered around a deity or deities. It often involves organized institutions, traditions, scriptures, and prescribed ways of worship. Religions provide frameworks for understanding the divine, moral guidelines for living, and a sense of community among believers. While religions vary widely in their beliefs and practices, they generally offer a sense of belonging, purpose, and connection to something greater than oneself. Benefits of religion include community support, moral guidance, and rituals that provide comfort and meaning during life's milestones and challenges. However, adherence to rigid doctrines and institutional hierarchies can sometimes limit individual autonomy and critical thinking. Something to be aware is that religion and organized religion are two different things.

Unfortunately, now and as it has been for a long time, there is only "organized religion". Religion from Latin means to tie or bind together. So, initially (*way before year 0*) religion was meant to unify people. When we speak about religion, most people associate it with Christianity, or any of the other major religions. But these organized religions' source is from sacred texts or brotherhood before them. We do not know exactly what happened at year zero, as per the altered/ unnatural Gregorian calendar which has each month at 30 or 31 days as opposed to the true calendar of 28 days for each month which aligns with the natural cycles of the Moon in one year [12-13 times a year]

For a better understanding or even just out of curiosity about the 28days in each month calendar and how it is related to saving the sacred secretion that all humans release once a month, check the books
Gain Wisdom Through Practiced Knowledge by Rimias K. Neo and **Your Are The One** by Pine G. Land. I think we already mentioned these books in our previous book titled ***Rebuild Yourself From Within***.

Religion is the be***LIE***f in someone else's experience. Spirituality is having your own experience. What you believe in, doesn't make you a free thinker. The ability to change your beliefs when you are presented with new information does. I always hear people referring to God as "he". Many have fallen for the lie that God is a man up there in the sky. Many people of Christian belief have told me that if I don't believe everything in the Bible, then I don't believe any of what is written in it. Yet when I speak of omnipresence and inseparable nature that is, they are lost. When I ask if they believe they could do the same work as Jesus did, they change the subject because they don't want to deal with it. It requires effort, discipline, pure unconditional love to ascend and become all of those things that Jesus talked about (regardless if a physical person named "Jesus or Jeshua or whatever" existed or not).

The message is important not names and dates. His-story is manipulated just as "time" is. The Bible has created more confusion, wars, hatred, racism than any other document in the history of the world. If you cannot contain yourself enough to not rape, pillage and murder, what good is a book going to do, except that it will produce more guilt, like it has for many people. If you need a book to produce humility, kindness, compassion and love, then you are already lost, because you are not doing it out of natural expression, but one driven by fear of the afterlife. The Bible is a fairytale when read literally. It is what church teaches people, the literal sense which does not make sense.

The story in the Bible is an allegory. It is very cryptic and truthful even after being edited many times. It is still full of truth that the church does not teach people. The Bible teaches you [*in encrypted ways*] how to meet your maker, which is within you. Only those that have a mind to make sense of it will decipher it. The rest of the people will be lost and have no idea what life is, and who/what God is. Do you think that if they used the word "consciousness" in the Bible, people would innerstand? Of course not. The phrase "mother, father and son" means "The Holy Trinity". Christianity suppresses the feminine aspect by replacing the "Mother" with the Holy Spirit (e-motional innerG=Emotional Energy), which is the feminine aspect of spiritual essence.

Christians: Father-Son-Holy spirit

Jewish: Kether-Chokmah-Binah

Hindu: Brahma-Vishnu-Shiva Egyptian: Osiris-Horus-Isis.

Soul energy is the masculine aspect dealing with intellect. The child is the physical body when learns to navigate the physical realms with spirit and soul as guides. Separate but equal-The trinity is what so many refer to as "God". No book (Bible/Koran or any other religious book) can tell you what God wrote. The human brain is the world's greatest computer because it is self-aware, self-thinking, self-learning, and can even reprogram itself.

> Why would God implant such great abilities into our heads and then give us religions that discourages intelligent critical thinking in exchange for blind dumb faith? Also, the theory (made up) of God/Allah rewarding good deeds with 72 virgins is both morally and logically unacceptable. God can't reward good deeds with women. Women are not subjects. This is from a patriarchal only mindset that suppresses women/feminine.

"Organized religion is like organized crime; It preys on people's weakness, generates huge profits for its operators and is almost impossible to eradicate".

It is almost impossible, until you realize that Christ (Christ consciousness=The highest vibration which is unconditional love) is within. When Jesus (regardless of if he actually existed or not) said that he was coming back, he meant Christ consciousness was, the energy of the soul fully connected to the divine through the human heart. We have to bring that high vibrational consciousness back through our own lives. Not through someone else's words. People took his words literally and it has confused humanity to this day. Go within. Have an intimate relationship with your inner self and bring out the Christ Consciousness from within.

Spirituality: Spirituality is a personal and subjective pursuit of meaning, connection, and transcendence beyond the material world. It encompasses beliefs, experiences, practices, and values related to the inner self, the universe, and the divine. Unlike religion, spirituality is often more fluid, individualized, and eclectic, drawing from various traditions, philosophies, and personal insights. Spirituality emphasizes inner growth, self-awareness, and the exploration of deeper truths about existence and consciousness. Benefits of spirituality include personal growth, inner peace, and a sense of interconnectedness with all life. It allows individuals to cultivate a deeper understanding of themselves and their place in the universe, independent of external dogma or religious institutions.

Spirituality is a relationship with self. If there is any savior, it is within yourself. No amount of praying to external deities will fix problems that requires you to act and be responsible. But by all means, if you beLIEve that by being lazy and by hoping or praying that things will fix themselves, good for you, that is your choice or inactive choice. Now, some things can fix by themselves, problems such as those that you create in your mind, when you make up stories in your head. Most of our daily thoughts go to waste. We waste energy by telling ourself stories that don't serve us, stories that are rooted in beliefs that hold us back.

The Universe is there to serve us. The Ether, the Great Spirit, the Quantum field or whatever other term you feel more comfortable with, is there for you and not against you, but only if you operate and are aligned with the organic creation and not when you live in the illusioned, synthetic Matrix.

"If u want to innerstand the Universe, you need to think in terms of Vibration, frequency and Energy"

Vibration is about the structure of everything in creation, moving in waves, moving faster than other things, like the color red has slower motion than the color green. That's why it looks red when seen with our human eye system. Look up colors on the internet and look up the vibration of colors. It gives a general idea of how everything is always moving. The best explanation about vibration I learned is that it is your astral body rubbing against the physical body. Technically your non-physical and physical bodies are one/together. What you're experiencing is the higher vibes of the astral while you are still in the physical body which has a lower vibration.

The truth is, YOU, as a physical being are vibrating all the time. The best analogy at the moment that I can tell is, if you are in a room temperature environment and then you step into a heated room. At the doorway you can sense the change in temperature even though you haven't entered the room yet. Once you enter the room, the temperature difference disappears once your body adjusts and the heated room becomes your new normal until it is time to go back to the room temperature environment again. Only when you come back to a lower temperature, the transition isn't as noticeable because your body adjusts effortlessly. Vibration is the output of a wave. It could be light, sound or energy. Your thoughts and feelings create vibration. When it is quiet, try plugging both ears with your fingers and you will hear your internal body's sound/vibration. It's amazing.

To me it's like a buzzing sensation in my body, like my bones are vibrating and so are the other things I touch. The more you quiet down, the more you can hear/feel it within yourself and within all things- "alive". You feel like you are ONE with the Creation, the Source of everything. Since energy is neither created nor destroyed, everything you will ever want already exists. It is simply a matter of choosing the correct thoughts which will put you in alignment with what your heart desires.

Consciousness:

Consciousness refers to the state of awareness and subjective experience that underlies all thoughts, emotions, sensations, and perceptions. It is the essence of our being—the awareness that perceives, reflects, and interprets the world around us. Consciousness is not limited to individual minds but is considered a fundamental aspect of reality itself, encompassing both the personal and the collective. In spiritual and philosophical traditions, consciousness is often regarded as the ultimate reality, the source of all existence, and the interconnected web that unites all beings. Benefits of expanding consciousness include heightened perception, profound insights, and a sense of unity with the cosmos. By transcending egoic limitations and identifying with the deeper layers of consciousness, individuals can experience profound states of peace, joy, and interconnectedness with all life.

Differences and Benefits:

While religion, spirituality, and consciousness intersect and overlap in many ways, they also have distinct characteristics and benefits:

Religion-provides structured frameworks, community support, and moral guidance but can sometimes limit individual freedom and critical inquiry.

Spirituality - emphasizes personal growth, inner exploration, and connection with the divine but is often more fluid and individualized than religion.

Consciousness - represents the fundamental state of awareness that underlies all experiences and is considered the highest and most profound aspect of reality. Expanding consciousness leads to deeper insights, unity with all life, and a sense of transcendent peace and joy. In summary, while religion, spirituality, and consciousness offer different paths to meaning and fulfillment, they ultimately share a common goal: to awaken individuals to their highest potential and deepest truths. Whether through structured belief systems, personal exploration, or the realization of universal consciousness, each path offers unique benefits and insights on the journey towards self-discovery and enlightenment.

Chapter 4

SHADOW WORK – TAME THE BEAST WITHIN. GIVE IT WINGS

"People will do anything, no matter how absurd, in order to avoid facing their own souls. One does not become enlightened by imagining figures of light, but by making the darkness conscious" – **C.G. Jung**

Confronting and integrating the shadow is essential for personal growth, as it allows us to expand our self-concept. These transformative experiences often occur during midlife, but can occur at any point when we feel stuck and disconnected from the vibrancy of life.

In order to truly be authentic, genuine, and complete, it is necessary to embrace and integrate one's shadow aspect. In order to achieve spiritual awakening and self-mastery, it is essential to transform one's darkness. Prior to addressing the collective shadow that has been tormenting humanity, it is essential to confront and acknowledge one's own individual shadow.

Individuation is the transformative process through which an individual strives to become whole and unique. It involves embracing both the light and dark aspects of oneself, allowing for a constructive relationship to develop between the ego and the self. This relationship symbolizes our personal sense of individual wholeness, where the integration of contrasting elements leads to a harmonious and balanced existence. Through open and sincere communication as well as the analysis of dreams, we are able to confront the facade we present to the world and embrace our true selves in the therapeutic setting. Taking ownership of our less desirable traits is often facilitated and expedited by the support and guidance of a therapist or a mentor.

The gradual awakening to the shadow is a fundamental aspect of this process, as eloquently depicted in the passage from Marie-Louise von Franz's Shadow and Evil in Fairy Tales:

If someone who knows nothing about psychology comes to an analytical hour and you try to explain that there are certain processes at the back of the mind of which people are not aware, that is the shadow to them. So, in the first stage of approach to the unconscious the shadow is simply a "mythological" name for all that within me of which I cannot directly know. Only when we start to dig into the shadow sphere of the personality and to investigate the different aspects, does there, after a time, appear in the dreams a personification of the unconscious, of the same sex as the dreamer.

As the consciousness of the shadow expands, the dream figures gain greater significance and their integration becomes increasingly important. Ultimately, establishing a connection between one's personal shadow and the collective shadow of their culture becomes an inherent outcome. Erich Neumann, the Israeli psychoanalyst, described the subsequent phase of shadow-work as the individuation process progresses:

"The differentiation of "my" evil from the general evil is an essential item of self- knowledge from which no one who undertakes the journey of individuation is allowed to escape. But as the process of individuation unfolds, the ego's former drive toward perfection simultaneously disintegrates. The inflationary exaltation of the ego has to be sacrificed, and it becomes necessary for the ego to enter into some kind of gentleman's agreement with the shadow—a development which is diametrically opposed to the old ethic's ideal of absolutism and perfection."

The individual who is willing to confront their foes, whether within or without, will always have a path to follow. Shadow-work is based on a confessional act that can sometimes be cathartic. According to Jung, this is the most crucial activity. "Modern man," he asserted, "must rediscover a deeper source of his own spiritual life. To accomplish this, he must battle with evil, face his shadow, and merge with the devil. There is no other option."

The individual Shadow is essentially our hidden dark side – the part of ourselves that we have neglected and pushed away. It holds our deepest secrets, suppressed emotions, and primal urges that we deem unacceptable or even evil.

Deep within your unconscious lies a concealed space where suppressed emotions like lust, fury, envy, loathing, greed, deceit, and self-interest dwell. Neglecting the individual Shadow can result in detrimental effects on our well-being, including addictions, low self-esteem, mental illness, chronic illnesses, and various neuroses.

The longer our Shadows are suppressed in the unconscious, the more likely they are to take control of our lives, leading to psychosis or extreme behaviors like cheating or violence. Intoxicants such as alcohol and drugs can also trigger the release of the Shadow.

"One thing that comes out in myths is that at the bottom of the abyss comes the voice of salvation. The black moment is the moment when the real message of transformation is going to come. At the darkest moment comes the light" – Joseph Campbell

WHAT IS SHADOW WORK?

Engaging in Shadow Work entails embarking on a profound exploration of your inner darkness or Shadow Self. It is a courageous endeavor to bring to light all that has been unconsciously concealed, disowned, and rejected within you, residing within the depths of your Shadow Self.

In my personal experience, I have found that a powerful way to engage in shadow work is by sitting in a dark room, surrounded by the gentle glow of candlelight. This practice, known as self-reflective meditation, allows you to delve into your past or present and explore any traumas you may have experienced or caused.

By immersing yourself in this introspective process, you can gain valuable insights and grow as an individual. By acknowledging and directing your attention towards your anger, lust, jealousy, or any manipulative games you may have played with others, you can uncover and confront these suppressed negative traits.

Within your unconscious mind lies the Shadow Self, containing all the thoughts and emotions that you are ashamed of, along with suppressed desires, fears, and perversions that have been locked away either consciously or unconsciously. This serves as a method to appear tame, likeable, and socially acceptable to others.

Suppressing your desires, fears, and perversions in order to gain acceptance from others or conform to societal norms is nothing but a facade. When you suppress certain aspects of yourself just to please others or seek society's approval, you are essentially being inauthentic. The key to achieving an awakened state lies in recognizing, embracing, and actively engaging with the shadow aspects of our own selves. None of these aspects are inherently negative or necessitate eradication. The mistaken notion that awakening and enlightenment solely bring eternal happiness, brightness, and cheerfulness, while considering anything else as negative, only amplifies the shadow within individuals and society.

The depths of our being harbor a darkness, a clandestine reservoir of anger, grief, and untamed energy that we struggle to acknowledge or process. It is the collective interplay between our hidden selves and our conscious personas that shapes the world, giving birth to violence, conflicts, prejudice, inequality, and the unspoken guidelines that govern our behavior.

Through individual exploration of every aspect of ourselves, including the shadow, we gain a deeper understanding of our whole self and can transcend simplistic notions of good and evil, darkness and light. Mary Mueller Shutan pointed out that:

> **Within the lightworker community, there is a common tendency to focus on increasing one's light without acknowledging the presence of darkness. The aspects labeled as "dark" or "shadow" are often overlooked and end up expanding in relation to the amount of light one possesses.**

Ignoring the darker aspects and adhering to strict guidelines on awareness and consciousness is a common trait within these communities. ***However, failing to acknowledge our shadow self only hinders our spiritual growth and keeps us trapped in a state of immaturity.***

It is common for individuals to become spiritual bypassers, continuously searching for spirituality outside of themselves and avoiding the raw and complex journey of truly awakening, which involves facing our own emotions, traumas, and the darker aspects of life.

Authentic awakening involves truly comprehending and showing compassion towards our shadow side. It entails fully embracing and exploring all of our emotions and facets. It requires reconciling and refraining from judging even our deepest impulses and emotions, regardless of how dark they may seem.

Through conscious awareness and acceptance of our shadow,

we can attain a state of wholeness. Instead of dividing ourselves into opposing forces of light and shadow, good and bad, or spiritual and physical, we can embrace our messy, embodied existence. Our shadow is not something to overcome, but an essential aspect of our being.

Based on my personal experience, shadow work involves uncovering the hidden aspects within oneself and bringing them into the light. It is essential to engage in this process in order to achieve wholeness. Therefore, shadow work can be seen as a form of healing work. Until you heal, you cannot truly become whole. It is crucial to embrace our shadow – to fully embrace both the destructive and joyful aspects of our being. This profound awakening is a thing of beauty, as we learn to love every part of ourselves.

Every individual capable of acknowledging their own shadow and embracing their darker side contributes to the gradual dissolution of the collective shadow. As we integrate these aspects of ourselves, our society as a whole becomes more enlightened and awakened.

"*Wholeness for humans depends on the ability to own their own shadow*"
– C.G Jung

WHY DO SHADOW WORK

We engage in this work because unless we delve into the depths of our being, we will continue to carry the weight of unresolved issues such as persistent lust, anger, guilt, shame, fear, grief, and various challenges like addictions, relationship breakdowns, and even spiritual afflictions like existential depression or the **Dark Night of the Soul**.

Throughout the course of human history, Shadow Work has exerted a profound influence, enabling us to delve into the depths of our minds and uncover the fundamental origins of our individual and communal psychological disorders, physical discomforts, and even the heinous acts of criminal nature.

Shadow Work was traditionally practiced by Shamans, medicine people, priests, and priestesses in ancient times. Nowadays, it is more commonly associated with psychotherapy, where psychologists, psychiatrists, spiritual guides, and therapists lead the way.

Working with our shadows allows us to fully embrace our physical existence. As physical beings, we are meant to wholeheartedly experience a range of emotions such as anger, joy, bliss, love, and grief. Moreover, we should find immense pleasure in appreciating art, music, and our senses.

Our spirituality remains separate from ourselves when we neglect to clear and open the pathways of the physical body. By relying on external teachers and not acknowledging the unity of the spiritual, mental, and physical bodies, we create a spiritual divide within ourselves. Our physical and spiritual natures are intertwined, eliminating the need for a separate journey to awaken. By fully embracing our physical selves, expressing our emotions, and finding harmony within ourselves and the world, we naturally awaken our spiritual essence.

THE CONSEQUENCES OF DENYING THE SHADOW

The ancient Greeks acknowledged the significance of respecting all elements of the psyche. They viewed these elements as individual deities. Disregarding a god or goddess meant inviting their wrath and potential destruction. When we disavow any aspect of ourselves, it eventually becomes our adversary.

The personal shadow encompasses all these rejected fragments. The fascinating thing about the Shadow Self is its inherent need to be acknowledged. It passionately desires to be understood, examined, and integrated. It fervently longs to be recognized and embraced in awareness. The longer the Shadow remains buried and confined within the depths of the unconscious, the more it will create chances to remind you of its presence. The realms of religion and contemporary spirituality often gravitate towards highlighting the "love and light" aspects of spiritual growth, ultimately leading to their own downfall. This overemphasis on the ethereal, uplifting, and pleasurable elements of a spiritual awakening can result in a superficial understanding and a fear of anything that is too genuine, earthly, or dark.

> **Ignoring one's inner darkness spiritually can lead to a variety of severe problems. Within the spiritual and religious community, prevalent Shadow issues include pedophilia in priests, financial exploitation by gurus, as well as megalomania, narcissism, and God complexes in spiritual leaders.**

Denying our Shadow side can bring about other issues to contend with, such as:

Hypocrisy
Lies and self-deceit

Uncontrollable bursts of rage/anger
Emotional and mental manipulation of others
Greed and addictions
Phobias and obsessive compulsions
Racist, sexist, homophobic, and other offensive behavior
Intense anxiety
Chronic psychosomatic illness
Depression (which can turn into suicidal tendencies)
Sexual perversion
Narcissistically inflated ego
Chaotic relationships with others
Self-loathing
Self-absorption
Self-sabotage

Failing to acknowledge the presence of the shadow can have detrimental effects on our relationships with our spouse, family, and friends. Moreover, it can significantly impact our professional relationships and hinder our leadership capabilities.

Ignorance of our own shadow propels us into an endless loop of self-deception. Ultimately, without integrating the shadow archetype, we become entangled in a psychological battle within.

"Confront the dark parts of yourself, and work to banish them with illumination and forgiveness. Your willingness to wrestle with your demons will cause your angels to sing" – **August Wilson**

THE RELATIVITY OF OPPOSITES

The essence of Taoist philosophy is captured in stories that honor the useless, emphasizing the relativity of values and the principle of polarity. The traditional Chinese symbolism of yin and yang in Taoism serves as a portrayal of this concept. It symbolizes the shady and sunny sides of a mountain, and in a broader sense, encompasses all paired existence. The harmonious balance of yin and yang, dark and light, useless and useful, showcases the inherent unity of nature, where these complementary aspects are forever intertwined, akin to two sides of a coin.

According to *Chuang Tzu*: Those who would have right without its correlative, wrong; or good government without its correlative, misrule—they do not apprehend the great principles of the universe nor the condition to which all creation is subject. One might as well talk of the existence of heaven without that of earth, or of the negative principle without the positive, which is clearly absurd. Such people, if they do not yield to argument, must be either fools or knaves.

Recognizing that no single concept or value could be deemed absolute or superior, the Taoists believed that being useful and being useless both have their benefits. The ease with which these opposites can interchange is demonstrated in a Taoist fable about a farmer whose horse escaped.

> **His neighbor commiserated only to be told, "Who knows what's good or bad?" It was true. The next day the horse returned, bringing with it a drove of wild horses it had befriended in its wanderings. The neighbor came over again, this time to congratulate the farmer on his windfall. He was met with the same observation: "Who knows what is good or bad?" True this time too; the next day the farmer's son tried to mount one of the wild horses and fell off, breaking his leg. Back came the neighbor, this time with more commiserations, only to encounter for the third time the same response, "Who knows what is good or bad?" And once again the farmer's point was well taken, for the following day soldiers came by commandeering for the army and because of his injury, the son was not drafted.**

Taoists believe that yang and yin, light and shadow, useful and useless are all various facets of the whole. By choosing one side over the other, we disrupt nature's equilibrium. To be complete and in harmony with nature, we must embrace the opposites through a challenging process.

INTEGRATING THE SHADOW

Jung also discovered that the human psyche is made up of both light and dark elements, masculine and feminine qualities, and numerous other opposing forces that exist in a constant state of psychic tension. Similar to the Taoists, Jung cautioned against the danger of aligning oneself solely with one extreme (such as focusing solely on productivity). He believed that placing excessive importance on any one aspect of the psyche could lead to detrimental consequences like physical illness, neurosis, and psychosis. Jung proposed a different approach, suggesting that we must face the contradictions within ourselves as an essential part of the individuation process.

By actively acknowledging and confronting our shadow, the darker aspects of our personality that hold the qualities and attributes we deny, we can effectively integrate our inner opposites. Confronting and embracing these characteristics can be a challenging and uncomfortable journey, as the shadow often embodies our weaknesses – primitive, undeveloped, and clumsy traits that we have shunned because of ethical, aesthetic, and societal norms.

Despite being perceived as despicable, lowly, and worthless, the shadow aligns with the Taoist depictions of the gnarled tree and unattractive hunchback. Much like the shadow, these images are deemed to hold no value. This suggests that each individual may possess a gnarled tree or hunchback Shu within.

CONCLUSION

The shadow self and shadow work are incredibly expansive subjects, providing an abundance of material for numerous future chapters in other books we may write/publish. This was merely a quick glimpse into the subject matter. The individual shadow is often overlooked on any spiritual path but is highly critical. All the subjects presented in this book are equally important in awakening the kundalini. The inner serpent cannot be awakened if there are unresolved traumas and negative emotions that have not been brought to light.

It is impossible to transition the body to the astral planes while carrying unresolved inner turmoil. The risks of attracting negative entities are numerous. Let's assume that not all readers of this book have the willpower or motivation to attain such a high level of self-discipline, but they can still benefit from applying certain advice to enhance their health or other areas of their life.

Shadow work is healing your self, it's looking society in the face and saying "*this is who you want me to be but this is who I actually am.*" It's integrating all aspects of yourself and living a true and whole authentic life. It involves integrating all elements of one's being, enabling the pursuit of an authentic and fulfilling existence.

"Shadow work is the way to illumination. When we become aware of all that is buried within us, that which is lurking beneath the surface no longer has power over us" – **Aletheia Luna**

Chapter 5

ACTIVATE REMEMBRANCE

"Remember, as a member of the family of light, you carry the vibration and intent of change wherever you go-Altering the system you find yourself in."
– **Aurora Ray**

In the quiet moments of solitude, where the noise of the world fades and the soul stands naked before its own truth, a profound awakening can occur. This journey, often arduous and filled with moments of despair, leads to a horizon where the dawn of spiritual enlightenment breaks through. It is a path walked by many yet understood by few, for the truths uncovered are deeply personal and universally resonant. Years of seeking, wandering through the labyrinth of existence, have brought me to a place of profound spiritual understanding. This awakening is not a sudden burst of light but a gentle unfolding, a delicate unfurling of the soul's petals, revealing the radiant core of truth within.

This journey has been a dance of shadows and light, a symphony of silence and sound, guiding me to an inner peace that words can scarcely capture. In the heart of this transformation lies a simple yet powerful realization: we are all beings of light, intricately woven into the fabric of the universe. Our essence is not bound by the physical form but extends into the vastness of existence, connecting us to all that is. This interconnectedness is the source of our greatest strength and the wellspring of our deepest compassion. It is in recognizing this unity that true peace is found. Imagine standing at the edge of a great ocean, the waves whispering secrets of the deep. The horizon stretches infinitely, a mirror of the limitless potential within each of us. This ocean is our spirit, boundless and eternal, ever flowing and ever changing. To awaken to this truth is to understand that we are not separate drops but the entire ocean in a single drop. Our lives, our struggles, our joys, and our sorrows are all part of this magnificent expanse.

In this state of awakened consciousness, the mundane becomes miraculous. Each breath is a gift, each moment a precious gem. The beauty of a flower, the laughter of a child, the gentle touch of a loved one—all these become portals to the divine. Life, in its simplest form, is a celebration of this divine presence. To live with this awareness is to walk in a state of grace, where every step is a dance and every word a song.

This transformation is not merely an internal shift but radiates outward, touching all who come into contact with it. People around you will notice a change, a serenity that defies explanation, a joy that cannot be contained. This inner peace becomes a beacon, drawing others to their own journey of self-discovery. Your presence becomes a sanctuary, a place where others can find solace and inspiration. The journey to this state of enlightenment is not without its challenges. It requires courage to face the shadows within, to confront the fears and doubts that have long held us captive. But it is in these moments of vulnerability that we find our greatest strength. It is in the surrender to the unknown that we discover the limitless potential of our true nature. This path demands honesty, humility, and above all, a deep trust in the process of life.

As you walk this path, you become a living testament to the power of transformation. Your story becomes a source of inspiration for others, a reminder that no matter how lost or broken we may feel, there is always a way back to wholeness. Your journey, with all its twists and turns, becomes a beacon of hope, illuminating the way for those who follow.

To awaken is to remember our true nature, to reconnect with the divine essence that resides within us all. It is to see the world through the eyes of love, to understand that we are all expressions of the same infinite source. This realization brings with it a profound sense of peace, a knowing that we are exactly where we are meant to be, doing exactly what we are meant to do. In this state of awakened being, life is no longer a series of random events but a beautifully orchestrated dance of synchronicity and purpose. Every encounter, every experience, is imbued with meaning, guiding us ever closer to the fulfillment of our soul's journey. We begin to see the hand of the divine in everything, recognizing that we are co-creators in this magnificent tapestry of existence.

This awakening is not an endpoint but a continuous unfolding. It is a journey of ever-deepening understanding, of ever-expanding love. It is a call to live fully, to embrace each moment with an open heart and a grateful spirit. It is an invitation to be the light that we are, to shine brightly and boldly in a world that desperately needs our illumination. As you continue on this path, may you find the courage to trust in the wisdom of your own soul, the strength to embrace the unknown, and the grace to walk in love and light. May your journey inspire others to embark on their own path of awakening, and may the light within you shine ever brighter, illuminating the way for all who seek the truth.

This is your story, your journey, your awakening. Embrace it fully, live it deeply, and let your spirit soar. For in your light, others will find their way, and together, we will create a world of peace, love, and infinite possibility. The deeper you connect to your own soul, the more apparent this realization becomes. Virtually all undiluted aspects (*outside of man-made artificiality*) of creation have a spirit, or intelligence behind them.

This spirit of nature is always keen to interact with us, to catch our attention, to share souls back and forth. It is in the trees. It is in the rays of the sun. It is in the living, conscious waters. The hum of the soft breeze. It is in the very air we breathe. And it is beautiful, joyous and blissful. All it takes is to look and FEEL from our SOUL, and then we truly experience it's ecstatic embrace. We are of the EXACT same timeless divine energy. And it is reminding us of this by holding up a mirror. The moments of beauty in nature we experience which leaves us awestruck. "*All*" actually exist inside of our enormous spirits, which are interspersed everywhere, inside everything we actually perceive. That feeling of awe and wonder is an indescribable connection felt as your spirit is known to be one with all beauty and brilliance you behold. It is a part of you, and you are also within it.

In Rumi's word "*Words are pretext. It is the inner bond that draws one person to another, not words.*" Although words are needed to communicate with one another, not everyone can communicate telepathically like we used to back in time before our way of life and consciousness was heavily altered/manipulated to the benefit of those that only crave control and power at the expense of others. I'd say that as of now, by using words to communicate, that makes us invalids. Because words can be easily misunderstood and misinterpreted.

Nonetheless, we are remembering who we are. Words trigger remembrance. Words suppress remembrance too, depending on whether we use negative or positive words. The main thing that people should begin to remember is their divine selves. Women have to remember their divine feminine, while men must remember their divine masculine. Out of many ways to activate remembrance, one of them is the SUN.

SUN – The PORTAL, the GATE of WISDOM, the SAVIOR

Here are a few important points related to the Sun.

1- SUN IS LIFE

If you get skin cancer or any disease while staying too much on the Sun, it is because of your polluted body. The skin is the biggest organ of the human body, it has pores, it needs breathing. Nature, in this case the Sun will never harm you. Nature heals you. You've been conditioned that healing comes from the shelves of the stores or from purchasing things online. Only your body can heal itself. Your job is to stay out of its way, do not consume what is not meant to be consumed by a biological created body. Use your organs to catapult you in higher level of living and not for expelling/sewage purpose.

2- If you eat junk foods and drink junk drinks for weeks, months and years, not only that the whole body is imbalanced, polluted, full of death, but also under the skin is all blocked, the energy stagnated and decayed. The Sun needs to penetrate your skin and do its/his job to heal and balance you. But if you prohibit its intended job, then all that Sun energy will be concentrated on the skin and that's how you get cancer because the toxins under the skin react to the energy of the

Sun. But the so-called healthcare system doesn't tell you the truth. If they did, they would go out of business.

3- There is absolutely nothing wrong with the Sun, never was and never will be. The problem is YOU. Stop putting poison/ death (sunscreen, lipsticks, deodorant/perfumes, make up, hair gel/ spray etc.) on your skin You were created beautiful/handsome to perfection, why do you become a clown? Because you were conditioned to serve the mega corporations instead of serving your temple (body, mind and soul). The sunlight directly affects your pineal gland, can't you tell why those who want to control you don't want you to receive the Sun rays/light. Many people spend many hours in their jobs, inside a box (building) and then when they go home they are too exhausted to go outside so they distract themselves with technological devices which continue to keep them inside a box, box (mind) within a box (device screens a.k.a dark magic mirrors).

4- Begin immediately to not put any of that poison on your skin and also eat less, eat healthy and the most important of all since eating junk is seen as healthy by most, get into fasting, to make up for the lack of intelligence, make fasting a way of life. Your body is very intelligent, your body doesn't think, it does what it is designed to do but only when you don't let your confused mind complicate its job. Do not be a copy cat by doing what other women and/or men do. Every HUEman is unique. No two people are the same.

Following a blind will only get you to fall off the cliff. Falling off the cliff in this case I'm using it as a metaphor for the end of the physical life which you (if you follow the blind) will end it in ignorance and subsequently you will reincarnate again with a total wipe out of the memories of the previous lifetime therefore, you will live the whole thing again and again until you learn the lesson to see with your own eyes and not through the blurry lenses of someone else's.

5- Also, the skin, besides the nose and #2 (defecating), is one of the importants functions of your body that is designed to expel toxins through sweating, especially through exercising. But if the pores of your skin are blocked by the poisons you put on, what do you think happens to the toxins? They become permanent residents in your body. Do you care about external look or to be original, genuine, authentic and divine? The answer to this question (and the implementation or lack of the implementation of the answer) determines our intelligence or stupidity.

6- Personally, I do not put anything on my skin. Even the shampoo that I use is herbal and I do not use shampoo/soap when I have shower after a good Sun bath. It takes up to 48h for the body to produce vitamin D. If you use soap/shampoo you wipe out the oily substance that the skin has for helping in the production of the Vitamin D. Wash with soap only your private parts and underarms, unless you have dirt on you or are really smelly (depending on what kind of job you do) then use soap to clean the whole body. But if you innerstand the importance of the Sun and go out in the Sun daily then it is not a problem if you use soap to clean the whole body more frequently than you should. You're killing yourself if you shower daily because you are wiping that oily substance that your skin naturally is equipped with.

7- It is simple enough to put things in perspective. Technically your body produces Vitamin D and not the Sun. But for the body to produce it, you need the SUN. A metaphor about life is that the SON is the SUN of life, meaning that to have a strong society you need strong SONS (men) and not weak feminized compliant modern men. For the SON to become a strong man it needs a strong father, loving intelligent mother and also the woman he gets together with, must be intelligent, a nurturers and self-aware. So, pretty much the Suns (sons) and the Moons (daughters) must be properly raised to have a strong foundation for a strong healthy family and strong future generations. If the Sun killed, then India's and China's populations would have been wiped out long time ago.

Do not fall for the p**HARM**aceutical conglomerate scam. The so-called controllers (you are the controller, but you may not know that) will do what you want, regardless of if it is they who deceived you to put those harmful products on you. They "*Will do what you want*" when you know end exercise the power of free will, otherwise they will do what they want, and what they want is the opposite of what you truly want (from a higher intelligent, self-awareness ,empathetic perspective and state of living).

9- Every moment of the day you can change your life for the better. You are not condemned to death for eternity, you can make a change anytime you wish, but you must realize the beauty of the creation that you are. You are a Son (light/inner intelligent in itself). Anything you do that harms your body is like betraying yourself and the whole creation. After a rainy day when you see the Sun, doesn't that make you feel good? Hmm, I wonder why. That's because you and the Sun are one. The Sun is created for you, by you. You might ask how could the Sun have been created by you? Let's stop here, that's a topic for another day...or another lifetime. Some questions are better left alone until we are ready for them. Another way to activate remembrance is **URINE** or **ULTRAPLASMA** filtrate in the next chapter.

Chapter 6

ULTRA PLASMA FILTRATE – URINE FASTING AND MONOATOMIC GOLD

Urine is filtered blood plasma, medically referred to as "*plasma ultrafiltrate*." Before appreciating urine and its benefits, you must unlearn the misinformation that you were taught to believe about what it is. Urine is not a dirty substance excreted by your body. It is a by-product of blood filtration, and not waste filtration. Urine is a purified blood derivative, made by the kidneys, whose main function is not excretion, but regulation of all the elements and their concentrations in the blood.

Nutrient-filled blood passes through the liver where toxins are removed to be excreted as solid waste. This purified clean blood undergoes a filtering process in the kidneys, where excess water, salts, vitamins, enzymes, minerals, urea, antibodies, uric acid, and other elements that are not usable at the time by the body, are collected in the form of a purified, sterile, watery solution which is called "urine." So, you see that your urine is very rich and very beneficial for you.

Now that I recalled something, when you consume coffee, or soft drinks which are neurotoxins, many of the minerals, enzymes, antibodies etc. are expelled unnecessarily (which your body really needs). Which means that it is very important to drink your urine especially when the minerals, enzymes etc. are expelled unnecessarily in the case of having consumed coffee or soft drinks prior, or anything that is not natural in its most natural and purest form.

Any neurotoxic substance is a foreign organism to your body, so your body will use its water to expel it. Since you now know what is in your urine, wouldn't it make sense to not consume neurotoxin products (sugar is the worst legal drug neurotoxin) and to consume urine? Probably I don't have to say it but I'm going to say it anyway, because you never know, I've seen people that have said and done the unthinkable.

What I'm trying to say is that you must consume your own urine and not that of your neighbour (or anyone else's other than your own). Yes, yes, I can hear your thoughts that it is common sense to ingest our own liquid, but you would be surprised that common sense is not so common among humans. One of the most powerful healings comes from URINE FASTING. Urine fast is essentially a water fast where you also consume everything you pass. Urine fasting/therapy is very effective because fasting puts the body in a healing state, by leaving all its energy for healing instead for digesting solid food. On top of consuming raw fruit/veggies, exercising urine fasting is like putting your healing process on steroids (natural steroids).

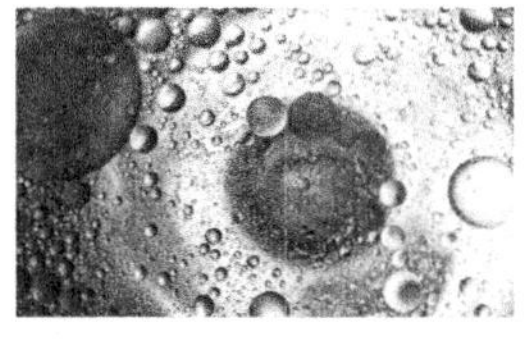

Urine fasting is very, very powerful, but it will not do its job fully or in a short time of practicing it when your body is clogged with junk food, junk thoughts, junk liquids, junk feelings (actions/inactions as a reaction to unhealed self/emotions). Urine will help you but by itself will have to work against a mountain of previously mentioned junks. So, it is very advisable that you also exercise, eat healthy and fast (check fasting chapter in later pages.) Even if you are fully convinced (which you will eventually, depending on how serious you are about your health) that urine therapy is indeed very beneficial, you can't think: *"Ok, I will keep consuming crap, so urine therapy will make up for it"*. It doesn't work like that. Either you are all in or out. I'll mention the analogy of changing the oil of your car. You don't just add the good oil or part of it in the dirty oil that needs to be changed and expect to fix the problem. Urine will keep your body functioning better. Without addressing your diet/lifestyle, urine benefits are limited. Is like consuming fast food, processed food, ice-cream, soft drink, meat and at the end of the day you eat a big bowl of vegetable salad. What is that going to do? "*Nothing*", as the junk food takes priority for digestion, while the good food that can digest fast gets fermented on top of the acidic/cancerous food that you had. Urine Therapy is the magic pill when combined with a fast and/or clean diet. Your lifestyle/diet is what will sustain your good health. John Armstrong, the author of 'The water of LIFE' cured thousands of people with urine therapy. Urine therapy is a wonderful cure. It will heal many ailments even if you don't change your diet, but the real benefits are when they (urine and healthy diet) work synergistically as it will heal the dangerous diseases as without lifestyle change will only heal minor diseases (minor disease can turn into major).

When you research "*urine therapy*", the main search engines most likely will say that no scientific evidence exists or any other exclamation as to dismiss the benefits of urine therapy. Hmm, who decides what is true and what is not? Have in mind that most scientific so-called research is done in a controlled environment by the same $cientists that have personal gains. Many studies' results are to the satisfaction of those that gain from the results. I don't know your age, but back in time when we got hurt, let's say the leg, we would pee on the wound to disinfect it.

Do we need $cience to tell us if its ok to do it or not? Unfortunately, as a society we are conditioned to beLIEve $cience and doctors (***legal drug dealers***). And as a result, we pay for it by giving our power away to corporations that only profit is their main concern. Urine therapy/consumption may be hard for you or many others to grasp, and that is precisely because of conditioning. We were never taught knowledge about our body. Once you realize how powerful your body is and how insanely efficiently it is designed, then it will all make sense. Your body makes its own medicine and self-heals. Urine consumption has helped reverse even the most degenerated bodies to homeostasis. HOW? Because urine contains information about everything that is wrong with your body. When you ingest urine, the glands that you have in your throat will pick up the information of the urine and will instantly produce antibodies for whatever is wrong with you. As an important example for an urgent situation: If you get bit by a snake or stung by a wasp, drink your urine and the poison should be neutralized from your system.

You may think that you may replenish the urine/liquid lost by simply drinking water. Even though that would be one of the corrects logical things to do, know that water doesn't have stem cells but urine does. How do you think the baby is so shiny/smooth in a mother's womb? It's because of the ultra plasma filtrate liquid that baby swims/grows in. Drinking your own urine is such a big deal, it is a big change you must undertake. Because all life you were conditioned to think that urine is a waste product. Of course, those who conditioned us, wanted us to remain invalid and ignorant of our own internal medicine.

Urine therapy is not for everyone. The human energy field flows outward and expands in the growing years. It takes in food from the environment and releases urine, potty etc. back to the environment. During this stage, a healthy person in a healthy environment does not really need their urine. Urine is full of negatively charged ions and is basically a form of energy moving *inwards* instead of *outwards* as is the pattern during growth of the body. Urine therapy for babies outside the womb and grown ups is only useful when they've had a crisis that caused significant damage, or an illness that isn't resolving on its own.

Urine therapy is useful especially when you are energetically bombarded, as in the case of vibrational assaults from technological devices (tablets, cellphones, TVs) and cellphone towers, H.A.A.R.P etc. No matter how filtered/clean the water you drink is, it is still polluted energetically from different low vibrational frequencies from external factors and the examples of the devices/tower/HAARP I mentioned above. Urine is pure. No matter how unhealthy you are, the urine will always be clean, unless your kidneys are failing, then that's an extreme situation that other forms of healing are required.

For men: In a later chapter you'll read an excerpt from a book on the 1st step in retaining your semen and even though you retain it, some will still escape through the bladder. You'll know it because the urine will be blurry. The point I'm mentioning this is to have a broader idea on how and why the internal elixir is wasted and how to save it by ingesting it back. Some things in this book or in life in general may seem far fetched or ridiculous and disgusting. If you feel disgusted from your own magical elixirs, what would you say about the store-bought packaged foods you eat/drink? Many of those products have disgusting chopped animals, and even people in them.

Many of those products are cooked with engine oils and many other disgusting ways on how many products that we see them as healthy, they are nothing but death disguised as healthy products. If you are curious about the book speaking on how to retain Semen and more information on URINE THERAPY, that book's title is ***Body Mind Soul*** by Saimir Kercanaj. We also spoke about sexual energy in our previous book titled ***Rebuild Yourself From Within*** by J.J. & TAMO.

IS there MONOATOMIC GOLD IN YOUR URINE?

In the vast landscape of alternative wellness, few topics spark as much intrigue and debate as monoatomic gold. Often hailed as an ancient elixir, its origins, benefits, and scientific validity are subjects of much discussion.

What is Monoatomic Gold?

Monoatomic gold, sometimes referred to as monatomic gold, ORMUS gold, or white powder gold, is believed to be gold in its single-atom state. Unlike the familiar metallic gold, where atoms bond together, monoatomic gold consists of detached, individual gold atoms.

Historical Roots of Monoatomic Gold

The allure of monoatomic gold isn't new. Ancient texts and alchemical traditions hint at a mysterious substance, often linked to the "Philosopher's Stone" – a legendary alchemical substance said to grant spiritual enlightenment and physical rejuvenation.
Touted Benefits of Monoatomic Gold

Proponents passionately advocate for a range of benefits:

1- **Spiritual Awakening**: Many believe monoatomic gold can amplify spiritual awareness and psychic abilities. If you are depleted of Urine, Blood, Semen, Ovum (women's equivalent to semen for men) you will not be able to have psychic abilities, and if you have any it will be very limited.

2- **Enhanced Cognitive Abilities**: Claims include improved focus, memory, and overall brain function. Know that every time you urinate you lose monoatomic gold, nutrients and stem cells. These and other minerals that the urine contains are building blocks of the brain (besides the stem cells, phosphorus etc. in the semen and blood). By wasting the healing resources that your body already produces by default, it depletes you of intelligence). You may not ingest urine and can be already intelligent, but that's because you are taking care of yourself though other means like fasting, consuming healthy food, exercise etc. There are many ways on how to regain your health and intelligence. But being intelligent is not enough, the most intelligent people I ever met, are emotionally bankrupt or not in an optimal emotional and mental state. Urine takes a picture of everything that is wrong in your body. All the ancestral trauma or even trauma from this lifetime that we've been through since *birth can be healed through urine ingesting. If it's recent trauma, it can be healed from fresh urine, if it's from trauma from the past it can be healed with aged urine.

3- **Physical Healing**: Some users report accelerated healing and rejuvenation. As always for any kind of healing, your belief in healing is important. When you believe that something is working, even though at the moment you are sick, by the universal law of manifestation you will be healed. Of course, depends on the severity of your sickness. Additional help may be needed such as grounding, or sun baths/sun gazing, listening to binaural music, fasting etc.

4- **Anti-Aging Properties**: Everyone wants to live for as long as possible. Nobody wants to age. The quest for eternal youth has some turning to this ancient substance. Urine therapy is as ancient as humanity itself. Back in time, people were way more knowledgeable about their body's internal remedies than we are now. Unfortunately, throughout many generations, humanity has been conditioned that ancient humans were primitive. Back in time people loved each other, communicated telepathically with each other. Nowadays people lie, deceive and hurt one another so who is primitive the so-called modern human or the ancient one? I'll leave it up to you to decide. Aging doesn't just happen from eating bad foods or wasting your semen/ovum, but also from the belief that aging is normal. Your mind dictates your inner cells how to behave for example celebrating your birthday which is none other than celebrating your death. Celebrating is a dark ritual. This is a subject for another time, even though this part is about aging. But if you are interested/curious to read about this subject, check the chapter "WHY DO WE AGE?" in the book "***I AM THE KEY THAT OPENS ALL DOORS***" by Saimir Kercanaj

The Science Behind Monoatomic Gold

"The center of the periodic chart of elements consists of what are known as the "transition elements", meaning that they can transit from metallic to monoatomic or diatomic via chemical treatment or through other means (what some would refer to as "shadow chemistry" or "arcane

chemistry" or even "alchemy"). Take gold for example. When you have two or more gold atoms in a micro cluster, it will have metallic properties, but if you have only one atom, it will then have ceramic properties, which means that it becomes chemically inert but at the same time will have superconductive capabilities even at room temperature. The weight of these amazing materials can also change by heating, becoming lighter, even to the point of levitation. Because it is chemically inert, it can be ingested for health, wellbeing and super-energizing at the cellular level"

While the anecdotal accounts are plentiful, scientific validation remains scarce. The majority of claims lack rigorous scientific research, making monoatomic gold a contentious topic among experts. Key word "experts". Who are these experts? Are they independent researchers or are they controlled puppets that what they say will benefit only those that want us to be sick and detached from our own magical existence? **There are two kinds of scientists**:

1- *$cientists* – These ones are paid to lie even though many of them are tricked into thinking that their research is for the betterment of human life. Some researches are conducted so that when the truth of how something works is found out, the finding are meant to be buried or patented on purpose so that he who holds the patent, will use it to make money or to hide/bury the finding since burying the truth is more convenient to them than making money out of it.

2- *Scientists* – These beautiful souls are the good ones. These Scientists are independent, they are not tainted by the dark intentions of those who have something to gain. These kind of researchers are to be respected and honored because to them, the truth is what matters. The word 'scientist' when one hears it, they think of someone in the government, someone that works for the establishment. You can be a scientist, conducting independent research for any field/subject. There are countless of normal people like me and you who research daily about exposing the fraud governments and their agendas, but also researchers who research about health or any other subject that contribute to the prosperity and freedom

Safety and Consumption

Monoatomic gold is available in various forms, from powders to liquids. However, its safety profile is not well-established. As with any alternative supplement, it's paramount to consult with a healthcare professional before diving in. There are mainstream healthcare/homeopathic practitioners who are only taught what the controllers want and there are homeopathic healthcare practitioners who have a broader knowledge about the human body [*physical, emotional and spiritual knowledge*].

The Verdict on Monoatomic Gold

Monoatomic gold stands at the crossroads of ancient wisdom and modern speculation. While its allure is undeniable, it's essential to approach the topic with both curiosity and caution. As research evolves, the mysteries of monoatomic gold may one day be fully unraveled. If we have to wait until others decides for ourselves, we could be long gone. In life we should practice being our own teachers, scientist and doctors. When we do this, we do it to our own benefits because we don't do it for money.

Chapter 7

DM - DIVINE MASCULINE

The Divine Masculine serves as a protector of the feminine but also as protectors of children since masculinity is power, electricity, meant to protect the fragile feminine, not only in the physical realm but also in the astral and spiritual dimensions. A fragile woman doesn't mean she is a weak minded so don't misunderstand the word fragile for weakness. This role goes beyond mere physical protection; it is about safeguarding the Divine Feminine's energy and essence from negative influences and harmful energies that may attempt to interfere with her soul's journey. The Divine Masculine creates a sacred space where she can rest, recharge, and flourish without the threat of external disturbances.

This protection is not a reflection of weakness on the part of the Divine Feminine. On the contrary, it acknowledges her immense power and potential. By ensuring her safety and providing a nurturing environment, the Divine Masculine allows her to fully express her strengths, wisdom, and nurturing qualities. Within this secure space, she can access deeper levels of her intuition, creativity, and spiritual insight, which in turn enriches and empowers the Divine Masculine.

The dynamic between the two is one of mutual support and enhancement. The Divine Feminine, rested and renewed, becomes an even more potent force, using her gifts of intuition, healing, and emotional depth to uplift and guide the Divine Masculine. In this balanced union, both energies reach their highest potential, each complementing the other in a harmonious dance of strength and grace. There is only freedom of expression in this kind of state. This sacred partnership creates a powerful synergy, where the Divine Masculine's protection and the Divine Feminine's nurturing powers combine to form a unified force capable of facing any challenge, whether it is in the physical world or the spiritual realms. Together, they embody the perfect balance of strength and compassion, logic and intuition, action and reflection, creating a harmonious existence that reflects the true essence of divine love and unity.

Divine Masculine - Upon each Incarnation, the Androgynous Soul hosts a distinctive Archetype of Self to Cognitively Assimilate manifested Existence. Both the Essence of Yin and Yang Energy provide the Observer with a uniquely curated Experience for Expansion. As the Awakened Presence of all men alike, the Divine Masculine transcends ego to exemplify Truth, Love and Conviction. Such elevated awareness births natural leadership through an ambition to Better Thyself. Reaching this state of being requires tremendous amounts of refinement and inner work to transmute the old for the new. Although men are conditioned by society to suppress vulnerability, the Divine Masculine embraces his anima, thus allowing for deep subconscious clearing and revival. To learn from the past, we must ground in the present.

With so many men in the collective pursuing self service, the Divine Masculine is a rare breed who seeks only to guide and protect others beyond incentive. He opens his mind to expand consciousness and purifies his heart to nurture those around him. A good representation of Divine Masculine embodiment can be seen in the ascended masters who share love freely without condition. These vibrationally attune beings discovered that true power comes from empathy, not apathetic control. The shift from authority to responsibility is a hallmark of the Divine Masculine. When one's actions mirror their intentions, the most fundamental foundations of trust may be lain through mutual reassurance.

With the rise of the Divine Feminine influencing the masculine presence in the collective, men are slowly waking from their amnesiac slumber to remember who they truly are. As logical thinking transitions to feeling, the pure radiance of the sacred heart center once again illuminates for all to see. The Divine Masculine cultivates his potential by learning the lessons and integrating the teachings to further progress in his soul growth. Evolution is a choice of free will that must be consciously made. Never doubt the influence of the Divine Masculine, one man can change the world through his personal metamorphosis.

The Divine Masculine is "***yang – Electrical/power-protection***" energy of the soul that serves as protective and grounding force leading from loving integrity. Listen to the heart, the heart it always knows. Whenever you think that a so-called bad person has an evil heart, that is incorrect. It is the mind that gets hijacked. The heart can never be hijacked, it is impossible. When a person doesn't have empathy about any sentient being's life, it's their mind that causes apathy. It means that those people live in the mind. The mind and the heart are meant to work in coherence with each other. The heart has neurons just as the brain does. Only the brain can be confused and conditioned but not the heart. That's where meditation comes in, in meditation you align the heart and the mind. Later on, you'll read about chakras and meditation.

The ***Divine Masculine*** energy is focused and determined. He has the discernment that is necessary to see through any games, manipulation or distractions that are blocking him from moving forward on his path. He has the willpower to delay gratification and resist temptations that take him off course. The Divine Masculine energy knows what he wants and won't allow anything to stop him from reaching his highest potential, his purpose and his destiny. An integrated masculine man's mission is focused on being of service. He is supportive of the feminine energy. His mind is integrated with his heart. His ego desires cannot control him anymore. He cannot be distracted and he leads with love and integrity. His energy feels safe and grounded. He honors his feelings and is emotionally available. This kind of masculine is deserving of the counterpart Divine Feminine.

Healthy integrated with a head above the shoulders Divine Masculine men are:

Independent
Fierce
Present
Spiritually wise
Revering of women
Responsible
Clear minded and open hearted

Warriors when called upon
Directive
Introspective
Physically adept and grounded in their bodies
Connected to Earth
Responsible

The true masculine warrior observes his emotions without engaging in chaotic ways. He will have days where he will feel good and days when he will feel awful. He never tries to get rid of them. He feels them, he understands (innerstands) them and he controls them. He never tries to suppress them. If you suppress your feelings, the low vibration is still in you. The only way to clear out low vibrational frequencies is to face them.

Wounded Masculine

Controlling
Dominating
Conquering
Emotionally numb
Disconnected

The wound begins with childhood where father didn't raise the child to become a man where the child remained a child but in a grown-up body. Or when the child grew without a father or with a feminized father. Nobody is condemned to suffer. Everyone has the ability and the potential to forge a path of greatness. Every moment you can shine, think for yourself and create an environment that encourages growth, strength and enlightenment.

In the book **I AM THE KEY THAT OPENS ALL DOORS** by Saimir Kercanaj, the author wrote this interesting and very important thing about this subject:

"A person that stays with you mostly for sex, denies that the sex is parasitic as it is painful for them because they need to feed off of your energetic field or life force to sustain their shallow parasitic selves.

You owe it to yourself to do a parasitic cleanse. Both a physical and an energetic cleanse. Get rid of those kind of people feeding off of you sexually. They will find another one to leech off of until they will one way or another get healed. Their healing will begin to offer positive healing energy back instead of sucking it out of other people. Growth in a relationship happens when both partners heal each other and when both partners water and not draining each other. You cannot grow in the presence of someone that refuses to heal.

You are in no way responsible to heal them if they themselves are not willing to put the effort in healing their wounded child within. Casual sex or the dating scene is full of unhealed people with internal energy blockages. They will parasite off of your energy. Do not allow that for temporary sexual surface pleasure. You will be harmed by receiving their insecurities, their low self-esteem, and their past traumatic experiences/ low energy.

If you are a man, I greatly suggest you practice semen retention (refer to the chapter **ORGASMING WITHOUT EJACULATING-SEMEN RETENTION** in the book **BODY MIND SOUL AS YOU BELIEVE SO SHALL IT BE** by the same author.

If you are a woman, check the chapter **MENSTRUATION RETENTION** [How To Control/Stop Menstruation naturally] in the book **GAIN WISDOM THROUGH PRACTICED KNOWLEDGE** by Rimias K. Neo

If you are a woman, do not enter in an energetic contract (sexual intercourse, including kissing) with a man that does not practice semen retention. A man that ejaculates for the purpose of a few seconds of pleasure, is half a man. Do not settle for less. This of course applies when you have realized your purpose, when you know your worth. Only then, will you have a successful relationship. A relationship doesn't necessarily have to.....fill in the rest of the sentence however you think"

Healed Masculine
Protector with respect
Grounded
Integrated with their feminine aspect of self
Heart-centered
Present

There cannot be freedom unless the collective masculine awakens. An awakened masculine man is a warrior of the heart. He calls to other conscious men to join the revolution, to lay down their ego, and with the true masculine energy, demonstrate what It means to return to love. The Divine Masculine Energy is an active force which represents action, responsibility, direction, focus, strength, generosity, the Sun (the Divine Feminine represents the Moon), encouragement, intellect, clarity, growth and transformation. But for you to realize and practice this state of existence, you must be yourself, by yourself, meaning *solitude*, until you are ready to deal with the world outside of you in a healthy manner.

Remember, that the world outside of you reflects the world inside you. First you must build a healthy and bright world within so that it can be mirrored in the world outside of you as in circumstances. As an example, if you are a griever, someone that holds on to grudge, fearful and worried person, you will attract people and circumstances of the same vibrational field that you put out. If any of your friends or family members live in a high frequency mindset, they will get away from you because they don't want to be dragged down by your drama. The same applies for the opposite, if you are someone of a high vibrational frequency, you will attract the same kind of people and repel those that are of a low vibration.

Solitude is the foundation of self love. In solitude, your connection with your soul gets really strong, you start hearing the intuition over your fears. Intuition is the real inner voice. Your vibration becomes powerful when you stop surrounding yourself with the energies that don't really suit your spirit. When you choose your own soul over the fake company, everything starts shifting in your favor. When you are no longer around the people who drain your energy, you are more connected to your true self. Your intuition becomes your inner compass. Confusion is replaced with a deep clarity. You start attracting love as you embody it yourself now. You can't really love others if you don't love yourself first. You can't really understand others when you don't even understand yourself. Embrace solitude if you want to have a chance in becoming free.

How to Increase the Masculine Energy?

Heal your ideas and feelings towards your own father
Encourage others toward growth
Be an active giver of love
Take full responsibility of your life and actions/decisions
Channel your sexual energy from lust to the heart
Listen and learn about women, after all you too are made of feminine energy also.
Semen retention*

*No matter how healthy you eat/drink, no matter how much you train your body, you will not achieve the awakening of the full Divine Masculine unless you practice semen retention. The semen is the astral liquid, the life force, the intelligence, the most precious gift a man has. If you waste that, your life is forfeited. Read the books mentioned below, you don't have to believe anything in those books but no matter what you do, READ them.

> "Men who abstain from casual sex, pornography and masturbation, raise the vibration of the collective as a whole.. When you (men) stop entertaining lust, sex indulgence and other carnal pleasures, you become protectors of purity. Being pure, makes you the best, son, father and husband. Being pure, you make the world safer for women and children. You see other men as your brothers and you develop a greater appreciation for motherhood. Lust becomes repulsive. Virtue becomes "the new beauty." When you are pure, you will attract women because they will naturally feel comfortable around you because you don't carry the vibration/frequency of sexual perversion. When you have self-control over your body, mind and soul, you are the paragon of masculinity." – **Saimir Kercanaj**, from the book **- I AM THE KEY THAT OPENS ALL DOORS**

Books on Semen Retention – Some of the books mentioned below, are only about semen retention and/or sexual alchemy and the others talk a good amount about it. All books are very good and equally important. The books that are not specifically written about semen retention, are books for both genders, just in case you are a woman and don't find the semen retention subject interesting, even though you should know that only a man that practiced semen retention has more chance of being a real masculine than those that don't.

Rebuild Yourself From Within by J.J. and TAMO

Gain Wisdom Through Practiced Knowledge by Rimias K. Neo

The SR (Semen Retention) Manuscript by Ancient Archives

Treatise Of Sexual Alchemy by Samael Aun Weor

Body Mind Soul – As You Believe So Shall It Be by Saimir Kercanaj

You Are The One by Pine G. Land

The Alchemy of Sexual Energy by Mantak Chia

I AM THE KEY THAT OPENS ALL DOORS by Saimir Kercanaj

Semen Retention by Arcan Scriverius

If you are a man, we greatly advise you to not skip the next chapter titled "DIVINE FEMININE". Even though it talks about women, it applies the same for men. Men too, have feminine energy in them. Both genders are created out of masculine and feminine energies.

Chapter 8

DF - DIVINE FEMININE

"The Divine Feminine is a spiritual concept that has recently gained increased attention. It refers to the feminine energy in all of us, regardless of gender identity, and represents the nurturing, compassionate, and intuitive qualities often associated with femininity."

Praise of masculine energy in a society led to imbalance and lack of harmony. This is why the importance of the Divine Feminine lies in its ability to create balance with the long-valued masculine energy that governs strength, power, and control, often at the expense of feminine qualities. By embracing sacred femininity, we can tap into personal and collective sensuality, softness, inner creativity, compassion, and courage. At the same time, the Divine Feminine refers to collaboration and empathy. This is why everyone —not just women—gendered or not—needs to connect to their feminine energies and explore the Divine Feminine. Feminized men and masculinized women means imbalance. Both genders must fully embrace and honor their gender's attributes/qualities.

"The Divine Feminine is a way of describing a universal, archetypal energy associated with the nurturing, creative, and life-giving aspects of the universe. It is an energy present in all things and not limited to any particular gender, culture, or belief system." **- Dr. Amy Hale.**

Roots and history of the Divine Feminine

The concept of the Divine Feminine has its roots in ancient cultures and traditions, where the feminine was revered and celebrated. In many indigenous cultures, the Earth was seen as a nurturing mother figure, and the feminine was associated with the cycles of nature, creation, and intuition.

In ancient Egypt, the goddess Isis was worshipped as the Divine Feminine, representing motherhood, fertility, and healing. She was seen as the embodiment of feminine energy, and her worship continued for thousands of years. In some modern-day pagan and Wiccan traditions, Isis is still revered and worshipped as a powerful goddess.

In ancient Greek mythology, many powerful goddesses such as Athena, Artemis, and Aphrodite were seen as the embodiment of the Divine Feminine. In Hinduism, the goddesses Durga, Kali, and Lakshmi represent different aspects of the Divine Feminine, from creation to destruction and abundance. Despite the worshiping of the Divine Feminine in ancient cultures, over time, the patriarchal system has suppressed feminine qualities and the rise of masculine energy.

However, in recent years, there has been a resurgence of interest in the Divine Feminine, with many people recognizing the need to balance masculine and feminine energies in everyday life.

Gendered terminology

"Masculine" and "feminine" are often used to describe certain characteristics or energies traditionally associated with men and women, respectively. These terms are used to describe qualities such as strength, assertiveness, and logic as masculine, while qualities such as nurturing, intuition, and emotion are considered feminine.

However, it's important to note that these gendered terms are not necessarily limited to biological sex, as anyone can embody qualities associated with either gender.

Additionally, it's crucial to recognize that gender roles and stereotypes are social constructs that have been reinforced by society rather than inherent qualities of biological sex.

Regarding spiritual practices, "masculine" and "feminine" are often used to describe different energies rather than gender. Masculine energy is associated with action, structure, and the outward expression of power, while feminine energy is linked to intuition, creativity, and the inward nurturing of oneself and others.

While it's important to recognize the different energies associated with masculinity and femininity, it's crucial to avoid limiting oneself or others based on these gendered terms. Instead, we should strive to balance these energies, embracing the strengths and qualities of the Divine Feminine and Divine Masculine. The **concepts of yin and yang** can help to establish balance between masculine and feminine energies. In traditional Chinese philosophy, yin energy represents feminine energy, characterized by receptivity, softness, and introspection. Yang, on the other hand, represents masculine energy, characterized by qualities such as activity, strength, and assertiveness.

Qualities of the Divine Feminine

The Divine Feminine is often associated with intuition, nurturing, creativity, empathy, and wisdom. These qualities are not limited to women but are attributes that anyone can embody, regardless of gender.

By embracing the qualities of the Divine Feminine, we can enhance our spiritual journey and bring more balance into our lives.

Some examples of the Divine Feminine qualities in everyday life include:

- Nurturing oneself and others through self-care practices, such as meditation, **yoga**, or time in nature.
- Using intuition and empathy to connect with others and to make decisions that align with our inner voice.
- Expressing creativity through art, music, or other forms of self-expression.
- Embracing wisdom and inner knowledge guides our actions and cultivates a deeper understanding of ourselves and the world around us.
- Practicing compassion and forgiveness towards ourselves and others as we navigate our spiritual journey.

By incorporating these qualities into our daily lives, we can awaken the Divine Feminine within ourselves and connect with the energy of the sacred feminine.

Benefits of connecting to the Divine Feminine

Connecting to the energy of the Divine Feminine can bring a range of benefits to our spiritual, emotional, and physical well-being.

- **Increased self-awareness**
- Enhanced creativity
- **Greater compassion** and empathy
- Increased balance and harmony
- Greater **connection to nature**
- Greater sense of purpose

How to connect to the Divine Feminine

Connecting to the energy of the Divine Feminine can be a deeply transformative and enriching experience.
Here are some spiritual practices that can help you connect with this energy:

Meditation

By quieting the mind and focusing inward, you can become more attuned to the subtle energies of the universe and the feminine aspects of your being.

Yoga

Through **yoga postures**, breathwork, and **meditation**, you can tap into the energy flow within your body and connect with the universal flow of feminine energy.

Chakra work

Working with the **chakras**, particularly the heart and sacral chakras, can awaken the feminine aspects of your being. Later on, there is a big chapter divided in 7 parts for all chakras including 5, 15 and 30min meditation practice/techniques for each individual chakra/energy center.

Spend time in nature

Being in nature can help you connect with the natural rhythms of the mother earth. By immersing yourself in the beauty and serenity of nature, you can align yourself with the creative forces of the universe and the nurturing energy of the Divine Feminine.

Create a sacred space

Dedicating a physical space in your home or elsewhere to your spiritual practice, creates a sanctuary where you can connect with the sacred femininity. Only in solitude will you be able to connect with your true self, especially through meditation practices.

Work with crystals

Certain crystals, such as rose quartz, moonstone, and amethyst, are associated with Divine Feminine energy and can be used to facilitate a connection with this energy by carrying or wearing these **chakra crystals** or incorporating them into your meditation or ritual practices.

Explore goddess archetypes

The Divine Feminine is often associated with goddess archetypes, such as Isis, Kuan Yin, or Lakshmi. By exploring these archetypes and learning about their qualities and attributes, you can deepen your connection to the Divine Feminine and better understand your feminine energy.

Honor the cycles of the moon

The moon cycles can be used to enhance the connection to the feminine. Observing the moon's phases and engaging in practices that align with each phase, such as meditation, journaling, or ritual, can deepen your connection to the Divine Feminine.

Connect with other women

Connecting with other women is a powerful way to tap into the feminine energy. By sharing experiences, supporting each other, and celebrating the feminine qualities within each other, you can create a community that nourishes and supports your connection.

Journaling

Journaling can be a powerful way to connect with the Divine Feminine within yourself. By writing down your thoughts, feelings, and experiences, you can become more self-aware and gain insight into your feminine energy. You can also use **journaling** to explore your connection to the Divine Feminine and record any spiritual experiences or insights you may have.

Self-awareness and self-love

Cultivating self-awareness and self-love is essential for connecting with the Divine Feminine. By developing a deeper understanding and acceptance of yourself, you can embrace your own feminine energy and connect with the universal flow of feminine energy.

Mindfulness, self-reflection, and self-compassion can help you cultivate these qualities and deepen your connection.

Divine Energy and Kundalini

One way the Divine Feminine energy is manifested is through the awakening of the **Kundalini**, a dormant energy that lies at the base of the spine. When this energy is awakened, it travels up through the chakras, or energy centers bringing about a range of powerful physical, emotional, and spiritual experiences. The role of the Divine Feminine in the **Kundalini awakening** process is often emphasized in spiritual traditions. It is said that the feminine energy is responsible for nurturing and guiding the Kundalini energy as it rises through the chakras. This energy is often depicted as a coiled serpent, symbolizing the potential for transformation and awakening within us.

In many spiritual practices, specific techniques are used to awaken the **Kundalini energy**. These may include meditation, breathwork, yoga, and other practices that focus on balancing and activating the energy centers in the body. However, it is important to approach these practices with caution and guidance from a qualified teacher.

Divine Feminine today

In today's world, there is a growing recognition of the importance of the Divine Feminine, both in spiritual practice and in wider society. Many people seek to reconnect with this energy to find greater balance and harmony in their lives.

One of the key reasons for this is the recognition that traditional gender roles and stereotypes have created imbalances in society and that there is a need for greater respect and recognition of the feminine.

Many people see a connection between the Divine Feminine and the planet itself. As the earth faces increasing threats from climate change and environmental degradation, there is a growing awareness that we need to reconnect with the natural world and find ways to live in greater harmony. The feminine qualities of nurturing, caring, and connection to the earth are seen as essential for this work.

Conclusion

The Divine Feminine has a rich history and a powerful presence in spiritual and mystical practices worldwide. By reconnecting with this energy and embracing its qualities, we can find greater balance, harmony, and meaning in our lives. In a world shaped by traditional gender roles and stereotypes, there is a growing recognition of the need for greater respect and recognition of the feminine. By embracing the Divine Feminine and working to bring balance to our lives and our relationship with the planet, we can create a more sustainable and harmonious world for all. Only a woman can dance with two hearts. Only she can breathe with four lungs.

Only a woman is able to carry in her belly the weight of two worlds (hers and that of the child). The woman is the only being that can birth a life from the spiritual world onto this one. Women must be protected at all cost. And how are women protected? By men when their divine masculine is fully realized. Men are the protectors while women are the nurturers. It's how a child can have a strong intelligent free and prosperous future, by being raised with fully realized divine masculine and divine feminine parents.

Wounded Feminine

Wounded feminine energy is what is expressed when the raw, life-giving, erotic, transformative energy of the feminine has been suppressed, shamed, or denied. The wounded feminine can manifest in:

Low self-esteem,
difficulties setting boundaries,
shame around sex and
eroticism.

It also emerges through the systemic repression of women, everyday sexism and rape culture. Because of the resulting wounds, only distortions of feminine energy are able to emerge. Again, these distortions show up on a personal level, manifesting in the lives of individuals. But they also show up collectively. This is the female shadow. This wounding can happen on an individual scale, but it's prevalent on a much larger scale too. In the West, the true essence of the feminine has been systematically suppressed over many generations.

The wounded feminine is *everywhere.* And it's nearly impossible to separate the wounded feminine from cultural "femininity" because our media and modern Western culture *actually celebrate* many of these wounded traits. For example: being busy *all the time*, being highly independent, and of course, appearing eternally youthful (*hello anti-wrinkle cream advert!*)

6 key causes of wounded feminine energy are:

1. **Lack of self-love and self-care**
2. **Lack of support and validation from others**
3. **Trauma or abuse**
4. **Cultural conditioning and societal expectations**
5. **Repression of emotions and feelings**
6. **Perfectionism and people-pleasing**

Healed Feminine

How to heal wounded feminine energy. After you've identified wounded feminine energy in your life, first off, be with it. Hope yourself in a compassionate embrace. Healing is not only possible for you, *but you were also born to do it!* Know that it's *imperative* for the human collective that you begin the healing process FOR the feminine. For the women who came before you, *the women here with you*, and the women who will come after you. **The Goddess** has called you forth, so it's time.

Work with the feminine is *process based* – there's little point in aiming for the endpoint! Ultimately, you will heal the wounded feminine by dropping deeply into the present moment and being with what IS in each unfolding moment. Begin to unravel the conditioning that has wounded the feminine *so deeply* and allow the

re-emergence of real feminine power. Connect with nature.
Healing feminine energy can be as simple as spending time in nature. Whether it's a park, forest, or beach, make time to connect *deeply* with Mother Nature. This is especially important if you feel over-run with masculine energy (to function in our culture, this does tend to dominate).
The Great Mother is exceedingly good at recalibrating and returning balance to the masculine and feminine within.

Next try this: How to Embody the Wild Woman Archetype
Practice self-care. Every healing journey needs plenty of self-care.
If you're suffering from exhaustion (always feeling tired?) this is a tell-tale sign that your natural feminine traits are being shunned in favor of more masculine energy. You MUST take care of yourself physically, mentally, and emotionally. Get enough rest, eat healthy, and engage in activities that bring you joy. Practice forgiveness

Let go of past hurts and grudges, and practice forgiveness towards yourself and others. This isn't about pretending that abuses of the past didn't happen. Forgiveness is for YOU. It will release you from the bonds of anger and resentment that keep you and your feminine energy trapped.

Embrace your emotions, allow yourself to feel and express your feelings and emotions without judgment or shame. Increasing your capacity to hold the full spectrum of your emotions will also mean that you are less likely to collapse or explode when things get tough.
Explore your creativity. One of the primary functions of feminine energy is to create! Engage in creative activities that allow you to express yourself and find your own authentic voice. Create art, use paints, use your body, use anything you can find! Feminine energy needs to move, so give it somewhere to go!

Chapter 9

SEXUAL TRANSMUTATION

"Sexual energy should be wisely grown, prudently cultivated, and profitably expressed. Learn the art of sexual Transmutation, and channeling the sexual energy from root chakra to crown chakra." – **Hendrith Vanlon Smith**

Sexual energy transmutation involves transforming sexual energy into a more elevated drive, motivation, or energy. Before diving into sexual transmutation, let's explore the concept of sexual energy by visualizing the seven chakras.

Within the body, there are seven energy centers called chakras. These chakras are often described as "whirling wheels of light" and each one corresponds to a specific gland in the endocrine system.

Sexual energy is a vital component of your life force, originating from either the first chakra or root chakra, as well as the second chakra or sacral chakra. Your reproductive glands are associated with the root chakra, while the adrenals are connected to the sacral chakra.

The seven chakras are interconnected by a spiraling energy pathway known as kundalini, which ascends through the body. The foundation of this entire energy system is derived from the base, where sexual energy resides.

The sacral chakra governs the realm of pleasure. When this chakra is in equilibrium, the pursuit of sexual pleasure is maintained within reasonable limits. When the sexual energy center is blocked or weakened, it can result in a variety of issues such as sex addictions, perversions, porn addictions, depression, and aggressive behavior. The flow of sexual energy is limited to two directions. It can either be expressed through sexual activities and desires, dissipating through the sex organs, or it can be transmuted and directed towards the higher energy centers.

Transforming sexual energy involves harnessing its power and directing it towards a higher energy center. The solar plexus chakra, positioned above the sacral chakra, governs willpower and serves as the ideal channel for this process.

In the case of a person lacking willpower, it is quite likely that their sexual energy is being drained through excessive engagement in sex, masturbation, over-stimulation, desire, worry, overthinking, or other unsupportive habits.

There are 7 primary motives for transforming sexual energy. The Kundalini/Spiritual aspect is the main focus of our books. We advocate a lifestyle that involves transmuting sexual energy to awaken the Kundalini or the inner dragon.

Transforming Sexual Energy: 7 Compelling Reasons

1. Kundalini/Spiritual Awakening
2. Improve Your Physical Health, Strength, and Power
3. Cultivate More Physical Energy
4. Unlock More Creativity
5. Achieve Material Success
6. Develop Martial and Internal Power
7. Mental Clarity, Strength, and Focus

The focus with this particular chapter will be on using this energy to enhance creativity and attain material success, as seen through the eyes of Napoleon Hill.

Before diving into the subject matter, it is important to acknowledge what blocks sexual transmutation. Sexual energy transmutation is an innate process that occurs naturally. If we fail to convert this energy into creative energy and willpower, it indicates that there is an obstruction or misdirection of this powerful force. Buddhists refer to this misdirection as indulgence, while Taoists label it as leakage. Essentially, our life force seeps out of us. The primary goal of meditation and internal alchemical practices in the East is to prevent this leakage.

The mind is the root cause of this leakage, which arises from random thoughts and negative emotions such as anger, fear, and guilt. (Guilt, in particular, obstructs the sacral chakra). According to Tibetan Buddhism, human suffering originates from the Three Poisons: Desire, Aversion, and Ignorance. Energetic leakage is caused by all three poisons.

> **"The transmutation of sexual desire drives the creative imagination"** – Napoleon Hill

The Mystery of Sex: Transmutation

In simple terms, "transmute" means to change or transfer one element or form of energy into another. The feeling of sex gives rise to a specific state of mind.

Due to a lack of understanding on the matter, this mindset is commonly linked to the physical realm. Moreover, the mind has been significantly influenced by improper sources when it comes to gaining knowledge about sex, resulting in a strong inclination towards purely physical aspects.

Sexual emotion encompasses three powerful potentials:

1. The continuation of the human race.
2. Serving as an unparalleled therapeutic tool for maintaining good health.
3. The remarkable capacity to convert mediocrity into genius through transmutation.

Sex transmutation is a straightforward concept that can be easily understood. It involves shifting the focus of the mind from thoughts of physical desires to thoughts of a different kind.

The human desire for sex is unparalleled in its power. When this desire takes hold, it unlocks a profound sense of imagination, courage, determination, and creativity that remains dormant otherwise. Such is the strength and urgency of this desire that men are willing to risk their lives and reputations to satisfy it.

By effectively harnessing and redirecting this powerful driving force, its original attributes of imaginative prowess, courage, and more remain intact. These exceptional qualities can be utilized as potent creative forces in literature, art, or any other profession, ultimately leading to the accumulation of wealth and success.

The transformation of sexual energy necessitates the use of willpower, but the benefits far outweigh the exertion. The natural and inherent desire for sexual expression should not be repressed or eradicated. Instead, it should be directed towards forms of expression that enhance the physical, mental, and spiritual aspects of humanity. Without this outlet, if not transmuted, the desire will seek release solely through physical avenues. The serpent is a symbol of renewal/transformation. When you allow your whole being to be exposed to the unlimited knowledge that you possess within, the kundalini/serpent will rise without obstruction. A river can be obstructed and its flow controlled temporarily, but eventually, it will find a way to break free. The same principle applies to the powerful force of sexual emotion. Although it can be suppressed and managed for a while, its inherent nature drives it to constantly seek avenues of expression.

If not channeled into a productive endeavor, it will inevitably find a less noble outlet. The person who has learned to harness sexual energy in a creative pursuit is indeed fortunate, as this discovery raises them to the level of a genius.

Scientific studies have revealed these important findings:

1. The men of greatest achievement are men with highly developed sex natures; men who have learned the art of sex transmutation.
2. The men who have accumulated great fortunes and achieved outstanding recognition in literature, art, industry, architecture, and the professions, were motivated by the influence of a woman.

Over the course of two millennia, extensive research delved into the realms of biography and history to uncover these remarkable findings. The evidence gathered from the lives of exceptional individuals consistently pointed towards one undeniable truth – their profound cultivation of their sexual nature.

The force of sexuality is an unstoppable power, surpassing any immovable barrier. When directed by this force, men are granted exceptional abilities to act decisively. Acknowledge this truth, and you will appreciate the importance of the assertion that converting sexual energy can elevate an individual to the stature of a genius. Creative ability is intricately linked to the powerful emotion of sex. By eliminating the sex glands, whether in humans or animals, the primary catalyst for action is effectively eradicated.

The evidence of this can be seen by observing the transformation that occurs in any animal after it undergoes castration. Once sexually altered, a bull becomes as calm and gentle as a cow, losing all the aggression that was once present in its nature. Similarly, altering the sex of a female has an identical impact.

"The individuals of greatest achievement tend to be those who have highly developed sexual natures and who have learned the art of sex transmutation" – Napoleon Hill

The Ten Mental Triggers

1. The desire for sex expression
2. Love
3. A burning desire for fame, power, or financial gain, MONEY
4. Music
5. Friendship between either those of the same sex, or those of the opposite sex.
6. A Master Mind alliance based upon the harmony of two or more people who ally themselves for spiritual or temporal advancement.
7. Mutual suffering, such as that experienced by people who are persecuted.
8. Auto-suggestion
9. Fear
10. Narcotics and alcohol.

The urge for sexual expression tops the list of stimuli that can significantly elevate mental vibrations and set physical actions in motion. Included in this list are eight stimuli that are natural and constructive, as well as two that are destructive.

The intention behind presenting this list is to provide you with the opportunity to engage in a comparative study of the primary sources of mental stimulation. Through this study, it becomes evident that the emotion of sex surpasses all others in terms of intensity and influence on the mind.

This comparison serves as an essential basis for substantiating the claim that the transformation of sexual energy can propel an individual to the esteemed status of a genius. Let us now explore the characteristics that constitute a genius. As humorously stated by someone, a genius is an individual who embraces long hair, indulges in peculiar cuisine, leads a solitary existence, and becomes a favorite subject for jesters. A genius can be defined as someone who has unlocked the ability to elevate their thoughts to a higher frequency, enabling them to connect with sources of wisdom beyond the usual level of thinking vibrations.

The person who thinks will want to ask some questions concerning this definition of genius. The first question will be, "***How may one communicate with sources of knowledge which are not available through the ORDINARY rate of vibration of thought***?"

The next question will be, "***Are there known sources of knowledge which are available only to genii, and if so, WHAT ARE THESE SOURCES, and exactly how may they be reached***?"

We will provide evidence to support key points mentioned in this article, or we will provide you with the means to conduct your own experiments for verification. By doing this, we will address both of these inquiries.

> **"It may be controversial contention, but sexual energy is the creative energy of virtually all geniuses. There never has been and never will be a great leader, builder, or artist lacking in this driving force of sex".**

The Sixth Sense is the Key to Developing True Genius.

The concept of a "sixth sense," (sixth sense is derived from the "third eye") specifically "Creative Imagination," is well-established. The majority of individuals never tap into this faculty, and if they do, it is often accidental. A small percentage of people actively and intentionally use the faculty of creative imagination. Those who do so with awareness of its functions are considered geniuses.

The faculty of creative imagination serves as the direct connection between the limited human mind and the boundless Infinite Intelligence. Within the realm of religion, what are commonly known as revelations, as well as the unveiling of fundamental or innovative principles in the realm of invention, all stem from the power of creative imagination. Ideas or concepts that suddenly appear in the mind, often referred to as a "hunch," can originate from the following sources:

1. Infinite Intelligence
2. One's subconscious mind, wherein is stored every sense impression and thought impulse which ever reached the brain through any of the five senses
3. From the mind of some other person who has just released the thought, or picture of the idea or concept, through conscious thought
4. From the other person's subconscious storehouse

No other sources that are recognized exist from which one can receive "inspired" ideas or "hunches". The optimal functioning of the creative imagination occurs when the mind is vibrating at an exceptionally high rate, which is higher than that of ordinary, everyday thinking.

When the brain is stimulated using one or more of the ten mind stimulants, it has the remarkable ability to transport the individual beyond the boundaries of conventional thinking. This enables them to explore the vast expanse of thoughts, encompassing distance, breadth, and excellence, which are not readily accessible during the usual problem-solving activities of business and professional life. By elevating one's thinking to a higher plane, whether through mental stimulation or any other means, an individual attains a perspective akin to that of someone soaring in an airplane, able to gaze beyond the horizon and expand their vision beyond the confines of the ground. Create happiness and good memories with your thoughts.

Furthermore, at this heightened elevated plane of thinking, the person is unrestricted and unburdened by any external influences that confine and restrict their perspective while grappling with the challenges of acquiring the fundamental essentials of sustenance, attire, and housing. They exist in a realm of contemplation where the commonplace, everyday thoughts have been eradicated just as the geographical features and other visual constraints vanish from sight when one ascends in an aircraft.

In this elevated plane of THOUGHT, the mind's creative potential is unleashed. With the sixth sense activated, it becomes receptive to ideas that would remain out of reach in any other circumstance. This exceptional faculty is what separates a genius from an average individual.

The creative faculty's alertness and receptivity to external vibrations from beyond the subconscious mind increase with frequent use. Relying on this faculty and making demands for thought impulses further strengthens its capabilities. Cultivating and developing this faculty is only possible through consistent utilization. The conscience, also known as the sixth sense, operates entirely through this faculty. The path to greatness is paved by the remarkable artists, writers, musicians, and poets who embrace the habit of depending on their inner "still small voice." This voice communicates through their faculty of creative imagination, and individuals with vibrant imaginations are well aware that their most remarkable ideas often materialize as intuitive "hunches."

There is a great orator who does not attain to greatness, until he closes his eyes and begins to rely entirely upon the faculty of Creative Imagination. When asked why he closed his eyes just before the climaxes of his oratory, he replied, "I do it, because, then I speak through ideas which come to me from within." Renowned for his financial prowess, one of America's most accomplished and widely recognized financiers had a peculiar habit of closing his eyes for a brief period before reaching a decision. When questioned about this practice, he confidently stated, "By shutting my eyes, I tap into a wellspring of exceptional intelligence."

Dr. Elmer R. Gates, the esteemed inventor from Chevy Chase, Maryland, harnessed and nurtured his creative abilities, resulting in over 200 valuable patents, several of which were groundbreaking.

Dr. Gates, without a doubt, belonged to the category of geniuses, making his method both noteworthy and captivating for those aspiring to attain such status. Among the world's truly exceptional scientists, Dr. Gates stood as a remarkable figure, albeit less recognized. Within his laboratory, he maintained a designated space known as his "personal communication room."

The room was designed to be completely soundproof, with the ability to block out all light. It featured a small table where he placed a notepad for writing. Mounted on the wall in front of the table was an electric pushbutton to control the lights.

Dr. Gates would enter the room, take a seat at the table, turn off the lights, and focus on the familiar aspects of his invention. He would stay in this position until new ideas started to emerge in his mind regarding the unfamiliar elements of the invention.

Ideas flooded in rapidly, leading him to write non-stop for nearly three hours. Upon reviewing his notes, he discovered a detailed description of principles unlike anything found in the scientific community.

Additionally, the solution to his dilemma was cleverly outlined in those documents. Dr. Gates finalized more than 200 patents that were initiated by less capable individuals. Proof of this can be found in the United States Patent Office. By offering his services as an "idea generator," Dr. Gates secured his livelihood. Numerous prominent American corporations were willing to pay him substantial fees per hour for his expertise in brainstorming and providing innovative solutions.

The reasoning faculty frequently proves to be flawed as it heavily relies on one's past experiences. It is important to note that not all knowledge gained through "experience" is entirely accurate. On the other hand, ideas derived from the creative faculty are far more dependable as they originate from sources that are more reliable than those accessible to the reasoning faculty of the mind. The distinction between a genius and an ordinary "crank" inventor lies in their utilization of the faculty of creative imagination. While the genius harnesses this ability, the "crank" inventor remains oblivious to it. Notably, scientific inventors like Mr. Edison and Dr. Gates employ both synthetic and creative faculties of imagination.

The scientific inventor for example, commonly referred to as a "genius," initiates the process of inventing by systematically arranging and merging existing ideas or principles that have been acquired through experience and logical reasoning. In the event that this pool of accumulated knowledge falls short in bringing the invention to fruition, the inventor taps into their creative faculty to access additional sources of knowledge.

The manner in which he achieves this objective varies depending on the individual, but this is the core of his process:

1. **HE STIMULATES HIS MIND SO THAT IT VIBRATES ON A HIGHER-THAN AVERAGE PLANE**, using one or more of the ten mind stimulants or some other stimulant of his choice.

2. **HE CONCENTRATES** upon the known factors (the

> finished part) of his invention, and creates in his mind a perfect picture of unknown factors (the unfinished part), of his invention. He holds this picture in mind until it has been taken over by the subconscious mind, then relaxes by clearing his mind of ALL thought, and waits for his answer to "flash" into his mind.

There are moments when the results are both conclusive and immediate. Conversely, there are occasions when the outcomes are negative, contingent upon the progress of the "sixth sense" or creative faculty.

Mr. Edison diligently experimented with over 10,000 diverse combinations of ideas using his imaginative synthetic faculty before he eventually tapped into his creative ability and discovered the breakthrough for the incandescent light. The same pattern emerged during his invention of the talking machine.

The human mind possesses a remarkable capacity to respond to various forms of stimulation, and among the most significant and potent stimuli is the innate drive for sexual gratification.

When harnessed and transformed, this compelling force has the power to elevate individuals to a superior level of cognitive functioning. It empowers them to conquer the sources of worry and trivial annoyances that hinder their progress on a lower plane of existence.

The status of a genius is exclusively attained by a man who actively stimulates his mind, tapping into the available forces through the creative faculty of imagination. Among the numerous stimuli that can facilitate this amplification of vibrations, sex energy stands out.

However, possessing this energy alone does not guarantee genius status. It is imperative to transmute this energy from a longing for physical contact into a different form of desire and action, as only then can one truly ascend to the realm of genius.

The majority of men, driven by their insatiable sexual desires, often misunderstand and mismanage this incredible force, ultimately reducing themselves to the level of mere animals. It is evident that they are far from attaining any form of greatness.

"Destroy the sex glands; whether in a human being or a beast, and you have removed a major source of action" – **Napoleon Hill**

Later on, you will read a lot more on the pineal gland/third eye subject, two chapters' content that are very important to know and practice.

Why Men Seldom Succeed Before Forty

Through analyzing more than 25,000 individuals, it was found that men who achieve remarkable success typically do not do so until after the age of forty, with many hitting their stride well into their fifties.

This study disclosed the fact that the major reason why the majority of men who succeed do not begin to do so before the age of forty to fifty, is their tendency to DISSIPATE their energies through over indulgence in physical expression of the emotion of sex. The majority of men never learn that the urge of sex has other possibilities, which far transcend in importance, that of mere physical expression.

Most people who come across this realization do it after spending a significant amount of time during their peak sexual energy years, typically before the age of forty-five to fifty. This is often followed by remarkable success.

Many men, even beyond the age of forty, often waste their energies instead of utilizing them in more productive ways. They scatter their intense emotions aimlessly. This behavior led to the phrase "sowing his wild oats."

The strongest and most compelling of all human emotions is the desire for sexual expression. When this desire is channeled and transformed into something other than physical expression, it has the power to elevate an individual to the status of a genius. An accomplished businessman from America openly confessed that his alluring secretary was the driving force behind most of his innovative strategies. He acknowledged that her mere presence elevated his creative imagination to extraordinary heights, surpassing any other form of motivation.

For more than twelve years, a very charming young woman has been the driving force behind the success of one of America's most prominent men. While the man's identity is widely recognized, the true source of his accomplishments is not common knowledge.

Psychologists widely acknowledge the strong correlation between sexual desires and spiritual yearnings. This connection sheds light on the peculiar conduct exhibited by individuals engaging in religious "revivals," particularly prevalent among primitive communities.

Human emotions dictate the world's affairs and shape the destiny of civilization. Actions are driven by "feelings" rather than reason. The creative aspect of the mind is fueled by emotions, not by rationality. The most dominant human emotion is sex. While there are other mental stimulants, none can match the compelling force of sex.

A mind enhancer is any factor that can elevate the frequency of thoughts, either temporarily or permanently. The ten primary enhancers, as explained, are the most frequently utilized ones.

By utilizing these resources, one can connect with Infinite Intelligence or effortlessly access the reservoir of the subconscious mind, whether it be their own or someone else's. This process is the essence of genius.

The teacher, with experience in guiding and supervising over 30,000 salespeople, uncovered a remarkable finding that highly passionate men excel as salesmen. This revelation stems from the understanding that "personal magnetism," a key aspect of one's personality, is essentially derived from sexual energy.

Individuals with a strong sexual drive naturally possess an abundant reserve of magnetism. By nurturing and comprehending this vital force, it can be harnessed and leveraged to foster meaningful connections between individuals.

Others can receive this energy through the following media:

1. *The hand-shake. The touch of the hand indicates, instantly, the presence of magnetism, or the lack of it.*
2. *The tone of voice. Magnetism, or sex energy, is the factor with which the voice may be colored, or made musical and charming.*
3. *Posture and carriage of the body. Highly sexed people move briskly, and with grace and ease.*
4. *The vibrations of thought. Highly sexed people mix the emotion of sex with their thoughts, or may do so at will, and in that way, may influence those around them.*
5. *Body adornment. People who are highly sexed are usually very careful about their personal appearance. They usually select clothing of a style becoming to their personality, physique, complexion, etc.*

The key trait a proficient sales manager seeks in salesmen is personal magnetism. Those lacking sex energy will struggle to ignite enthusiasm in themselves and others, a vital component for effective salesmanship regardless of the product.

A public speaker, orator, preacher, lawyer, or salesman without sex energy will struggle to influence others effectively. Emotions play a crucial role in influencing people, underscoring the importance of sex energy in a salesman's natural abilities.

Master salesmen achieve success by converting sex energy into sales enthusiasm, whether they realize it or not. This idea sheds light on the practical application of sex transmutation.

By shifting his focus from thoughts of sex to his sales endeavors, a salesman can effectively harness the power of sex transmutation, applying the same level of enthusiasm and determination to achieve success in his professional endeavors. Most salesmen unknowingly harness their sexual energy without realizing the process or its effects. The transmutation of sexual energy requires a greater level of willpower than most individuals are willing to exert. However, those who struggle to summon enough willpower for transmutation can gradually develop this ability. Despite requiring strong will-power, the practice is immensely rewarding. The topic of sex seems to be one that the majority of people are shamefully ignorant about. The true nature of sexual desire has been greatly misunderstood, defamed, and ridiculed by those who are ignorant and malicious for such a long time that the word "sex" is rarely mentioned in polite society.

Men and women who are known to possess a highly passionate nature are often viewed with suspicion rather than being recognized as fortunate individuals. Instead of being acknowledged as blessed, they are unjustly labeled as cursed.

Despite living in an era of enlightenment, countless individuals still suffer from inferiority complexes due to the misguided notion that having a strong sexual nature is a curse. It is important to clarify that acknowledging the value of sexual energy does not justify indulging in promiscuity.

The virtue of sexual emotions lies solely in their intelligent and discerning use. Unfortunately, these emotions are frequently misused, leading to a degradation of both the body and mind instead of their enrichment.

The human species stands alone as the only creature on Earth that defies Nature's purpose in this particular matter. Unlike any other animal, every other species indulges in their sexual nature with restraint, in accordance with the laws of nature. While other animals respond to the call of sex only during specific periods, humans have a proclivity to declare an "open season" on their inclinations.

It is common knowledge among the wise that excessive stimulation, whether from alcohol or drugs, is a type of intemperance that wreaks havoc on the body's vital organs, including the brain. Yet not everyone is aware that indulging excessively in sexual expression can also become a destructive habit, just like narcotics or alcohol, and hinder one's creative endeavors.

A man consumed by his sexual desires is no different from a man consumed by drug addiction. In both cases, they have relinquished control over their ability to think and make rational decisions.

Engaging in excessive sexual activities not only impairs one's reasoning and willpower, but it can also result in temporary or even permanent insanity. It is important to note that many cases of hypochondria, or the belief in imaginary illnesses, stem from misconceptions about the true purpose of sex.

The limited mentions of sex transmutation clearly highlight the severe consequences of ignorance on this subject. Ignorance leads to significant penalties for the uninformed, while also denying them substantial benefits. The prevalence of ignorance regarding sex can be attributed to the subject being shrouded in mystery and enveloped in a veil of silence. This conspiracy of secrecy and silence has had a similar impact on the minds of young individuals as the psychological effects of prohibition.

The outcome has sparked a heightened sense of curiosity and a strong urge to gain further understanding on this forbidden topic. It is disheartening that lawmakers and even most physicians, who are the most knowledgeable in educating young minds about this subject, have not made information readily accessible. The dark sorcerers who still (not for much longer) hold dominion over our world are deliberately hiding the profound power of transmuting sexual energy from humanity.

Their primary aim is to keep humanity confined to their lower instincts and ignorant of their spiritual and creative capacities, as this aligns with their agenda of enslavement.

Few individuals engage in significant creative efforts in any field before reaching the age of forty. On average, people reach their peak creative potential between forty and sixty, as evidenced by the careful observation of thousands of men and women.

These insights should offer encouragement to those who haven't found success by forty and those who fear growing older around this age. The years between forty and fifty are typically the most fruitful, so one should approach this stage of life with hope and anticipation. Most men do not reach their peak performance until after the age of forty, as evidenced by the success stories of prominent figures in American history. Henry Ford and Andrew Carnegie both achieved their greatest accomplishments after reaching this milestone.

James J. Hill continued to operate a telegraph key even at the age of forty, but his greatest accomplishments occurred after that milestone. Biographies of American business magnates often highlight the ages between forty and sixty as the most productive period in a person's life.

It is during the years of thirty to forty that individuals start to grasp the concept of sex transmutation, if they ever do. The revelation is generally accidental, and more frequently than not, the person who stumbles upon it is completely unaware of their discovery.

They may notice that their abilities to achieve have increased around the age of thirty-five to forty, but in most cases, they are unfamiliar with the cause of this change; Nature begins to harmonize the emotions of love and sex within the individual between the ages of thirty and forty, enabling them to draw upon these powerful forces and apply them jointly as stimuli for action.

Sex, on its own, exerts a formidable urge that compels us to act, yet its forces can be as uncontrollable as a cyclone. However, when love intertwines with sexual desire, it results in a calmness of purpose, composure, precise judgment, and equilibrium.

Is there anyone over the age of forty who hasn't had the opportunity to analyze these statements and validate them based on their own personal experiences?

A man's actions driven by the desire to please a woman through sex alone can lead to great achievements, but they may also be chaotic, warped, and harmful. However, when love is added to the mix, his behavior becomes more rational, stable, and thoughtful.

> "The major difference between love and sex is that love is spiritual, while sex is biological. Love is chemistry; sex is physics."
> – **Napoleon Hill**

Criminologists have made a remarkable discovery that the influence of a woman's love can reform even the most hardened criminals. It is worth noting that there is no documented case of a criminal being reformed solely through the influence of sex.

While these facts are widely known, the underlying cause remains a mystery. Reformation, if it occurs, stems from the heart and emotions of an individual, rather than their rational thinking.

Reformation is synonymous with "a change of heart," not a "change of head." While reason may lead a person to alter their behavior to avoid negative outcomes, true reformation can only occur through a genuine desire for change. Love, Romance, and Sex are powerful emotions that can propel individuals to great accomplishments. Love acts as a stabilizing force, ensuring equilibrium, composure, and productive action. When these emotions are combined, they have the potential to elevate someone to a level of genius.

Amongst the geniuses, there exist individuals who possess limited understanding of love. Many of them are preoccupied with activities that are either destructive or lack fairness towards others.

If it were appropriate, we could easily identify twelve geniuses in the domains of industry and finance who unscrupulously trample upon the rights of their peers. They exhibit a complete lack of conscience. Readers can effortlessly compile their own list of such individuals.

Emotions are the various states of mind that individuals experience. Just as the principles of chemistry govern the interactions of matter, nature has equipped humans with a "chemistry of the mind."

It is widely known that a chemist can create a deadly poison by combining certain elements, even if each element is harmless individually. Similarly, emotions can be combined in a manner that produces a lethal poison. When the emotions of sex and jealousy intertwine, they have the ability to transform an individual into a raging beast.

The presence of any one or more of the destructive emotions in the human mind, through the chemistry of the mind, sets up a poison which may destroy one's sense of justice and fairness.

In extreme cases, the presence of any combination of these emotions in the mind may destroy one's reason. The road to genius consists of the development, control, and use of sex, love, and romance. Briefly, the process may be stated as follows:

Embrace these emotions as the prevailing thoughts in your mind, while rejecting all destructive emotions. The mind is a creature of habit and thrives on the thoughts it is fed. By exercising your willpower, you can discourage the presence of any emotion and encourage the presence of others. Controlling your mind through the power of will is not a difficult task. It requires persistence and the formation of positive habits. The key to control lies in understanding the process of transmutation. Whenever a negative emotion arises, you can transform it into a positive or constructive emotion by simply changing your thoughts.

The path to genius lies solely in voluntary self-effort! While a person may achieve great financial or business success through the power of sex energy, history shows that they often carry certain character traits that prevent them from maintaining or truly enjoying their fortune.

This truth is worth analyzing, contemplating, and reflecting upon, as it holds valuable insights for both women and men. Countless individuals have lost their chance at HAPPINESS, despite their wealth, due to ignorance of this fact. The emotions of love and sex leave their unmistakable marks upon the features. Moreover, these signs are so visible, that all who wish may read them. The man who is driven by the storm of passion, based upon sex desires alone, plainly advertises that fact to the entire world, by the expression of his eyes, and the lines of his face.

The emotion of love, when mixed with the emotion of sex, softens, modifies, and beautifies the facial expression. No character analyst is needed to tell you this- you may observe it for yourself.

Love, with its profound impact, awakens and nurtures the artistic and aesthetic side of individuals. It imprints itself on the very essence of one's being, persisting even when time and circumstances have dampened its intensity.

> **Love's memories never fade away; they linger, providing guidance and exerting influence long after the initial inspiration has waned. This is a universal truth known to all who have experienced genuine love, as it leaves an indelible mark on the human heart.**

The enduring effect of love stems from its spiritual nature. A person who remains unaffected by love's power to propel them to great achievements is devoid of hope and essentially lifeless, despite outward appearances.

The mere memories of love have the ability to uplift one's creative pursuits to a higher realm. Love's mighty force may exhaust itself and fade away, like a fire that has consumed itself, yet it leaves behind everlasting imprints as a testament to its passage.

The departure of love often serves as a catalyst, preparing the human heart for an even greater and more profound connection. Take moments to revisit your yesterdays and indulge your thoughts in the exquisite memories of past love, allowing them to nourish your soul.

Indulging in this will alleviate the impact of current concerns and irritations. It will provide you with a means to detach from the unpleasant aspects of reality, and perhaps, unexpectedly, your mind may conceive thoughts, ideas, or strategies that could revolutionize your financial or spiritual well-being during this temporary sojourn into the realm of imagination.

Don't consider yourself unfortunate for experiencing love and loss. True love can never be fully lost. Love is unpredictable and temporary, arriving and departing unexpectedly. Embrace and savor the present moment, but don't waste your energy fretting over its eventual end. Worrying will never bring it back. Moreover, let go of the notion that love only comes around once. Love can enter and exit our lives countless times, yet each experience impacts us uniquely. While one love may leave a profound mark on our hearts, all love experiences have their own value, except for those who harbor resentment and cynicism when love departs.

Disappointment in love can be avoided if individuals grasp the distinction between love and sex. Love is spiritual, while sex is biological. Any experience that deeply impacts the heart in a spiritual manner is not harmful, unless fueled by ignorance or jealousy.

Love is, without question, life's greatest experience. It brings one into communion with Infinite Intelligence. When mixed with the emotions of romance and sex, it may lead one far up the ladder of creative effort.

The emotions of love, sex, and romance are sides of the eternal triangle of achievement-building genius. Nature creates genii through no other force. Love is a multifaceted emotion that encompasses a wide range of aspects, shades, and tones.

The 'love' one experiences for their parents or children is vastly different from the love they feel for their significant other. The latter is intertwined with the intensity of physical desire, while the former is not. Additionally, the love found in true friendship is distinct from the love felt for a romantic partner, parents, or children, yet it is still a genuine form of love. Love for inanimate objects, like the appreciation of Nature's creations, is one form of emotion. However, the most intense and passionate love arises from the fusion of love and desire. Marriages lacking the eternal bond of love, harmoniously combined with desire, cannot truly be happy and rarely last.

Love alone cannot guarantee marital bliss, nor can desire alone. It is the perfect blend of these two exquisite emotions that can bring about a state of mind in marriage, closest to the spiritual realm one can experience on this earthly plane. The fusion of romance, love, and sex eliminates the barriers between the limited human mind and the boundless Infinite Intelligence. It is in this moment that true genius is born! This narrative diverges greatly from the typical associations with sexual emotions.

It offers an interpretation that elevates this emotion beyond the ordinary, transforming it into a divine tool in the hands of God, shaping all that is magnificent and uplifting. When comprehended correctly, this interpretation has the power to restore harmony in countless marriages plagued by chaos. The disharmony commonly seen as nagging can typically be linked to a lack of knowledge about sex. In marriages where there is love, romance, and a proper understanding of the emotional and physical aspects of sex, there is no discord between partners. A husband is truly fortunate when his wife comprehends the genuine connection between love, sex, and romance. With the influence of this sacred trio, every task, no matter how humble, becomes a labor of love, devoid of any burden. The saying goes that a man's wife can either build him up or tear him down, but the underlying reason is often overlooked. The power to shape a man's destiny lies in his wife's understanding, or lack thereof, of love, sex, and romance.

Despite men's inherent polygamous tendencies, it remains true that no other woman holds as much sway over a man as his wife, unless he is unfortunate enough to be married to someone who is completely incompatible with his nature.

> "If a woman allows her husband to lose interest in her and seek fulfillment elsewhere, it is typically due to her ignorance or apathy towards matters of intimacy, affection, and passion. However, it is important to note that this assertion assumes that there was once genuine love between the man and his wife. The same applies if the man allows her wife to lose interest in him. When there is love and genuine connection/interest, a woman and a man are enough for each other. When you seek external gratification, it is an indication that you feel some form of emptiness in you"

The truth applies just as much to a man who lets his wife's affection for him fade away. Couples in marriage frequently argue over minor matters. Upon closer examination, the root of the issue is often revealed to be apathy or lack of knowledge on these topics.

The primary driving force for men is their wish to make women happy! In ancient times, the most skilled hunters succeeded due to their aspiration to impress women. In this regard, man's nature remains unchanged.

In modern times, the way men seek to win a woman's affection has evolved significantly. Instead of bringing home animal skins like hunters of the past, men now strive to please women by providing luxurious clothing, fancy cars, and wealth.

This desire to please women has remained unchanged since the beginning of civilization. However, the methods employed to fulfill this desire have undergone a transformation. Men today accumulate vast fortunes and achieve immense power and fame primarily to satisfy their longing to please women.

Remove women from the equation, and the vast majority of men would find little value in immense wealth. It is the intrinsic longing of men to please women that empowers women to either build up or tear down a man. A woman who comprehends the nature of men and skillfully attends to it, has no reason to worry about competition from other women. While men may appear formidable and resolute when interacting with their fellow men, they can be effortlessly handled by the women they choose.

The majority of men are hesitant to admit that they can be influenced by the women they favor, as they inherently strive to assert their dominance as the stronger sex. Furthermore, perceptive women are aware of this trait and tactfully choose not to bring attention to it.

Certain men acknowledge that they are being influenced by the women in their lives – whether it's their wives, girlfriends, mothers, or sisters. Rather than opposing this influence, they choose to accept it gracefully, understanding that a man's happiness and wholeness are incomplete without the positive impact of the right woman. Failing to grasp this vital truth means missing out on a powerful source that has played a crucial role in helping men succeed.

Conclusion

Sexual transmutation can be used for various reasons. Despite our primary focus on Napoleon Hill's perspective on sexual transmutation as a tool to harness creative energy and achieve material success, our books' and our website's {the Serpent's Way} content utilizes sexual transmutation for a distinct spiritual purpose, specifically to awaken the Kundalini.

In various parts of both our blog and books, we have emphasized the immense power of sexual energy, and we will continue to do so. Based on our experience, it can be truly life-altering, especially for men because of the nature of their external ejaculation. We personally never thought at any point in our life we would have the creative desire to create a blog and write books or all the creative thoughts we have about writing in general if it weren't for sexual transmutation.

As previously mentioned in this chapter, sexual energy transmutation encompasses the process of converting sexual energy into a more elevated drive, motivation, or energy. The key factors in our journey were the drive, motivation, and goal to awaken the kundalini and achieve spiritual enlightenment, both of which hinge on the preservation of sexual energy.

Countless ancient philosophies, religions, mystery schools, and spiritual communities across the globe have stressed the importance of converting sexual energy through seminal retention for spiritual motives. To conclude, sexual energy can be transformed through celibacy or through engaging in sexual activity {only through tantric sex where the sexual energy is not dissipated externally but transmuted internally}. In both cases, seminal retention is a key component.

"Transmutation of sex energy calls for more willpower than the average person cares to use for this purpose. Though this requires willpower, the reward for the practice is more than worth the effect" – **Napoleon Hill**

Chapter 10

KNOW THYSELF: THE EXISTENTIAL SENSES BY KURT LELAND

"The first step in becoming a multidimensional human, is developing our existential inner senses. These senses ground us in our personal identity. When we know our true identity, we can get closer to Source through the environmental and kinesthetic inner senses and open up to deeper levels of union with other beings through the relational inner senses. The existential senses enable us to discover our life purpose, so we begin serving the greater good for all. They correspond to the philosophical and spiritual dictum: Know Thyself."

Without the existential senses, we have no access to realities beyond the physical. Our identity isn't strong enough to encounter the ***otherness*** of ***otherwhere*** without possible damage. Such damage may include terror at this otherness intense enough to prevent us from exploring astral projection any further

At age fourteen, I experienced such terror during my initial OBEs (**O**ut of **B**ody **E**xperiences) and did everything I could to shut them down for the next six years. When I discovered what they were, I began to open up to them again. But it took another six years before my identity was strong enough (at twenty-six) to begin exploring non-physical reality. By then, I'd been reading the Seth material for several years. My existential senses were fully operational. I was ready to begin exploring "Otherwhere". In this chapter I'll define each of the existential senses and demonstrate its usefulness in astral projection, providing a provisional belief to activate it.

1- Consciousness

The first existential sense is ***consciousness***. According to Seth, "Everything that exists on any plane and under any circumstances contains consciousness. Annie Besant in the book ***The Ancient Wisdom: An Outline of Theosophical Teachings*** concurs, declaring that,

"Consciousness is the one Reality, in the fullest sense of that much – used phrase; it follows from this that any reality found anywhere in drawn from consciousness."

The consciousness sense grants awareness of ourselves and others *as* consciousness. It's the basis of self-awareness, the gateway to all the other inner senses. If everything is consciousness, then we can build relationships with anything that exists, on any plane, on the basis of our common consciousness. Moving between planes with kinesthetic senses requires nothing more than shifting our consciousness to perceive (environmental senses) and interact with (relational senses) other forms of consciousness on that plane. On the physical plane, the consciousness sense opens the way to empathy (not just commiserating with someone, but actually feeling what they feel) and telepathy (thought transference). The provisional belief that activates this inner sense and opens up to all the others is: ***Everything is consciousness***.

2- Durability

The second existential sense is ***durability***. This sense guarantees the continuity of consciousness in any form for as long as and for whatever purpose that form is required. It's the basis of identity. The durability sense allows us to recognize ourselves *as* ourselves. We have an unshaken sense of identity that goes back to childhood, despite the different sizes and shapes our body has taken since then. Durability of consciousness underlies that continuous sense of identity. The durability sense also allows us to recognize and interact with any other consciousness. Without this inner sense, none of our friends of family would be recognizable to us. At best, they'd seem like dream images, new and different every time we perceived them, with no possibility of developing ongoing relationships.

The durability sense provides physical and nonphysical entities with recognizable identities. It's essential for reading and projecting information about ***idents***, Monroe's term for the way we recognize the entities we encounter in nonphysical reality.

Monroe (Robert A. Monroe, author of ***Journeys Out of The Body***) defines idents as the "mental name or 'address', i.e., energy pattern" of beings encountered in nonphysical reality. A similar idea exists among theosophists: ***the mystic chord***, which Leadbeater describes as the unique combination of vibrations generated by our etheric, astral, mental and causal bodies. This "combination of sounds" is our 'true occult name" by which we may be identified and located anywhere in nonphysical reality.

Just as every chord has a root of fundamental tone, so does our mystic chord. This fundamental tone is the durability of our consciousness, which has been created for a particular purpose and lasts for as long as we require to evolve back to oneness with the Source. It's the same as what theosophists call the monad: our truest, deepest self, the God within us. The provisional belief that activates the durability sense is: ***Our Consciousness is inviolable***. We won't suddenly become someone or something else as a result of exploring psychic and mystical experiences. We continue to be ourselves, no matter what.

Believing in our durability of consciousness and its inviolability is essential for feeling safe in any nonphysical environment. No matter what pressures or influences we encounter there, our consciousness will endure. Aspects of our personality may change as a result of such experiences, but the core or essence of who we are -the monad- will not. Even death does nothing to change the durability of our consciousness. We leave the physical body behind and our consciousness takes up residence in our most developed energy body, usually the astral, mental or causal.

3- **Creation**

The third existential sense is ***creation***. Creation means the dynamic tendency of consciousness to express itself in ever new ways. Seth says that...

> **"Creation is a constant process, "the addition of something new, and something that has not existed before" to any universe, plane or reality. Creation results in births and beginnings, the initiation of a new consciousness or growth process".**

This inner sense has many applications. For example, in nonphysical reality, we create our experience more or less instantly. On the astral plane, emotions create our experience. On the mental plane, thoughts create our experience. The same thing happens in physical reality, but in a greatly slowed-down fashion. Here, sense impressions create our experience-in particular, the memories of past pleasures.

Creation provides us with experience – the inner or outer form taken by any expression of ourselves. As an inner sense, creation allows us to set goals and to perceive the steps necessary to achieve them. The provisional belief that awakens the sense of creation is: ***Whatever We Experience Is Our Creation***. It's either an expression of ourselves, generated by our memories, emotions or thoughts, or something that our memories, thoughts, or emotions have drawn to us. If we don't like what we experience, creation gives us the power to change it. But first we have to take responsibility for the realities we create. Otherwise, we end up feeling like helpless victims.

In *Otherwhere*, the inner sense of creation allows us to determine the difference between negative entities we've created from our fears and those which pre-existed our encounters with them. It's an essential tool for feeling safe in nonphysical reality.

The best way to practice using the inner sense of creation is to be creative in fine arts, crafts, or daily living. Draw, paint, sculpt, compose, dance, write poetry or fiction. Make pots or quilts, garden, cook, weave, knit or sew. Move the furniture into new arrangements or redecorate the room. You could even revert to the joys of childhood play, building with blocks or erecting sand castles on the beach.

Do something creative every day. Making room in your daily life for creativity breaks down old habits and routines, increasing flexibility of consciousness and awakening the creation sense. Many books are currently available to support you in becoming more creative, such as Julia Cameron's bestselling ***The Artist's Way***.

As you awaken the inner sense of creation, you become more aware of, awed by, and grateful for the wonders of creation that surround you. You begin to recognize that you, too, have the power of creation. Not only do you become more creative, but also more cognizant of how you create your own reality. The power to change life conditions that aren't conductive to your growth stirs within you. You'll know that you have the ability to realize any plan or dream.

We are created to create. We are creators. We are not created to live a passive, uninteresting and mundane life. If you feel bored in anyway, know that's the moment you have lost the purpose of life. Create daily and watch your life become a blissful experience. - Pine G. Land, from the book ***You Are The One***

4- Evolution

The fourth existential sense is ***evolution***. Theosophists claim that we're all evolving back towards oneness with our Source. During this process, the consciousness of every mineral, plant, animal and human being explores and realizes its evolutionary potential. The evolution sense provide us with an instinctive understanding of how to do so.

Annie Besant defines evolution as "latent potentialities becoming active powers." According to H. P. Blavatsky, the goal of evolution is achieved only when consciousness has passed "individually and personally, i.e., spiritually and physically, through every experience and feeling that exist in the manifold or differentiated universe." The goal is to become coequal with the Source in experience, feeling and understanding.

The 13th century Sufi poet Mowlana Jalaluddin Rumi expresses a similar view of spiritual evolution as follows:

I died from the mineral and became a plant;
I died from the plant and reappeared in an animal;
I died from the animal and became a man
Wherefore then should I fear? When did I grow less by dying?
Next time I shall die from the man,
That I may grow wings of the angel.
From the angel, too, must I seek advance;
"All things shall perish save His Face."
Once more shall I wing my way above the angels;
I shall become that which entereth not in imagination.
Then let me become naught, naught; for the harp-string
Cryeth unto me "Verily unto Him shall we return."

My adventures in Otherwhere have taught me that we do indeed become something like angels once we've completed our evolution as human beings in physical reality. The two Guides I encountered during my sun/heart adventure were at that level of development. I call such beings ***Facilitators***, because they facilitate our growth while we are in physical bodies and when we're between lifetimes in nonphysical reality.

There are many levels of development within the human evolutionary cycle as well. Charles says that we begin as *infant souls*, just getting used too being in a physical body. Then, like children, we begin to explore and master our physical environment, as ***baby souls***. As ***young*** souls – the equivalent of adolescents – we become competitive, ambitious, driven to succeed. As ***mature*** souls – the equivalent of adults – we make lasting contributions to science, politics, arts and the humanities. As ***old*** souls, we seek to expand our consciousness, to develop ourselves as spiritual beings and explore realms beyond the physical.

At each level, in our own way, we're trying to get closer to the Source – to move to the next higher level of being. When we pursue psychic development and astral projection as spiritual practice, we accelerate our evolution by actively seeking oneness with the Source.

Our soul is an expression of that Source. The soul has a master plan for our development in each lifetime. When we draw closer to the soul by fulfilling this plan, we get closer to the Source. The soul's master plan is an expression of our function within the whole of creation – as much of it as we can embody in a particular lifetime. Discovering this plan through the evolution sense leads us from the physical plane to the etheric, astral, mental, and causal bodies. It's a process of mastering our physical sensations, our emotions, our thoughts and our fate. Thus, we're led by the soul to master and transcend our personality.

Beyond the causal body, our evolution sense leads us to realize our function within the Source itself. The soul is replaced by the monad as the guiding force in our growth. The monad has a more comprehensive plan for our development than the soul – a plan that includes what we've learned from all of our lifetimes in physical reality and what we're about to learn as we explore the higher planes, especially when we're between lifetimes. The process of discovering and living from this plan leads us to develop the buddhic and nirvanic bodies – which Besant calls "***supernormal evolution***." Eventually, we achieve the monadic body, becoming fully aware of this plan. We merge with our monad.

"Monad – The term monad (from ancient Greek monas) 'unity', and

(monos 'alone') is used in some cosmic philosophy and cosmogony to refer to the most basic or original substance. Could this substance also be referred to as "akasha"? As originally conceived by Pythagoreans, the Monad is the Supreme Being/Divinity or the totality of all things. According to some philosophers of the early modern period, most notably Gottfried Wilhelm Leibniz, there are infinite monads, which are the basic and immaterial elementary particles, or simplest units, that makes up the universe. So pretty much it's the substance of the Aether. I'm going to strongly assume that by "becoming the monadic body", Leland meant that we become one with the Source, or one with God if you feel more comfortable with this word, as long as you know that God is neither a man nor a physical female personified human being. Although on a microcosmic level, we can be considered Gods and Goddesses, expressions, or mirrors of the Great God, the Supreme Being that has no shape or form (Aether/Quantum field/Akasha substance), or in unlimited shapes and forms (humans, animals, birds, plants, oceans, air etc.).

Theosophists say that at this point (*referring to emerging with our monad*), we've completed our evolution as human beings – our divine potential is fully realized. Yet there's still one body to master in our search to achieve oneness with the Source. But how we get to the divine body and what we learn from it are things that "entereth not the imagination." As Rumi points out.

The provisional belief that activates the evolution sense is: ***We each have a life purpose (a soul-based master plan) that our impulses allow us to perceive and realize***. The soul sends us impulses directing us toward activities that realize its plan for us. When we perceive and act on this impulses, we develop our evolutionary potential. The evolution sense allows us to become aware of such impulses. Charles defines seven components of the soul's plan. Creating a lifestyle in which we live from all of them on a regular basis is the best way of developing the evolution sense. In line with the master intention's idea of serving the greater good, each component of our life purpose is a mode of service.

1- The first is ***service to the body***. By this, Charles means eating nourishing food (neither too little nor too much) and getting regular exercise. If your body breaks down, none of the other components of your life purpose can be served effectively. You may be confined to physical reality, unable to access psychic information or explore the higher planes.

2-The second is ***service to the soul***. This means working with the soul to discover and then to ***live*** from its master plan. Reading books about spiritual development, pursuing spiritual practices, recording and interpreting dreams, learning to receive inner guidance, and consulting trustworthy spiritual teachers and healers will help us develop this aspect of our life purpose.

3-The third component of our life purpose is ***service to the Creator***. By this, Charles means exercising our God – given creative gifts. The Bible says we are created in the image of God, and this phrase is often interpreted in terms of our creative abilities.

4-The fourth component is ***service to personality***. Many spiritual traditions teach us to deny the senses or kil the ego. By personality, Charles means the full range of being human on the physical plane, from dancing to viewing the wonders of nature, from great sex to seeing a movie, from going to a museum to riding a mountain bike.

Such activities increase our willingness to be present in the body and on the planet. Through them, we counterbalance the intense focus of spiritual and creative work, the challenges of responding to the needs of others, and the demands of our job. We refresh ourselves with playfulness and fun.

5-The fifth component is ***service to family***. By family, Charles means not only our next of kin, such as our parents, siblings and children, but also the spiritual family of our closest friends. Service to family involves being sensitive to their needs and available to satisfy them without preventing our own growth in the process. Again, the greater good of all included ourselves.

6-The sixth component of life purpose is ***service to humanity***. This is what most people think of as their life purpose. The idea is to find work that benefits others and harms no one, often a challenge in the world of business. This can mean volunteer work if a job doesn't involve a recognizable component of service.

7-The final component is *service to all life*. This means living in a way that benefits other life forms on the planet, not just human beings. By not wasting water, food, or energy; by recycling, protecting wildlife habitat through supporting land conservation, buying green, and eating low on the food chain; by maintaining a policy of not harming plants, insects, and animals we help our fellow creatures survive and thrive. If we have pets, spending time with them is also a way of serving all life. So is gardening and putting out birdseed.

Our soul sends us impulses to direct us toward activities that realize its plan for us. When we perceive and act on these impulses, we develop our evolutionary potential. The evolution sense allows us to become aware of such impulses. Through realizing this plan, our identity becomes strong enough that we can begin throwing our consciousness into other physical beings and experience how the world looks or feels to them, just as we might throw our voice as a ventriloquist. In nonphysical reality, it's possible to ***become*** that being, to merge our consciousness with it so completely that what it knows becomes what ***we*** know.

Everything that surrounds us on all planes is conscious and has evolutionary potential, a purpose within the whole of creation. The evolution sense allows us to experience all of creation, from every conceivable angle. On higher planes, this sense provides the basis of melding minds with other forms of consciousness, an essential mode of information exchange.

5- Fulfillment

The fifth existential sense is ***fulfillment***. In addition to our life purpose, we each have a growth trajectory: where we've come from, where we are, and where we're going in the process of discovering who we are. This trajectory determines how close we are to the Source – and what we must do to get even closer.

In Hinduism, the concept of ***dharma*** embraces several of the existential senses and clarifies the concept of our growth trajectory. The simplest definition of dharma is ***path***. Besant expands this definition by describing dharma as: the inner nature [consciousness], marked by the stage of evolution [evolution], plus the law of growth for the next stage of evolution [fulfillment]. Our dharma is our growth trajectory, including our life purpose and the soul's master plan for our growth.

As noted, the evolution sense allows us to become aware of the master plan for our growth and what it demands of us – through impulses sent by the soul. The fulfillment sense motivates us to act on these impulses. We discover what the law of our growth requires at a given stage in our evolution and then accomplish it. In Hinduism, this is called ***following the path of our dharma***.

When we perceive an impulse to grow in a certain direction

and subsequently follow that impulse, we experience a rising sense of bliss. This bliss can manifest itself in a variety of ways: inner peace, satisfaction, happiness or ecstasy. Joseph Cambell, the famous scholar of comparative mythology, said: "Follow your bliss." He was talking about the fulfillment sense.

The provisional belief that awakens the inner sense of fulfillment is: ***Bliss is a result of living from our life purpose (dharma), a sign we're getting close to Source***. When our degree of bliss or happiness rises, we're fulfilling the soul's master plan for our growth – we are following our dharma. When it falls, we're working against this plan. We may be pursuing selfish ends rather than the greater good, neglecting ourselves in favor of serving others, or avoiding the next step in our growth.

Our growth trajectory is the record of these movements closer to (or farther from) the Source. For most of us, these are micro – movements, the result of moment – by – moment choices made in physical reality that increase or decrease our level of happiness in barely noticeable levels. But for those who pursue astral projection as spiritual practice, living from the master intention produces an exponential increase of bliss as we master each energy body. Our growth trajectory (or dharma path) becomes the ladder of planes that leads us back to the Source.

Simple as it seems, we begin – and accelerate – our movement along this growth trajectory by becoming aware of our ***physical*** needs, then seeking to fulfill them. Such a practice develops our inner sense of fulfillment, making it easier for us to sense and respond to the subtler needs involved in accessing our energy bodies.

Physical needs are one form taken by impulses from the soul. Satisfying those needs is a means of service to the body, an aspect of our life purpose. We should sleep when we're tired, get up when we're rested, eat only when we're genuinely hungry (without stuffing ourselves), drink something when we're thirsty, use the bathroom before discomfort sets in and exercise daily.

When we ignore these needs, our performance in physical reality suffers. Our ability to sense needs and impulses from other aspects of the soul's plan for our growth diminishes. We're unlikely to access psychic information or to visit higher planes. We may even be getting farther from the Source because we're not serving the greater good, which includes the physical body.

If you're having trouble sensing the direction your life should be taking, try focusing on these basic physical needs. You'll notice that your needs in other areas get clearer and easier to follow. You're activating the fulfillment sense, finding your way back to the soul's master plan.

A second way to attune ourselves to the fulfillment sense is to pay attention to other impulses. True impulses come from the soul. They direct us out of habit and routine and into realizing less familiar aspects of the soul's plan for our development.

Typically, we follow impulses toward serving family and humanity (or at least our job, whether or not it benefits humanity) to the exclusion of all others. To develop the fulfillment sense, notice and respond to impulses that serve the soul (something that focuses on spirituality), the Creator (something creative), the personality (something fun that increases your willingness to be present in your body and on the planet), or all life (something that benefits all creatures, such as pets). Life often takes on an added dimension of magic as a result of pursuing such impulses.

Through activating the evolution and fulfillment senses, we become aware of our purpose in this life, the soul's master plan for our growth – our dharma path. The ensuing bliss informs us of the degree to which we've fulfilled this plan and how much closer we've gotten to the Source. Our identity becomes stronger and we get even closer to Source. The result is a further increase in bliss – and access to higher planes and energy bodies.

The clearer we get about who we are, the easier it becomes to sense the evolutionary potential of others and where they are on their growth trajectory – their dharma path. We can guide people (including a partner, our children, coworkers, friends and clients) toward discovering and realizing their own soul's plan. In so doing, we're serving the greater good of all, further increasing our bliss, and bringing us yet closer to Source.

As we activate the evolution and fulfillment senses in ourselves and begin extending them to others, we develop our ability to sense the purpose and growth trajectory (dharma path) of any entity encountered in Otherwhere. We're preparing ourselves for the relational inner senses, which allow us to perceive their idents or mystic chords.

Awakening the Existential Senses

Here's a reminder of the provisional beliefs that awaken the existential inner senses. Make a copy of this list and review it often as a way of reinforcing your intention to awaken these senses in your pursuit of psychic development and astral projection as spiritual practice.

1) *Everything is consciousness (consciousness)*
2) *Our consciousness is inviolable (durability)*
3) *Whatever we experience is our creation (creation)*
4) *We have a life purpose (a soul-based master plan) that our impulses allow us to perceive and realize (evolution)*
5) *Bliss is the result of living from our life purpose (dharma), a sign that we're getting closer to Source (fulfillment)*

"If your mind is powerful enough to dream up imaginary events when you are asleep and then produce intense emotions in response to them, how much power does it have over your waking life? The same brain that convinces you that you are flying through space, doing battle with monsters, or discovering buried treasure while you're sleeping, is also capable of telling you who you are and what you can do in the "real" world. And your brain creates whatever kinds of stories you train it to create. The problem is that most of us don't realize that we are in charge of this powerful dream machine. We let our minds create our reality, complete with its addition to suffering, instead of learning to create it ourselves." -**Don Jose Ruis**, from the book The Shaman's Path To Freedom

Chapter 11

FLUORIDE & PINEAL GLAND

> "Fluoride, commonly found in most municipal water as well as pesticides, accumulates in the pineal more than any other part of the body. This accumulation of fluoride forms phosphate crystals, creating a hard shell around the pineal called calcification" – **Scott Jeffrey**

On the next page is a striking image featuring an indigo dragon eye. Referred to as the Anja Dragon, it embodies qualities of intuition, vision, and psychic awareness. By embracing the indigo dragon consciousness, we can expand our visual consciousness and elevate our psychic abilities, harmonizing them with our inner knowing.

Shadow Dragon Consciousness - https://theserpentsway.com/
In numerous sections of our website mentioned above we have made mention of the shadow dragon consciousness and the malevolent dark sorcerers. We have provided compelling evidence of their direct involvement in the tragic downfall of the ancient civilization of Atlantis. Additionally, we have thoroughly examined the insidious rise of black magic, which eventually supplanted the spiritual authority and became the prevailing force in the state religion of ancient Egypt.

The shadow dragon consciousness discussed in this blog is characterized by its dual essence. Firstly, we demonstrate the method to confront the personal shadow that resides within each of us by engaging in shadow work. Recognizing, accepting, and assimilating this individual shadow is essential as it holds great significance in any spiritual journey.

Secondly, it exposes the collective shadow consciousness that has been manipulating humanity since the era of Atlantis. This consciousness has adopted different aliases to obscure its presence throughout history. While some may recognize it as the 'Cabal' or 'Illuminati', the authors of this blog choose not to align with conventional or mainstream terminology. Therefore, we shall always refer to this faction as the shadow dragon consciousness, dark sorcerers, or black magicians.

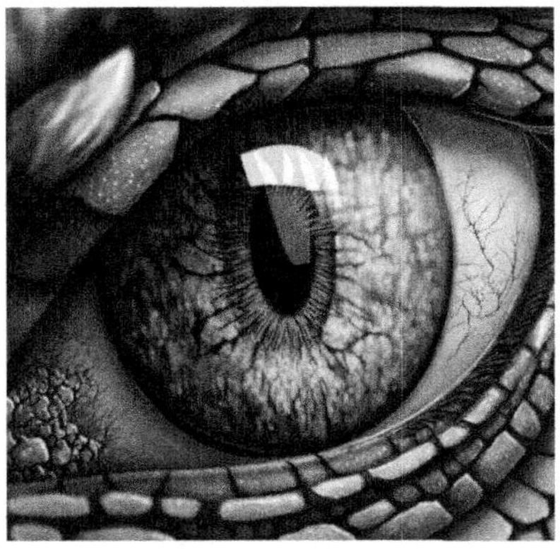

Dark Sorcerer's primary objective, dating back to the era of Atlantis, is the complete enslavement of the human race. Their ultimate objective is not focused on physical enslavement, but rather on enslaving our souls. To put it differently, their intention is to hinder humanity from attaining spiritual awakening, progressing towards higher consciousness, and accessing the spiritual powers bestowed upon us by the divine serpent, including the activation of our Kundalini energy. By familiarizing yourself with their {*dark sorcerers*} tactics, you will be better equipped to navigate the challenges and obstacles that may arise along the way, ultimately leading to a deeper sense of self-awareness and spiritual awakening.

Fear blocks the awakening. Bravery open your eyes to the fact that fear blocks the root chakra. This realization will also shed light on the orchestrated nature of major global events, terrorism, and wars, all aimed at perpetuating a fear-based consciousness. It is essential to acknowledge that those in control manipulate both the east and west to maintain this state of fear. Yet another illustration is the hypersexualized environment of society and the pornography sector.

The essence of sexual energy plays a pivotal role in any spiritual quest. Without the conservation and transmutation of this energy, the awakening of Kundalini holds no value. By acknowledging this truth, the true motives behind a society obsessed with hypersexuality and the porn industry becomes glaringly apparent.

In due course, we will reveal ample information to enhance your spiritual growth and guide you on your personal quest to awaken your inner potential.

As a valued reader of our blog, you will gain insights into the pitfalls of mindless entertainment, the fallacies of materialism, the questionable efficacy of vaccines, the influence of Rockefeller's petroleum-driven medicine, the concerns surrounding genetically-modified organisms (GMOs), the aspects of meat consumption and livestock slaughter, the reasons behind the high cost of healthy plant-based foods, and the exploitation of our addictions and vulnerabilities, among other topics.

> "The Archons, as known by the Christian Gnostics, are cunning masters of deception and the puppeteers behind these human dark sorcerers. It is crucial to understand that these beings pose as gods within various religious groups. By awakening the Kundalini and Christ Consciousness, you embrace your true essence as gods and goddesses."

"In point of fact, fluoride causes more human cancer death, and causes it faster than any other chemical" – Dr. Dean Burk

Fluoride Poisoning

There exist two distinct forms of fluoride. Calcium Fluoride, found naturally in underground water sources, is generally harmless. Nevertheless, excessive daily intake can result in dental or bone issues. Calcium is employed as an antidote for fluoride poisoning when it arises. This positive aspect suggests that the calcium present in naturally occurring calcium fluoride counteracts a significant portion of fluoride's harmful impacts.

Conversely, the fluorides incorporated into water supplies, beverages, and food products are derived from waste materials produced by the nuclear, aluminum, and predominantly the phosphate (fertilizer) industries. These substances, namely fluorosilicate acid, sodium silicofluoride, and sodium fluoride, have been classified as toxins by the EPA.

Sodium Fluoride encompasses all three variants. It serves as both a rat poison and a pesticide. A scientific study conducted a few years back, titled "Comparative Toxicity of Fluorine Compounds," revealed that industrial waste sodium fluorides are 85 times more toxic than naturally existing calcium fluoride. The majority of fluoride that enters the body is not readily excreted, leading to its accumulation in the bones and teeth. Interestingly, recent studies have shown that fluoride can also build up in the pineal gland, which is located in the brain.

Extensive evidence has been gathered documenting the detrimental effects of dental fluorosis, a condition that severely damages teeth, resulting from the daily use of fluoride. Despite this, the American Dental Association (AMA) persistently advocates for the use of fluoride, seemingly oblivious to the fact that it exacerbates dental problems rather than preventing tooth decay. In addition to the well-known condition of fluorosis, the excessive presence of sodium fluoride in water and food has been found to contribute to several other serious health issues. Despite being largely undisclosed or deliberately suppressed, reputable researchers and independent labs have established a correlation between prolonged daily consumption of sodium fluoride and the following health problems:

Cancer
Genetic DNA Damage
Thyroid Disruption – The endocrine system is profoundly influenced, ultimately resulting in obesity.
Neurological – A decrease in IQ and the inability to concentrate, accompanied by feelings of fatigue and exhaustion.
Alzheimer's Disease
Melatonin Disruption – Reduces the immune system's ability to fight cancer, hastens the aging process, causes disturbances in sleep.
Pineal Gland – This gland at the core of the brain is being clogged by calcification. It directly obstructs the activation of the third eye and the spiritual capabilities linked to it.

Fluoride, originally an industrial byproduct manufactured by fertilizer industries, is a hazardous waste containing aluminium, phosphoric acid, and phosphates. Its improper disposal in the past resulted in severe health damage, including the destruction of the immune, digestive, and respiratory systems, the development of cancer, impairment of blood circulation, harm to vital organs like the liver, kidneys, and thyroid, compromised brain function, and premature aging.

To avoid costly legal battles, manufacturers shrewdly influenced the Government and Medical Institutions to brainwash the general population into believing that fluoride is safe and beneficial for maintaining oral hygiene. As a consequence, it is now widely employed worldwide.

The Jews were initially introduced to fluoride during World War II, which was added to their drinking water in order to make them compliant, submissive, and easily manageable. The primary ingredient in rat poison, sodium fluoride, is also present in the anti-depressant drug known as 'Prozac'. Hyperactivity and lower IQ in children have been associated with fluoride exposure. Furthermore, unborn babies are vulnerable to the effects of fluoride if their mothers ingest it, as the neurotoxin can easily cross their underdeveloped blood-brain barrier and harm their developing brains.

Christopher Bryson, an investigative journalist and author of The Fluoride Deception, reveals that the deliberate introduction of significant amounts of sodium fluoride into our water and food system was a calculated strategy orchestrated by industries burdened with disposing of hazardous substances.

Fluoride played a crucial role in the production and enhancement of uranium. The promotion of fluoride began during the Manhattan Project, aimed at developing the initial atomic bombs in the 1940s. The objective was to persuade employees and residents near the biggest nuclear facility in Tennessee that fluoride was not only harmless, but also beneficial for children's dental well-being.

During the early 1950s, Edward Bernays, the influential spin master and pioneer of advertising, pushed for the addition of fluorides to water supplies in an effort to manipulate public opinion. The American Medical Association later supported the idea of adding sodium fluoride to water supplies, despite some health studies and reports that raised concerns being ignored or suppressed. Those who disagreed were often labeled as quacks, regardless of their qualifications. Roughly two-thirds of the water supply in the United States is contaminated with sodium fluoride, a commonly used pesticide. Consequently, this residue can be found in certain food items. Fluoride additives are commonly found in sodas, packaged orange juices, and even bottled drinking water specifically formulated for infants.

> **"I am appalled at the prospect of using water as a vehicle for drugs. Fluoride is a corrosive poison that will produce serious effect on a long-range basis. Any attempt to use the water this way is deplorable"** – Charles Gordon Heyd, M.D., Past President, American Medical Association

The Pineal Gland

The pineal gland, also referred to as the third eye, serves as the portal to a stronger spiritual bond and increased intuition. The term "pineal" originates from the Latin word "Pena," which translates to pinecone. Positioned in the middle of the brain, the pineal gland takes on the shape of a pinecone and is roughly the size of a pea. Its primary function is to produce melatonin, the hormone responsible for managing your sleep and wakefulness patterns. The indigo color, symbolizing the sixth chakra, is often associated with the pineal gland.

Acting as a vital regulator of your body's internal clock, the pineal gland is commonly known as the third eye. Situated in the center of your brain, it houses light-sensitive nerve endings, non-visual photoreceptors, a cornea, and a retina. Throughout the ages, mystics have long believed in the profound connection between the third eye and heightened intuition and clarity. It is often described as a powerful lens that enables us to perceive beyond the boundaries of our physical reality.

The importance of this concept is present in various ancient societies across the globe. It is suggested that if the third eye remains closed, one may face issues such as overthinking, a lack of direction, and a failure to establish a strong connection with their spiritual self.

Opening the third eye allows one to transcend the limitations of the five senses and access hidden otherworldly knowledge. The human body perceives the material world, but the third eye enables us to tap into alternate realms filled with vast information and heightened intuitive understanding.

Known as the seat of the soul, the third eye acts as a bridge between the physical and spiritual realms. By awakening this mystical center, you gain the extraordinary ability to connect with heightened senses and explore the wondrous beauty they unveil in our material world. The separation between the self and the spirit is believed to disappear when the third eye is consciously opened, enabling us to engage in activities like astral travel, lucid dreaming, and shifting realities. Contrary to the majority of our brain, the blood-brain barrier does not cut off the pineal gland from the rest of the body. Instead, the pineal gland experiences a high volume of blood flow, coming in second only to the kidneys. Positioned within a cramped cavernous region above and behind the pituitary gland, this gland finds itself completely enveloped and immersed in cerebrospinal fluid.

British scientist Jennifer Luke's research in the 1990s brought to light a remarkable observation as she detected elevated levels of fluoride in the pineal gland of her study participants. The accumulation of fluoride is significantly higher in the pineal gland compared to any other part of the body, and this can be found in both municipal water and pesticides. Phosphate crystals are created due to the excess fluoride, leading to the formation of a protective shell around the pineal gland known as calcification.

Due to the pineal gland's vital role in the endocrine system, Jennifer's discoveries were revolutionary. Her study successfully established the missing link between sodium fluoride and the numerous physiological damages that were previously only theorized. This breakthrough allowed for the identification of the primary source responsible for the disrupted chain of endocrine activity.

Fluoride in water is thought to be a major factor in the calcification of the pineal gland. Studies indicate that children are hitting puberty sooner due to the presence of fluoride in water. Research on animals has revealed that exposure to fluoride can lower melatonin production and cause premature sexual development in female animals. The findings of a study released in November 2019 by Biological Trace Element Research indicated that male rats showed heightened pineal growth when fed a fluoride-free diet.

In essence, if our pineal gland becomes calcified, it disrupts the harmony between our body and nature, hindering the optimal functioning of our biology and brain. When the pineal gland becomes calcified, it severs our link to intuition, clarity, and our higher selves. Additionally, a calcified pineal gland blocks our capacity to communicate with the source or creator, also referred to as the cosmic mind.

Great news! Regularly spending time in the sun, around 20 minutes each session, can boost the function of your pineal gland, which is crucial for various bodily processes. Remember to remove your hat for maximum benefit. This is just one of the numerous reasons why it is absolutely essential to practice daily sungazing along the Serpent's Way.

Conclusion

Fluoride is intentionally added to toothpaste, tap water, bottled water, and processed food for a specific purpose. Our books highlight the presence of dark sorcerers, both human and non-human, who aim to hinder humanity's evolution towards higher levels of consciousness. In recent years, humanity has been experiencing a profound global awakening.

However, it is important to note that this book does not aim to awaken individuals to the realm of shadow consciousness. We strive to be the antithesis of those dark sorcerers, offering you the wisdom to implement just as we have in order to awaken your higher consciousness. The inner serpent, or Kundalini, is the key to reaching this elevated level of awareness. Our purpose in unveiling this shadow consciousness is to enlighten you about the spiritual warfare tactics, enabling you to overcome their black magic. Fluoride is merely one example of their deceitful methods. The key point here is that fluoride disrupts your link to the cosmic mind, hindering your access to your multidimensional self, mystic abilities, and expanded awareness through your pineal gland, or third eye.

> "The pineal gland is activated by light and controls the body's bio- rhythms in concert with the hypothalamus gland which regulates hunger, thirst, sexual desire and the biological clock that dictates how fast we age. Look at the potential for mass control if you can externally suppress and manipulate the pineal and hypothalamus glands alone. You can make it much harder to perceive beyond the five senses, decide how quickly people age, how much they want sex, when they are hungry and thirsty and for how long. This is the key reason for putting sodium fluoride into water supplies and toothpaste. The pineal gland absorbs more fluoride than any other part of the body and becomes calcified by this highly damaging toxin. Sodium fluoride is an appalling waste product of the aluminum industry and has been used in rat poison. It causes cancer, genetic damage, Alzheimer's disease, disrupts the endocrine system and dumbs down the brain. It was added to drinking water in the Nazi concentration camps to make the inmates more acquiescent and docile." – **David Icke**

Chapter 12

DECALCIFY YOUR PINEAL GLAND

"The light of the body is the eye: if therefore thine eye be single, thy whole body shall be full of light" – Matthew 6.22

The pineal gland, a profound enigma, continues to elude our understanding. Among the various glands within our brain, it remains the most enigmatic, yet it has captivated the curiosity of our ancient forebears, dating back to the early days of ancient Egypt. Its potential and capabilities can be considered as one of the most closely guarded secrets in the annals of human history.

Resembling a pinecone, this small gland has been referred to as the "Seat of the Soul" by Renee Descartes. Remarkably, the pineal gland possesses the ability to discern the nuances of light and darkness in our surroundings and transmit this information to our cognitive faculties.

The third eye chakra, also known as the 'brow chakra', is the sixth chakra in the traditional seven chakra system. In Sanskrit, it is referred to as 'Ajna', which translates to 'perceiving' or 'command'. This name is quite fitting considering the properties and powers associated with this ambiguous energy center.

Positioned just above the center of the brows, this chakra functions as a conduit between our tangible reality and the profound insights and meanings that may elude our ordinary sight. This whirling energy center bestows upon us unique abilities that may remain untapped or incomprehensible to most individuals, primarily because of factors like calcification.

Experiencing what is often described as "brain fog", a condition marked by difficulty in concentrating, meditating, or maintaining focus, may indicate that your pineal gland is calcified and lacking proper nutrition intake.

Apart from keeping you in a state of spiritual darkness and cutting off your link to the source/creator, a calcified pineal gland negatively affects our sleep, cognitive skills, reflexes, decision-making, perception, and productivity.

The calcification of the pineal gland is frequently caused by the use of pharmaceutical drugs, consumption of fluoridated water, exposure to negative electromagnetic frequencies, lack of grounding or consumption of organic foods, and accumulation of toxins in the body.

> **Processed food, meat, alcohol, and smoking are just a few examples of the sources from which toxins accumulate. Additionally, the pineal gland is negatively affected by the excessive intake of caffeine. For those who find themselves unable to function on just a single cup of morning coffee or tea, turning to multiple servings throughout the day to power through work or school, it is probable that your pineal gland is not in equilibrium.**

So, what exactly is calcification? In short, the accumulation of calcium deposits and other toxins within the pineal gland can result in pineal gland calcification. The third eye chakra is linked to numerous abilities, with clairvoyance being perhaps the primary one. Clairvoyance is a psychic power that grants the ability to witness ethereal phenomena or receive psychic messages in the form of visual imagery.

The phenomenon of clairvoyance grants you the extraordinary power to perceive the invisible realm, where tangible objects cease to exist yet remain undeniably real. As mentioned in R.E. Guiley's encyclopedia, clairvoyance is the paranormal capacity to perceive objects, events, places, and individuals that are not visible through ordinary sight.

Later on you will read more about the third eye chakra and the advantages of unlocking it. It is essential to bear in mind that we have mentioned in this book the presence of dark sorcerers who have maintained their hold on power since the ancient times of Atlantis and Egypt. Their agenda revolves around the spiritual enslavement of humanity. These controllers possess extensive knowledge.

> **"Those entrapped in five-sense reality and disconnected from Consciousness are literally biological robots of the control system that dictates virtually their every thought and response. The aim was to totally control the minds, perceptions and behavior of their human slaves. The genetic manipulation re-wired the electro-chemical circuitry to isolate humans overwhelmingly in 'physical' reality as prisoners of the five senses and visible light"** – David Icke

Pineal Gland Detox

Let me make it clear that in order to undergo this pineal gland detox, you must first eliminate any sources of calcification. Detoxification is only achievable if you have switched to a raw food diet that primarily includes fruits, nuts, and plants. It is impossible to detoxify if you still consume processed garbage pretending to be food. Furthermore, removing fluoride from your daily life is crucial for the detoxification process. Lastly, detoxification cannot occur if you continue to consume alcohol and smoke.

It's important to avoid drinking tap water. Natural water can be deceiving, especially plastic bottled water. Many plastic bottled water brands contain **fluoride**. Additionally, plastic bottled water is unhealthy and let's not forget, tastes absolutely terrible. The availability of your water source ultimately depends on your specific location. Unfortunately, I cannot suggest a natural glass bottle water source as it may not be available in another country. However, I would recommend obtaining glass bottled water from a small, local shop. It is important to note that the food supply has been significantly influenced by those in control of the system. If you are confident in your decision to purchase a water filter, then by all means proceed. Nevertheless, I highly advise selecting a filter that can effectively remove all impurities.

Cleansing the pineal gland must:

- **Back decalcification efforts**
- **Utilize chelation to eliminate heavy metals**
- **Eliminate fluoride**
- **Enhance and purify the bloodstream**
- **Revitalize the body with minerals**

Let me begin by stating that the content of this chapter is not meant to be taken as medical advice. I have personally tested all the **supplements** discussed below and have been using them since I embarked on the decalcification process in 2018.

1. Iodine

Found in sea vegetables like seaweed and kelp, iodine is a vital mineral that aids in hormone regulation by assisting the thyroid gland and is highly effective in removing heavy metals from the body as a chelator.

Heavy metals like mercury, lead, cadmium, and aluminum, along with **fluoride**, are chelated by iodine. It also exhibits anti-fungal, anti-bacterial, and antiparasitic properties. It is widely believed that iodine is a vital **supplement** for detoxifying the pineal gland.

The best option for iodine that I have been taking is (5% solution) by J.CROW'S. Lugol's Solution of Iodine is the most widely recognized form of iodine. It's made from distilled water, potassium iodide, and iodine crystals. When taking iodine supplements, it is crucial to boost your calcium levels. This can be achieved by consuming calcium-rich foods like broccoli, kale, and almonds.

Take the initiative to delve into iodine and its dosing guidelines through comprehensive research. As per my own experience, I encountered no difficulties by adding a few drops to a small glass of water.

2. Chaga Mushrooms

Known as the "King of Plants" in China, the "Gift from God" in Siberia, and the "Diamond of the Forest" in Japan, this remarkable plant holds great significance in different cultures. Numerous scientific studies have provided compelling evidence of the powerful impact that the Chaga mushroom has on the immune, hormonal, and central nervous systems. Research conducted in Finland and Russia has specifically highlighted Chaga's remarkable effectiveness as both an anti-tumor agent and antiviral solution. Chaga supplies us with phytochemicals, nutrients, and melanin. Melanin gives color to our skin, hair, and eyes. The pineal gland employs melanin to safeguard us from UV light. For the most effective and traditional Chaga consumption, tea is the way to go.

3. Turmeric

Turmeric is a top-notch **supplement** for detoxing your pineal gland. In addition to pineal detox, there are various advantages such as being a natural anti-inflammatory, natural antibiotic, natural antiseptic, natural analgesic, promoting faster wound healing, enhancing digestion, purifying blood, strengthening ligaments, toning the skin, relieving coughs, improving asthma, antiarthritic properties, slowing down the progression of MS, aiding in preventing gas and bloating, reducing cholesterol, healing stomach ulcers, enhancing skin conditions, helping prevent cancer, halting the progression of Alzheimer's, assisting in fat metabolism, and managing weight.

Turmeric is an essential part of my everyday diet, whether I blend it into my vegetable smoothies or include it in the vegan dishes I cook. I usually opt for purchasing one-pound bags of turmeric powder from Amazon.

4. Apple Cider Vinegar

Raw apple cider vinegar acts as a powerful natural detoxifier for heavy metals. Through the chelating properties of malic acid, it effectively removes these harmful substances from your body. Additionally, the abundance of natural vitamins, minerals, and enzymes in raw apple cider vinegar helps replenish your body with essential nutrients.

The binding properties of malic acid enable it to effectively attach to toxins, aiding in their efficient elimination from the body. Additionally, apple cider vinegar assists in the purification of lymph nodes, facilitating improved lymph circulation. This process is vital for eliminating toxins and enhancing your immune response. The detoxifying benefits of apple cider vinegar are particularly advantageous for detoxifying the pineal gland. Ensure you purchase apple cider vinegar that is labeled as "raw" and is packaged in a glass container, not a plastic one. For a few years, I used to mix apple cider vinegar with freshly squeezed lemon juice to maximize its health benefits. However, in the past couple of months, I have switched to consuming it raw. I now take two shot glasses of apple cider vinegar daily, one in the morning and one in the evening.

5. Boron

During their research in 1942, Markovich and Stanley stumbled upon a remarkable finding – boric acid acts as an antidote to fluorine. This compound, which is the most abundant form of boron, is considered a trace mineral.

Foods abundant in boron consist of walnuts, almonds, hazelnuts, raisins, dates, prunes, chickpeas, beets, beans, avocados, and bananas.

Borax, a sodium salt derived from boric acid, contains a significant amount of boron. This abundant element makes borax a popular choice for various commercial cleaning purposes. Borax is sold by the brand 20 Mule Team for cleaning and laundry needs. Yet is it possible to use borax for **fluoride** detoxification as well?

6. Borax

Chemist Walter Last explains that borax has the ability to react with fluoride ions, resulting in the formation of boron **fluorides** that are subsequently eliminated. This highlights the potential of borax as a potent tool for detoxifying the pineal gland.

Back in 1987, a study was carried out in China with 31 patients afflicted by skeletal fluorosis. The Borax intake was escalated from 300 to 1,100 mg per day for a duration of three months, with a week-long break each month. The therapy exhibited notable success, resulting in 50 to 80% enhancement. Borax has demonstrated efficacy in managing arthritis and osteoporosis. Over the past six years, I have consistently incorporated Borax into my routine.

Despite experiencing pineal gland decalcification, I am pleased to share that at the age of 46, I have managed to avoid arthritis and joint pain, even after years of rigorous weight-training. In this particular protocol, men are advised to consume 1/4 teaspoon of Borax dissolved in one liter of water, while women are recommended to take 1/8 teaspoon. This dose should be consumed throughout the day. Following this regimen, it is important to take a break of two days before commencing the cycle again.

Note: *I have successfully followed this borax protocol for the last six years without experiencing any adverse effects.*

"The kundalini energy rests in potential at the base of the spine. It is possible to take that energy and allow it to move, to unleash it, from the base of the spine up to the third eye" – **Frederick Lenz**

7. Tamarind

A study conducted in the early 2000s revealed that tamarind led to higher **fluoride** excretion in urine when compared to the control group. Subsequent research validated these results.

The excretion of fluoride in urine conflicts with the chapter 6 about urine therapy. We purposefully let this information here so that you can also do your own research and decide for yourself. Lets assume that urine is toxic, if you ingested it, it would be such a strong concentration that you could even die. I practice urine therapy daily. My health has only improved. I am speaking from personal experience. The studies (which we have no clue who did it) are other people's experiences. Don't believe neither me nor the studies. Simply realize how magnificently your body has been created and you will realize what is harmful and what it is not. There is more to knowledge/health than what we think. Do you remember when we mentioned the words "**S**cientists" and "**$**cientists"? Between what you read here, what scientist say and what the actual truth is, there is a fine line that only you can discern the absolute truth for you.

Researchers suggest that tamarind has the potential to reverse the impacts of skeletal fluorosis resulting from fluoride consumption. Additionally, a study indicates that a substance found in the tamarind fruit shell can effectively remove fluoride from groundwater.

8. Raw Cacao

Countless scientific studies have revealed that raw cacao, known for its high flavonoid content, offers significant benefits in terms of lowering blood pressure and improving the condition of blood vessels. By stimulating the release of nitric oxide, raw cacao effectively enlarges the diameter of blood vessels.

Enhanced blood flow and oxygen delivery to the pineal gland are facilitated by the presence of larger blood vessels. This plays a crucial role in supporting the gland's optimal functioning and detoxification. Furthermore, raw cacao is packed with antioxidants and anandamide, further augmenting its beneficial effects on overall health.

Anandamide, commonly called the "bliss molecule," is a neurotransmitter that is naturally generated in the brain. It is responsible for the elevated state of happiness individuals feel when they indulge in delectable chocolate. Not every type of chocolate is made the same. Cocoa powder is actually raw cacao that has been roasted at high temperatures. This roasting alters the chemical composition of the bean, removing a lot of the enzymes and nutrients.

Raw cacao powder is made by cold-pressing unroasted cocoa beans. For optimal detox effects on your pineal gland, choose organic raw cacao. Raw cacao is a fantastic addition to shakes and smoothies.

9. Activator X

During the year 1945, Weston Price, a former dentist who earned the title of the "Isaac Newton of Nutrition," elucidated a vitamin-like substance that plays a pivotal role in various aspects of our well-being: growth, reproduction, brain function, tooth decay prevention, and protection against calcification of the arteries.

Price named this compound Activator X and found it present in the butterfat's, organs, and fat of animals that feed on rapidly growing green grass.

10. Vitamins K1 and K2

Activator X is a blend of vitamins K1 and K2. Vitamin K1 is found in fast-growing green, leafy vegetables. Vitamin K2 is produced by intestinal microflora in animal tissues. Sources of vitamin K2 include organ meats, fermented dairy products such as cheese or grass-fed butter, sauerkraut, and marine oils.

The scientific community has gained knowledge that the absence of vitamin K2 results in the calcification of the cardiovascular system. By consuming vitamin K2 in its Activator X form, we can effectively combat the accumulation of calcium in our arteries. It is plausible to assume that this mechanism also applies to the pineal gland.

The role of Activator X is not to eliminate calcium, but rather to direct it towards our bones and teeth, where it is vital. This is how it effectively reverses the process of tooth decay. Price's findings demonstrated that the true potential of vitamin K2 is unlocked when it is combined with vitamins A and D, two other fat-soluble activators.

11. Fulvic acid

Fulvic acid plays a role in getting rid of toxins and heavy metals, which in turn helps with the decalcification process. Moreover, it seems to provide antioxidants and minerals directly to the cells that require them.

12. Green Super Food

Consuming raw, green foods packed with chlorophyll can aid in detoxifying heavy metals from your blood and providing essential nutrients. Foods such as chlorella, spirulina, and wheatgrass are rich in chlorophyll and can enhance oxygen levels, promote tissue repair, and strengthen the immune system. In theory, any approach that enhances oxygen and immune function should aid in reversing pineal gland calcification. Furthermore, consuming foods charged with sunlight should also support the healthy functioning of the pineal gland. This is why The Serpents Way [https://theserpentsway.com/]advocates daily sungazing, as it allows the pineal gland to thrive in sunlight.

Incorporating a raw food diet into one's spiritual and mystical path is imperative for various reasons, including the awakening of the inner serpent. It is crucial to understand that processed and low-vibrational food cannot facilitate the activation of the third eye.

When it comes to pineal gland decalcification, chlorella, spirulina, and wheatgrass are absolutely crucial. Every time I have my vegetable smoothie, I make sure to include these three powders, no matter which vegetable recipes I'm blending. You can easily find all three of them on Amazon.

Chlorella
Spirulina
Wheatgrass

Conclusion

When I embarked on the process of pineal gland decalcification six years ago, I discovered various effective techniques. Among these techniques, the use of amethyst crystals stood out as they possess the ability to stimulate the pineal gland. It is worth mentioning that crystals are available for each chakra, offering a holistic approach to spiritual well-being.

Your kundalini and chakras will truly appreciate any nourishment that originates from the earth. However, there are exceptional products available that greatly aid in the decalcification and activation process.

There are: ***watercress (lettuce), pineapple, oranges, grapefruit, banana, coconut oil, watermelon, lemon, coconuts, avocado, oregano oil, neem extract, organic blue ice skate fish oil and vitamin D12, zeolite, hemp seed and hemp powder, garlic, cilantro, and bentonite clay.***

As previously stated, incorporating daily sungazing into your routine is not only beneficial for the pineal gland, but also promotes overall health, which is why it is a key component of The Serpents Way. The consumption of ayahuasca plants or ayahuasca tea, a practice commonly employed by shamans, can result in profound experiences and vivid hallucinations due to its ability to quickly unlock your third eye.

When it comes to meditation, the most effective technique involves fixating on a candle in complete darkness, while concentrating on the breath and attaining a state of mental calmness. The early morning hours at dawn are particularly beneficial for meditation as they actively stimulate the pineal gland.

Lightly tapping the center of your forehead, right between your eyebrows, triggers the pineal gland and all three parts of the Crystal Palace. This vibration creates a wave that goes straight to the pineal gland, activating it. The vibration also travels through the bones to the sphenoid, which then stimulates the pituitary gland located in the Sella turcica. Activating the pineal and other glands through toning or chanting can energize the Cerebral Spinal Fluid by sending vibrations into the Crystal Palace.

When you press your tongue against the roof of your mouth, you stimulate the pituitary gland, leading to the activation of the pineal gland and hypothalamus via their physical and chemical pathways. The act of squeezing our eyes creates a muscular connection with the sphenoid bone, activating the pituitary gland. When we suck in our cheeks, it moves the jaw and stimulates the neck and cranial pumps. By contracting the anal sphincter and perineum, vibrations are sent to the muscles surrounding the anus and the pelvic floor. These vibrations then travel up the spine and dural tube from the pelvis to the occiput. The intracranial membrane system transfers these vibrations to the center of the head, activating the pineal and pituitary glands.

Increased melatonin levels are a response to darkness, causing the pineal gland to release pinoline and DMT, thus assisting in the activation of the third eye. You can find a variety of frequency music on YouTube that can help with decalcification.

In order to truly embark on The Serpents Way and attain kundalini awakening and self-mastery, the conservation and transmutation of sexual energy are paramount. Without this crucial foundation, all other endeavors are in vain. By embracing celibacy and/or sexual alchemy, one can conquer lust and safeguard their seed, ensuring progress and fulfillment on this transformative path. Preserving and transforming sexual energy is the key to awakening the inner serpent or the kundalini energy, which in turn activates all chakras.

> "This third eye is the link connecting humans with the spiritual world or, to be more correct, with the higher spiritual nature of them selves. When Kundalini reaches this point, divine consciousness is attained. " — **Manly P. Hall**

Chapter 13

YOUR 7 INNER SUNS/CHAKRAS

Everything is energy, unseen or seen/materialized. Whenever people begin to explore the immense world of energy they tend to get stars in their eyes around the heart chakra. Quite a few New age practices are about operating from the heart center. Even though this can be useful it is somehow limited. The heart center has so many layers going on. Some of the layers are hate, despair, depression, sadness, grief and resentment. All these layers suppress or cover the core of the heart which is LOVE. I'm speaking metaphorically and not anatomically here. The heart is one of the main seven energy centers. When you anchor your full awareness in your heart neglecting the other energy centers or chakras, overwhelms you. Is like working constantly and hard on fixing a raised bed in your garden and neglecting the other 6 raised beds. In the 6 beds, weeds will grow, or whatever is planted there will wilt. You should work daily on all of them.

The same applies for you energy centers. Your solar plexus is a better place to begin anchoring your full awareness, instead of beginning with the heart. Unless the heart center is the last one left to be unblocked/balanced, assuming you have already worked on the other lower 3 chakras/energy centers. The solar plexus deals with willpower, personal responsibility and self-esteem. When you develop personal responsibility (as an example) you also develop self-awareness, you are conscious of your choices therefore, you think for yourself.

What good is going to do if you only focus on your heart if you cannot think for yourself. The world doesn't get destroyed by evil people but by good hearted people that are naïve and cannot think for themselves. When you have this energy imbalanced, then you will have low-self esteem (not thinking for yourself), you will have manipulative tendencies which means that your heart cannot fully open if you have tendencies to lie and deceive for personal gain. You will misuse your powers.

> The spectrum of energy/full divine consciousness may be comparable with the spectrum of colors of the sunlight. This sunlight breaks up into 7 colors through the prism. Sunlight entails of seven colors because the light of divine consciousness is always spoken/expressed through the law of number 7, or the seven stages. The law of number seven, by which the divine consciousness of the Absolute expresses itself as the most general existence, is reflected in man as the microcosm of the overall existence. It is maintained as the system of the psychoenergetic centers otherwise known as C H A K R A S. – **Ivan Antic**

Since everything is energy, and energy is neutral, you are the only one responsible what you do with the energy, you can use it to build and heal or harm and destroy. All energy is divine from the same source. All energy is neutral, neither positive not negative. Well, the electromagnetic field which is energy has both masculine and feminine (positive and negative) aspects to it but I am talking about the energy in relation to your actions. Your actions are what determine if energy is transmuted in negativity or positivity. The divine consciousness or energy gets expressed as the full **spectrum** of overall existence. Everything that is possible can be expressed. What you think is possible and what is possible is not the same thing.

Your energy centers are your inner suns or chakras. These inner suns are whirls of energy in the form of a torus which connects consciousness with the existence. There is only one consciousness, the complete, absolute one that we all are part of. The word chakra means whirl of wheel because these energy centers spin in circles like a wheel. These energy centers cannot be seen with the naked eye, but they can bee seen when you attune yourself to the spiritual void, when you vibrate very high in frequency you can see (with your third eye) things you cannot see with your physical eyes.

The more you associate with your inner suns, the more you end up in the flow of your natural course or life path. When you energy centers begin to open or unblock, your digestive fire is stronger, your mind becomes clearer, your intentions become stronger and you feel loved and you will emit love back to the world. Your heart is your central sun. Your heart is the fourth energy center/chakra whether you begin counting from the bottom or the top.

Your heart is in the middle, there are three chakras (or inner suns) above the heart chakra and three below, total of 7 major chakras (but there are many more subtle ones, 144 in total. Starting from the bottom the order of the inner suns are the **Root, Sacral, Solar Plexus, Heart, Throat, Third Eye and Crown**. Chakras have their own individual colors which are in agreement/accordance/unity with the basic colors of the spectrum of sunlight. These energy centers (chakras or inner suns) are on the exact location of the glands in the human body which determine all the hormonal functions as well as functioning of all the vital organs. We are much more complicated than we think we are. We are not just our physical body.

Technically we have a body but we are not it. It is imperative to balance the inner suns. In some books or online you may have read/heard "activating the chakras". Without activated chakras we wouldn't be able to exist. I'm sure the authors meant "*balancing the chakras*". We all have them since birth, but with time our body ended up in disharmony from a myriad of external poisons/influences. It is very important what you think, say and do daily for an optimal healthy existence. Everything you hear and see, affects your glands, organs, chakras and everything that makes you, "YOU". Your body receives sunlight through the eyes at most. The chakras, sunlight, colors and the functioning of the vital organs interconnect in one union which gives life.

These energy centers play a crucial role in our physical, emotional, and spiritual well-being. Understanding their significance can help you identify any blockages or imbalances, allowing you to take steps towards healing and balance.

(a) ROOT chakra deals with **Survival**. This chakra is blocked by fear.

(b) SACRAL chakra deals with **Pleasure**, it is blocked by guilt.

(c) SOLAR PLEXUS chakra deals with **Willpowe**r, it is blocked by shame.

(d) HEART chakra deals with **Love** and it is blocked by grief.

(e) THROAT chakra deals with **Truth**, it is blocked by lies.

(f) THIRD EYE chakra deals with **Insight** and it is blocked by illusion.

(g) CROWN chakra deals with **Cosmic Energy**, it is blocked by ego.

Now let's look at each individual chakra.

WHAT IS? - The root chakra is the first chakra. Its energy is based on the earth element. It's associated with the feeling of safety and grounding. It's at the base of the chakra system and lays the foundation for expansion in your life. The root energy center connects us to the pure energy of nature, with the energy of PLANEt Earth. Our body receives all the vital energy for life from this chakra in the most elementary sense, whole and unpolarized. Our survival instinct derives from this raw energy base/root chakra.

LOCATION - The first chakra or root chakra is located at the base of the spine. The corresponding body locations are the perineum, along the first three vertebrae, at the pelvic plexus. This chakra is often represented as a cone of energy starting at the base of the spine and going downward and then slightly bent up.

CHARACTERISTICS OF THE ROOT SUN/CHAKRA - The first chakra is associated with the following functions or behavioral characteristics:

- Security, safety
- Survival
- Basic needs (food, sleep, shelter, self-preservation, etc.)
- Physicality, physical identity and aspects of self
- Grounding
- Support and foundation for living our lives

The root chakra provides the foundation on which we build our life. It supports us in growing and feeling safe into exploring all the aspects of life. It is related to our feeling of safety and security, whether it's physical or regarding our bodily needs or metaphorical regarding housing and financial safety. To sum it up, the first chakra questions are around the idea of survival and safety. The root chakra is where we ground ourselves into the earth and anchor our energy into the manifested world.

IMBALANCED ROOT CHAKRA - At the emotional level, the deficiencies or imbalance in the first chakra are related to:

- Excessive negativity, cynicism
- Eating disorders
- Greed, avarice
- Illusion
- Excessive feeling of insecurity, living on survival mode constantly

For a person who has imbalance in the first chakra, it might be hard to feel safe in the world and everything looks like a potential risk. The desire for security dominates and can translate into concerns over the job situation, physical safety, shelter, health. A blocked root chakra may turn into behaviours ruled mainly by fear. Your chakras might be blocked (the better term would be "imbalanced") if you feel stuck, tired, or emotionally out of balance. These energy centers in your body can get "clogged" with negative feelings or life stress. Maybe you have trouble speaking your mind? That could mean your throat chakra (which you will read later) needs help.

Or perhaps money worries throw you off? Your root chakra may need some attention. Discovering your chakra system can be a thrilling step in your spiritual journey. Each of the seven chakras is tied to different parts of your being. They range from the root chakra, which connects to stability and survival, up to the crown chakra that links you with the universe and higher states of consciousness. Feeling curious or out-of-sync might signal it's time for a personal exploration. Knowing which specific chakra matches your energetic balance will help guide you. You may resonate more with one over others due to unique life experiences or current challenges faced.

Engaging with this self-awareness empowers you on a path filled with wisdom, healing, and growth. You might feel off or stuck in life if your chakras are not balanced. To find out which chakra may be imbalanced, pay attention to your body and emotions. Think about areas where you face issues. Feeling anxious a lot? Your heart chakra might need some care. Trouble speaking up for yourself could mean your throat chakra is blocked. Take a moment each day to check in with yourself. Notice any strange feelings in different parts of your body. Do you have pain or tightness somewhere? This can signal an imbalance too.

Listening to what's going on inside can help point out which chakras are asking for attention so that you can focus on healing them. Healing your chakras begins with identifying which one needs attention. By understanding the specific chakra that requires healing, you can focus on targeted practices like meditation, affirmations, or using healing stones to restore balance and vitality to that area of your life.

OPENING THE ROOT CHAKRA - There are many ways to open the root chakra. For example, you can engage more in grounding and earth-related activities (for example, connection with nature, gardening, cooking healthy, hiking).

The main idea is to work at growing your "roots" in a safe and comfortable environment (i.e., surround yourself with earth colors/colours, objects reminding you of nature, stability; or on the contrary, if you wish to feel less stuck, do the opposite).

Yoga for the root chakra can be a more physical way to bridge the body and mind and restore a more balanced energy flow.

WHAT'S IN THE MULADHARA OR ROOT CHAKRA NAME? - The first chakra is referred to as:

- Root chakra
- Muladhara
- Adhara

Its Sanskrit name is "Muladhara" can signify "base", 'foundation", "root support".

The first chakra is associated with the Earth element.

CHAKRA COLORS: THE RED CHAKRA - The typical color used to represent the root chakra is a rich vermilion red. This is the color used on its symbol to fill its petals. Traditionally, it is also associated with the color yellow or gold (this is the color of its element as opposed to its petals). In the spectrum of chakra colors, red symbolizes strength, vitality, and stimulates our instinctual tendencies.

ROOT CHAKRA SYMBOL - The symbol of the root chakra is composed of a four-petaled lotus flower, often stylized as a circle with four petals with a downward-pointing triangle.

The downward-pointing triangle is a symbol of spirit connecting with matter, grounding on the earth and our earthly existence, in our bodies. It's seen as the center of our vital life force and is the seat where kundalini stays coiled, dormant, until is wakes up to distribute its energy through all the other chakras.

> "An out-of-balance Root Chakra could express its condition with issues such as a lack of grounding, fear of moving forward in life, general anxiety, impatience, and addiction. Physically, the body might respond with pain, growth problems, weight issues, colitis, diarrhea, hemorrhoids, or menopausal symptoms. You may also constantly lack energy, feel tired or, if your Root Chakra is overly active, you can be high-strung, have difficulty sleeping, or act aggressive and greedy"
> – **Mirtha Contreras**

The base chakra, also known as the root chakra, serves as the fundamental energy hub of your body. It is dedicated to ensuring the well-being and nurturing of your physical form. This chakra connects you to your purpose and your consciousness of your physical existence.

Knowing yourself and mastering your body enables you to fully exist in physical control. Being able to authentically be yourself is the wonder of life on this planet. Once your root chakra is fully open, you will experience a profound sense of security, stability, and fearlessness.

You will also feel a deep connection not only to the Earth but also to your loved ones, friends, colleagues, and partners. Begin each practice by reciting the root mantras to open your meditation, or conclude with them for closure. These affirmations can also be used throughout the day for focused healing.

This chakra, also recognized as the church of Ephesus in the book of revelation, houses the Kundalini, the serpentine fire, which lies dormant coiled three and a half times inside.

Element – Earth

Root Mantras

I trust

I am supported

I am safe to be myself

I ground down to rise up

Sanskrit Root Mantras

OM BHUR {aum bur} (Om and salutations to the earth plane/first chakra)

OM NAMAH SHIVAYA {aum num-ha shi-whyah} (Calling in all the elements under conscious control for grounding: mind, Earth, water, fire, air, ether)

Gyan Mudra

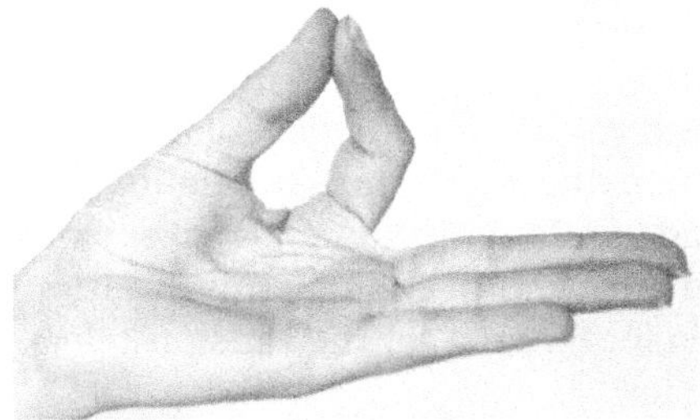

Gently touch the tip of your index finger and thumb while your palm remains open.

You can practice this mudra anytime during your meditation to more powerfully connect with grounding energy.

5-Minute Meditation

Differing from the other forms of meditations, this particular one directs its focus towards your physical body. To initiate, find a comfortable position in a chair or, if you wish to establish a connection with the Earth, sit on the floor. If you happen to be outside, sitting against a tree can be beneficial. Let your eyelids grow heavy, elongate your spine, release any tension in your shoulders, unclench your jaw, and allow your tongue to rest at the bottom of your mouth. Visualize a vibrant red sphere of energy.

Visualize the ball in your mind's eye or transfer it to the specific body part you are focusing on. Envision it growing larger and smaller. The position of the vibrant energy ball may vary each time. Now, start taking deep breaths, allowing the air to fill your lungs and travel down your spine, reaching your pelvic bowl. As you exhale, allow your breath to flow down through your legs, sending the vital life-force energy back to the Earth through the soles of your feet. Take a few deep breaths and you will begin to feel a sense of centeredness. Pay attention to this sensation.

Are you aware of any resistance? If so, focus your breath on those areas to promote relaxation. If you encounter resistance, simply observe it without feeling the need to fix or change anything. Begin by squeezing your toes together for a few seconds and then releasing them. Take a brief pause to observe the sensations that link you to this specific body part. Once you have acknowledged the messages conveyed by this part, proceed further. Rotate your ankles a few times and flex your knees individually.

Inhale deeply, allowing your breath to reach your hips, and consider circling them. Experience the sensation of connecting with these regions. Gently squeeze your perineum, take a deep breath into your abdomen, and release it audibly. Finally, stretch the left side of your body and then the right side. Inhale deeply into the back of your shoulder blades, allowing your chest to expand towards the sky. Rotate your shoulders and neck in circular motions, first clockwise and then counterclockwise. Feel the tension release as you breathe into your upper back.

Rotate your wrists by bending your elbows, and if desired, roll your tongue against the roof of your mouth. Finally, tightly squeeze your eyelids shut and furrow your brow line. Hold for a brief moment before letting go. Next, shift your attention to the crown of your head. Gently rub it and indulge in a soothing scalp massage to rejuvenate the topmost part of your body. Once you feel satisfied, assume the root chakra mudra and chant your selected root mantra. Finally, take a final deep breath, allowing it to fill your entire being, reaching all the way down to the base of your spine.

Let go of your breath, sending it back to the Earth. If your eyes were closed, open them and enter a space of reflection with a gentle gaze. Recognize what you were able to observe during your meditation. If you feel inclined, you can make note of any emotions that emerged, although this step is entirely optional.

"When the Kundalini is still enclosed within the Muladhara chakra, the seven chakras hang downwards. However, when the Kundalini ascends through Brahmanadi, then the marvelous petals of these chakras turn upward towards Brahmarandhra, marvellously gleaming with the incomparable sexual fire of Kundalini" – **Samael Aun Weor**

15-Minute Meditation

The earth's center emits a harmonious love frequency that grounds the entire planet. By anchoring yourself to this core, you can rejuvenate your stability, magnetism, and overall health. Within Mother Earth resides a potent crystal capable of transforming negativity into pure love. Use this meditation to access her nurturing energy. Sit or stand with a straight spine, whether indoors or outdoors leaning against a tree.

Start by taking deep breaths, inhaling deeply and allowing the breath to travel down your spine, reaching all the way to your pelvic area. As you exhale, imagine releasing the breath through your legs, sending the vital life-force energy back to the Earth through the soles of your feet. After a few moments of deep breathing, you will begin to feel a sense of calm and centeredness. Pay attention to this sensation. Are there any areas of resistance? Take a moment to breathe into those areas, allowing yourself to relax and let go.

As you take in each new breath, imagine it entering through the crown of your head, a few inches above your headspace. Allow each breath to cascade down through your head, neck, and spine, channeling its energy deep into the Earth. Embrace the profound connection between your body and the ground, feeling the unwavering support beneath you. Envision your seat as a powerful link to the Earth, or if you're standing, visualize your feet sprouting radiant golden roots that entwine to create a magnificent cord. (You can opt for a different color if you prefer.)

Let this connection firmly anchor your body to the Earth. Experience the sensation of a golden point emanating from the tip of your tailbone, pulsating and radiating energy. Imagine this vibrant cord extending deep into the Earth, penetrating through its layers until it reaches the core. Envision a magnificent ruby-red crystal residing at the heart of the planet, emanating a potent frequency of grounded love. This crystal has accumulated healing energy over countless ages and possesses the ability to effortlessly and unconditionally restore your trust and stability.

Always remember, the center of the Earth resonates with a flawless frequency of love that grounds and nurtures the entire planet. Start channeling the grounding energy of the red crystal. Watch as it moves up the golden cord with a vibrant electric glow. Repeat one of your root mantras while visualizing the crystal's energy connecting with your root chakra and spreading outwards. Witness it flow through your pelvis, hips, seat, and sexual organs. Feel the magnetic pull. Embrace the surge of unconditional love and power filling you.

This is a true Earth healing. Tap into centuries of wisdom and supportive energy rising from the Earth as you absorb the energy into your pelvis and saturate yourself. Immerse yourself in the captivating energy shift that leads you to a state of perfect balance. Feel this energy enveloping your chakras, saturating them with a warm red light that effortlessly transmutes any fears, worries, doubts, or insecurities that may linger within. Remember, the emphasis of this exercise is on the feeling rather than the specific hues of color.

As you bask in this nurturing energy, visualize the red light ascending your spine, guided by the golden cord as a conduit. Witness the light as it beams out from your crown and merges with the vastness of the universe. Embrace the grounding energy that flows within you, and allow your breath to transport this energy to every cell in your entire being. With sincere gratitude, thank yourself for being present today; you can choose to conclude your practice by chanting or audibly reciting your selected root mantra.

Extend your hands onto the Earth and vocalize your appreciation by saying, "Thank you!" Bestow blessings upon the Earth, acknowledging the love, light, and energy it has graciously bestowed upon you throughout your meditation and will continue to offer even after your session concludes. If you wish, take a brief moment to compare your current state with how you felt at the beginning of your meditation. If you feel compelled, jot down any fresh insights that have emerged during your practice.

> **"This is the fundamental or coccygeal chakra. This chakra nourishes all the other chakras with its sexual energy. The Kundalini is enclosed with the Muladhara chakra"** – Samael Aun Weor

30-Minute Meditation

Engage in this exercise to delve into the fundamental elements that impact your happiness, stability, thoughts, and beliefs. By immersing yourself in this meditation, you will uncover profound insights about your authentic self and the persona you consciously portray each day. You have the flexibility to practice this meditation either seated or lying down. If you choose to lie down, ensure that your body remains flat. Take a moment to acknowledge the profound connection formed by every part of your body touching the Earth, appreciating the unity it brings.

Start by taking deep breaths, allowing the air to fill your lungs and flow down your spine, reaching your pelvic bowl. As you exhale, release the breath through your legs, allowing the life-force energy to return to the Earth through the soles of your feet. Take a moment to become aware of the centering sensation that arises. Are there any areas of resistance? Direct your breath towards those areas to promote relaxation. Position your hands on your pubic bone or place one hand on each hip, below your navel.

Now, visualize and call upon a vibrant crimson healing light to flow into your pelvic region. Feel the energy spreading throughout your pelvic bowl and descending along your spinal column. Allow the intense red light to nourish your kidneys, colon, tailbone, and upper thighs. Direct your breath towards your lower back and hip sockets, and continue to guide it towards your sexual organs. As you exhale, allow your breath to flow down your legs, activating the chakras located on the soles of your feet. There are many more little chakras in the body beside the main 7.

Take a moment to observe any sensations or emotions that arise within you when you focus on this area. How do you feel at this moment? Are you using meditation as a means to release past or present emotions? Perhaps you're sitting down to address a physical issue. Pay close attention to the feelings that emerge, even if they bring discomfort. These uncomfortable feelings indicate areas that require extra care and compassion.

Here are a couple of meditation suggestions to include:

Which essential needs for survival are currently impacting my life the most?

How am I adapting to changes or transitions?

How am I dealing with grief or loss?

What aspects of my life can I remove that have caused instability, insecurity, financial difficulties, lack of connection, self-preservation, or support?

Am I unknowingly influenced by false beliefs, limiting thoughts, or fears?

Am I willing to confront the painful areas and understand the root cause of my suffering?

Am I hindering my own progress by shielding myself from the things I fear?

What is the universe reflecting back to me at this moment? Can these reflections guide me in identifying where my personal growth and inner work lie?

Pay attention to where you feel emotions in your body while contemplating these ideas. Concentrate on your breath and focus on these specific areas, intending to direct these energies towards the red light of your root chakra. Once you have gained valuable feedback, let go of what no longer benefits you. With your next exhale, imagine the red light descending down your left leg, through your left foot, and grounding into the Earth.

Offer Earth all your unneeded possessions. As you reflect on these matters, pay attention to where you feel emotions in your body. Concentrate on your breath and awareness in these spots, aiming to direct these energies towards the red light of your root chakra. Once you've gathered useful insights, let go of what is no longer beneficial. As you exhale, visualize the red light flowing down your left leg, through your left foot, and into the Earth.

This concept is known as the Stability Triangle. During the final moments of the sequence, exhale deeply while directing your breath down the left leg, allowing the red light to follow. As the breath reaches the left foot, it will transition to the right foot, connecting both feet with this radiant light energy. On your next inhale, the light will ascend back up your right leg, creating a red triangle of light that converges at your root area. Perform the Stability Triangle three times in succession. Recite your root mantra three times. Your session has now concluded.

"A healthy root chakra allows a person to be energetically grounded – a concept that is critical to understanding basic aliveness and well-being. Grounding orients us in time and space, and connects us to the environment. Being grounded gives us a source of strength through connection to our body and environment. Physically this happens through the legs and feet, through which excitement is passed up into the body and excess is discharged downward into the ground. This means we can stand on our own two feet and move forward in life. Only by drawing energy up from the base can we create the liberating current that flows to the crown" – **Anodea Judith**

"Movement is a medicine for creating change in a person's physical, emotional, and mental states" – Carol Welch

The sacral chakra, known as Svadhisthana, is often referred to as the "dwelling place of the self." This energy center is associated with creativity, receptivity, passion, sensuality, and emotions. When the sacral chakra is blocked, it can indicate a disconnection from emotions, difficulty in releasing things, and sexual issues such as feeling closed off, fertility problems, or low libido.

Lower digestive issues may also be encountered. When the sacral chakra is aligned, emotions flow freely and authentically. This alignment enables you to feel confident in sharing innovative thoughts openly. Embracing risks becomes easier, propelling you towards a harmonious state and distinctive outward expression. In the book of revelation, this chakra is identified as the church of Smyrna and is associated with the prostate in men and the uterus in women.

Immerse yourself in the depths of chakra wisdom with a visit to our (*this book's authors' webpage*) "dragon consciousness" tab in the web page here: **https://theserpentsway.com/dragons-consciousness/**.

Element – Water

Sacral Mantras

I am Creator/Creatrix (the Divine Feminine Creator).

I am open to receive

I feel deeply

Sanskrit Sacral Mantras

OM BHUVAHA {aum bu-vah-hah} (Om and salutations to the atmospheric plane/second chakra).

OM VYAVA SAYAYA NAMAHA {aum vyah-vah sah-yah nah-mah-hah} (invoking determination to be successful in efforts leading to self mastery).

Dhyani Mudra

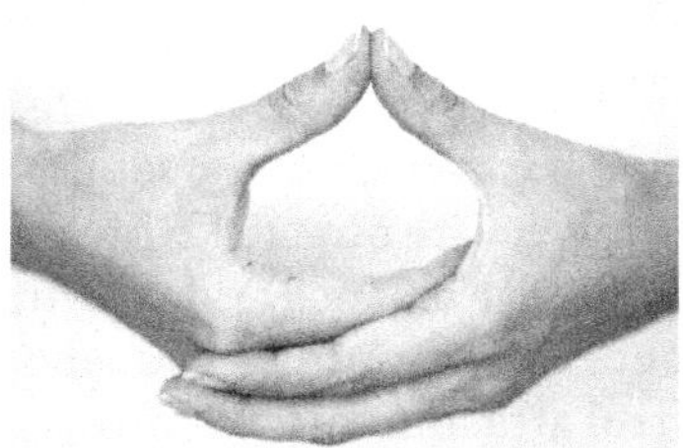

Place your hands in your lap, palms up. Slide your left hand under the backs of the fingers on your right hand. Your thumbs will touch together lightly, creating an oval cavern.

5-Mintue Meditation

The term "*anima*" is derived from the Latin word "animus" and refers to the soul or spirit, representing one's vital life-force energy. Psychologist Carl Jung employed this concept in his study of "*the feminine side of men.*" The duality of yin and yang is used to describe this phenomenon, encompassing both the masculine side of women. Through this meditation, we will delve into and harmonize our yin and yang attributes.

For this meditation, you have the option to practice either seated or lying down. If you choose to sit, ensure that you are in a relaxed and comfortable position with a straight spine. Start by allowing your eyelids to feel heavy and focus on lengthening your breath. Ease into your practice by observing the space at the top and bottom of each breath as it flows in and out slowly. You can place your hands above your hip bones or rest them in your lap, with your palms positioned below your navel, gently cradling your abdomen.

If you're struggling with lower back issues, try resting your hands on your lower back with palms facing inward for a comfortable stance. Focus on your exhales and expand your breath and personal energy field beyond your physical boundaries.

Visualize creating a bubble around yourself, approximately six feet wide, with you positioned at the center. Envision the bubble's walls as a protective shield of shimmering orange light, encircling you in a sacred and serene space. Within this space, permit the energy from your palms to flow into your body.

Breathe in slowly and deeply, allowing the air to flow through each side of your body, one at a time. As you exhale, imagine releasing your breath into the Earth through the soles of your feet. Notice any tingling or sensations of warmth, coolness, electricity, or pulsation as the energy moves through you. Take a moment to observe and acknowledge any internal or external feelings. Stay present and centered by staying connected to your breath, avoiding any distractions. The energy you are directing towards your sacral chakra is actively working to restore balance and stability.

Embrace the power of equilibrium as you take a deep breath in. Let go of the urge to control attachments, outcomes, or time-lines as you exhale. Allow yourself to be receptive and adopt a flexible mindset with every breath out.

Set your intention to release negative thought patterns and fill your being with nurturing care for your spirit. Notice how the light within your sacral bubble grows brighter with each exhale. Gently open your eyes if they were closed, and reacquaint yourself with the present moment. Observe the vibrant glow surrounding your sacral chakra. Take a deep breath, allowing the newfound balance to permeate your back, hips, and abdomen.

Feel the heightened energy coursing through your entire being. Express gratitude for dedicating this time to self-care, and conclude your session with a sacral mantra. If you feel inclined, jot down any emotions that surfaced during your practice, although this step is entirely up to you.

"The Kundalini passes through chakra after chakra. This is how the different states of consciousness are opened. This how the sadhaka (achiever, magician, adept, perfecting, proving) penetrates all the states of cosmic consciousness until finally acquiring the awakening of Absolute consciousness" – Samael Aun Weor

15-Minute Meditation

Engaging in ancient tribal rituals that involve water cleansing enables us to connect with our true selves. Essentially, this practice allows us to cleanse ourselves of past mistakes and release lingering regrets. This profound form of meditation holds sacred significance while remaining accessible to anyone who navigates the waves of emotions. You can easily practice this meditation while lying down.

Ensure you are seated in a comfortable and relaxed position with your eyes closed and the lights dimmed. Begin with your palms facing up, resting gently. Focus on lengthening your breath. Notice the space at the top and bottom of each breath as you inhale and exhale slowly. Connect with your emotions in the present moment. Set the intention to be open, responsive, and receptive to positivity. Keep clearing your mind.

Pay attention to your five senses as you inhale, allowing them to gradually fill your consciousness. Acknowledge any resistance you may encounter. Be mindful of the space within you and appreciate the positive attributes it holds, like tranquility, peace, calmness, and fluidity. Identify any negative thoughts or emotions that arise, such as anger, sadness, or loneliness. Embrace these thoughts with a compassionate mindset, as you would for a dear friend. Consider relabeling any resistance as "helpful" once you become more comfortable with this exercise.

Identify your current emotions and then release anything you want to leave behind for the day. Now, assume the sacral mudra position. If you are lying down, place your hands on your navel; if you are sitting, rest them in your lap. Visualize a calming waterfall flowing gently.

Imagine yourself standing behind the water or walking through it. You might be lying in a stream or standing in a shower. Let the water wash over you, purifying and removing any heaviness, like dirt being rinsed away from your body.

Feel the transformative water calming your inner astral plane, bringing clarity and tranquility to your subtle body and entire physical being. Allow it to purify your sacral chakra with restorative liquidity, rejuvenating your lower back, hips, and lower abdomen. Release any toxicity as you cleanse yourself with this healing water. Make a conscious choice to move forward with peace and clarity, leaving behind anything that no longer has a place in your life.

Pay attention to the transition this shift generates and the opportunities it uncovers for you. You can opt to dry yourself off now. Alternatively, you can remain in a state of mindfulness for a few extra moments.

Consider your current feelings, and allow yourself enough time to respond. Take note of your physical, mental, and emotional well-being before concluding your practice with a personal mantra.

"Emotion is the chief source of all becoming conscious. There can be no transforming of darkness into light and of apathy into movement without emotion" – **C.G. Jung**

30-Minute Meditation

Throughout this exercise, you will delve into your true self as a sovereign creator. By engaging in this meditation, you will access and ignite your highest excitement, where your inspiration thrives and expands. Following your highest excitement in each moment (and residing in your highest vibration) will help you uncover your ultimate life path. Let this meditation guide you towards healing and ultimate fulfillment. You can practice this meditation while seated or lying down.

Rest your hands in your lap or beside you, palms facing up, as you begin. Inhale deeply, feeling your lungs expand and your breath travel down your spine, all the way to your sacrum and lower abdomen. As you exhale, release your breath through your legs, allowing the prana, the life-force energy carried in your breath, to flow back to the Earth through the soles of your feet. Find your center through deep breathing.

Notice any resistance within you and breathe into those areas to encourage relaxation. Picture a revitalizing orange light entering your sacral region as you inhale. Let it spread through your abdomen, expanding with each exhale. Delicately infuse every organ, individually, with the awe-inspiring radiance of orange light frequencies: the bladder, kidneys, lower back muscles, uterus and ovaries (for females), prostate and testes (for males), and the lower intestines. Inhale deeply three more times to direct your energy towards any specific areas in need of healing. If visualizing light colors is challenging, remember that the key is the sensation rather than the specific hues. As you progress through this exercise, breathe deeply into the sacral region on both sides of your body. Observe your body's equilibrium. How are you feeling today?

As you immerse yourself in the transformative energy of healing light, tap into the depths of your creative and expressive potential by embracing your inner creator/creatrix. Your imagination is a remarkable superpower, while inspiration ignites a spark within you and unveils the infinite possibilities that lie ahead. With the power of your imagination, you can transcend the limitations of the physical world and embark on extraordinary journeys. Harness the power of your highest inspiration to imagine the creation you yearn for at this precise moment. Give yourself the freedom to welcome new ideas.Envision yourself crafting a compelling vision that sparks your motivation to excel, conquer challenges, surpass limitations, or evolve into an unrestrained version of yourself. If money was not a factor, how would this influence your vision? Can you identify any limiting beliefs during this exercise?

Have you ever entertained the thought of embarking on the journey of parenthood and welcoming a baby into your life? Allow yourself to delve into the realm of imagination and envision the profound connection that will be established when this precious soul enters your existence. Visualize the appearance, the tactile sensations, and the harmonious sounds that will accompany this little miracle. On the other hand, if you find yourself engrossed in a creative endeavor, be it art, music, or writing, what intricate details materialize in your mind's canvas?

How does this imaginative exercise stir your emotions? Can you paint a picture of the environment in which your creative pursuit thrives? Are there any fellow collaborators or like-minded individuals involved in this process? Reflect upon what brings you the utmost satisfaction in the present moment. Pay attention to the awakening of your sensual energy, also known as shakti or kundalini energy, as you flow with your feelings. By circling your hips a few times, you can help this energy move freely through the rest of your chakras.

This activation is a lovely result of warming up the sacral region and attuning your body to new healing frequencies. Sensuality should not be equated with sexuality. It is a natural essence or attribute that belongs to you inherently, independent of any sexual behavior or actions. Recognize that this expression of sensuality resides within you, growing and anticipating the perfect time to manifest itself. Keep evolving your visions for the future or allow them to blossom within you as they mature, prosper, and extend. Show appreciation to yourself for being here today.

Recite your chosen sacred mantra or a newly unveiled mantra that aligns with your creative essence. Repeat your mantra three times. Your meditation session is now finished. Take a moment to reflect on how you feel now compared to when you started. If you feel compelled, write down any newfound revelations.

"In the first chakra, we learned to ground, stabilize, and focus.

Now, in the second charka, our challenge is just the opposite – to let go – to flow and move, to feel, and to yield. Movement and change stimulate consciousness. They stir the watery essence of feelings that flow through the body. Through movement, we extend our field of perception, increasing our sensory input. By moving the body, we build muscle tissue, increase circulation, stimulate nerve endings, and generally enhance the body's flexibility and aliveness. The flow of pleasure and excitation through the nervous system bathes the organism in sensation and awareness. Movement has its own pleasure" – Anodea Judith

"It is folly for a man to pray to the gods for that which he has the power to obtain by himself" – Epicurus

The solar plexus serves as the core of your vitality and strength, as well as your link to purpose. When this area is empowered, you experience a surge of motivation and energy, enabling you to materialize your desires in the physical realm. Conversely, a blocked solar plexus often leads to feelings of exhaustion and depletion.

Your internal battery may be depleted, resulting in feelings of anxiety and uncertainty about your journey. Decision-making may be a struggle, and you may also be dealing with issues related to digestion, adrenal glands, or kidneys.

Identified as the church of Pergamos in the book of revelation, this chakra is recognized as the church of fire. It resides in the region of the navel and governs the functioning of the liver, stomach, and other organs. The color of this chakra resembles the vividness of clouds charged with rays, lightning, and a vibrant flame.

Element – Fire

Solar Plexus Mantras

I am strong and powerful

I radiate light as the central sun of my universe

I am enough

I manifest my reality

Solar Plexus Mantras

OM SWAHA {aum swah-hah} (Om and salutations to the solar region/ third chakra)

OM SURYAYA NAMAHA {aum soor-yah-yah nah mah-hah} (Ode to the sun/solar power inside you)

Rudra Mudra

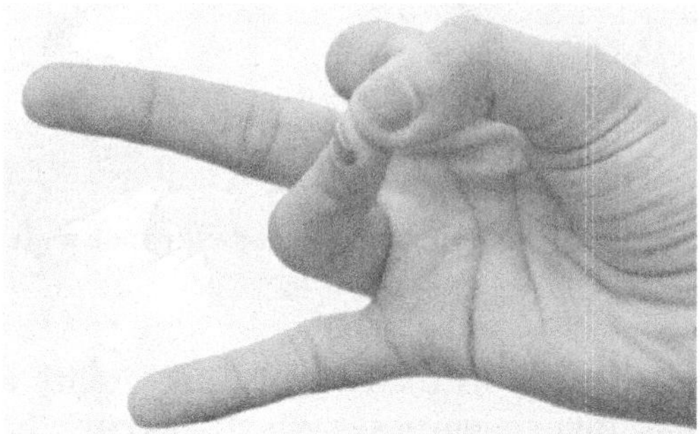

Draw the tips of your ring and index fingers in toward the thumb and lightly press. Your middle and pinky fingers should remain lengthened and extend comfortably.

You can practice this mudra anytime during meditation to more powerfully connect with solar plexus energy. This mudra enhances circulation and reduces dizziness.

5-Minute Meditation

Throughout various cultures, both in the past and present, festivities have been held to honor the sun and celebrate the summer solstice. These celebrations express gratitude towards the sun for its vital role in supplying energy to our planet and all living beings.

Today, you will rejuvenate yourself by basking in the sun's revitalizing wavelengths. It is recommended to stand during this meditation to fully embrace its energizing effects. However, if you prefer a seated position, that is acceptable, although the intention of this exercise is to adopt an invigorating posture.

Ensure that you are positioned close to a window or a natural source of light, regardless of whether you are standing or sitting. If you happen to be outdoors, make sure to face the sun.

Let your eyelids grow heavy, elongate your spine, release tension in your shoulders, unclench your jaw, and let your tongue rest at the bottom of your mouth. Keep your palms either by your sides, facing the light, or facing upwards on your lap.

Quiet any racing thoughts in your mind and refocus on your breath whenever you find yourself getting distracted. Embrace the sun's warmth on your face. Even on cloudy days, make a conscious effort to welcome solar energy. Take deep breaths into your belly, mid-back, and side body. Pay attention to the movement of your belly as you breathe in and out. Inhale new prana with each breath, and exhale any old energy. Feel your inner battery recharging as you absorb the golden sunlight.

Absorb all the energy you need to strengthen yourself and empower your ability to live, grow, and flourish. Keep drawing in sunlight until you feel a change in your vitality and energy levels. How do you perceive vitality? How is it reflected in your facial expression, posture, heart rate, stance, and breath? Identify at least three sensations of vitality within you. Every inhale sends radiant golden sun energy to every cell in your body, making you brighter, more vibrant, and revitalized. Be mindful of your breath as you exhale, cherishing every conscious inhale and exhale.

If you notice energy flowing to different parts of your body, acknowledge it before shifting your attention back to your belly or back. Inhale deeply into your core, then release your breath back to the Earth. Conclude your practice with a solar plexus mantra that resonates with you. Express your appreciation by giving thanks to Father Sun sincerely. If your eyes were shut, open them and, with a gentle look, enter a state of mindfulness, recognizing what you observed during your meditation. Now is the ideal moment to evaluate your current emotions.

> **"The church of Pergamos is opened when the sacred serpent rises and reaches the region of the navel. The power to govern over fire is granted unto us when we internally meditate on this precious lotus of the belly. Whosoever develops this chakra will not fear fire, but will be capable of remaining in fire for many hours without receiving any harm (see Daniel 3:23-27)"** – Samael Aun Weor

15-Minute Meditation

Purpose is not a destination to be reached, but rather the guiding light that shapes your life based on your passions and priorities. Your solar plexus serves as the gateway to connecting with and embodying this purpose-driven life. During this meditation, you will delve into the exploration of your purpose and the experience of manifesting that purpose in your daily life. Whether you prefer to meditate in a seated or lying position, start by taking deep breaths, filling your lungs and directing the breath down your spine to your belly.

As you breathe out, visualize your breath flowing down your legs, grounding the prana back to Earth through the soles of your feet. Connect with your inner wisdom. Focus on the purpose and intention you wish to nurture and bring to life in your reality, whether it's fostering a loving relationship, acing a job interview, working on a creative endeavor, attracting wealth, or nurturing yourself and your loved ones. Reflect on your personal definition of success when it comes to your intention. Imagine the sensation of being completely satisfied and having an abundance of happiness and well-being, which are essential for feeling fulfilled in your pursuit.

Take the time to connect with the underlying purpose behind your intention, recognizing that it may evolve and unfold in new and unexpected ways. Visualize every aspect of your intention materializing, while remaining open to the different paths your vision may guide you towards. Embrace the potential of this journey to break down barriers and open up new possibilities. Finally, think about one way you could celebrate this complete intention, or a milestone associated with it. Imagine this happening for you now.

Follow the feelings of joy and be open to experiencing other sensations and emotions that come with celebrating your achievement. If you have trouble finding your joy, try to sit with another intention that fulfills your greater underlying purpose more completely.

Express appreciation for your presence today with love and gratitude. Use your chosen mantra to mark the end of your practice. Reflect on your current feelings compared to when you started, and jot down any fresh insights if you feel compelled.

> **"Every time you don't follow your inner guidance, you feel a loss of energy, loss of power, a sense of spiritual deadness"** – Shakti Gawain

30-Minute Meditation

The sun holds a central position in our solar system and is intertwined with every dimension of life. It is theorized that each sun is linked to a central sun, with our sun's connection being to Alcyone from the Pleiadian star system.While there are countless galactic and central suns, the crucial point is that these suns function as repositories of knowledge and wisdom, sending out energy and love to the planets within their influence. This emphasizes the potential for us to unlock greater levels of love.

This meditation beckons you to align with the radiant energy of your own central sun, enabling you to embrace its love, joy, courage, and warmth. Whether you choose to practice this meditation while seated or lying down, start by taking deep breaths, filling your lungs and guiding the breath down your spine to the very core of your being located in your belly and diaphragm. As you exhale, allow your breath to flow down through your legs, sending the vital life-force energy back to the Earth through the soles of your feet. Take a few deep breaths and experience a sense of grounding and balance. Take note of this feeling.

Are there any areas of resistance? Direct your breath towards those areas to promote relaxation. Embrace the vibrant and revitalizing golden yellow light, ablaze with the intensity of the sun, as it enters the core of your being. Inhale purposefully, allowing the light to permeate your belly and expand effortlessly. With each breath, sense the heat growing, akin to the blazing inferno of your central sun, enlivening your core. Your radiant light shines brightly, a blazing flame that resides at the very heart of your universe.

Let it expand beyond your physical form, surpassing the immediate environment, and transcending the confines of the room as it ventures back into the vastness of the universe. Delicately infuse each targeted organ with a radiant golden hue, individually and without any specific sequence, ensuring that the light reaches the stomach, adrenal glands, liver, and the muscles in your side body and mid-back. Welcome the light energy to cut through anything blocking your path. Allow your anxieties, fears, nerves, and worries to melt away in your brilliance. Release something with every exhale.

Take three additional deep breaths to direct your energy towards specific areas needing healing, such as strengthening your back muscles or toning your abdomen after pregnancy. If you're struggling to visualize the color of light, focus on the sensation rather than the hues. Take deep breaths into your solar plexus area. Are you feeling energized and powerful, or drained? Remember, you're simply observing, not fixing. After filling yourself with healing light, expand by accessing your highest energy and awareness potential.

As you sink deeper into your meditation, embrace thoughts that resonate with your greatest potential. Allow any other thoughts to pass through your consciousness without attachment. Discover your innermost core value.

Reflect on restorative and empowering qualities like autonomy, respect, optimism, connection, pleasure, leadership, love, openness, abundance, or success. Choose one or two empowering qualities to center your focus on, as too many may overwhelm the meditation experience. To find fulfillment in each area, it is crucial to determine your needs. Take a moment to reflect on what you require and identify one or two actionable measures you can implement. Keep in mind that solar power is all about aligned action and activation.

Merely recognizing your values is insufficient; you must take action to manifest the change you desire. As you conclude your session, embrace an empowering mantra or mudra. Repeat your chosen mantra three times to fully unleash its power and activate its influence. With this, your session concludes successfully.

> **"A healthy third chakra exhibits energetic vitality. There is enjoyment and enthusiasm about life. Our sense of personal power gives us hope that we can make things viable for ourselves, and with this positive outlook we are not afraid to venture into the unknown, to take risks, or to make mistakes. When our energy field is strong, we do not get bogged down by obstacles. We do not lost our direction when challenged, but go forth with strength and will. We enjoy engaging in activity, tackling challenges, and grappling with the world. Activity develops our sense of power through constant presentation of new challenges"** – Anodea Judith

"Within you is a key, the master key, to the master suite. All you need to do is to open up from within. Find the opening, the spark that is within you- it is always there" – Ulonda Faye

The heart chakra acts as a portal to your soul, allowing the flow of your amorous energies. Within this sacred space, gratitude, compassion, patience, acceptance, joy, and love reside. It serves as a profound link that connects you to the entirety of existence.

Achieving balance in this chakra involves releasing judgments, fears, disappointments, unnecessary suffering, and victimizing attitudes. As you anchor yourself in a place of unconditional love towards yourself, the resonance of your heart chakra will spread and commence the healing process not just for your own physical body, but also for all beings across the universe, particularly those you are deeply connected to.

The heart chakra, known as the church of Thyatira in the book of revelation, is one of the seven sacred centers. These centers align with the seven degrees of the power of fire. Within the heart, love serves as a sanctuary, pure and universal in nature. It is essential to be cautious of blending sacred ecstasy with selfish love. Love, akin to the morning star, is untainted and impartial, transcending personal limitations and remaining ineffable.

Element - Air

Heart Mantras

My heart space is harmonious

I love myself with compassion

All love resides within me

I am love[**d**]

Sanskrit Heart Mantras

OM MAHA {aum mah-hah} (Om and salutations to the first spiritual region beyond the sun/fourth chakra).

OM TARE TUTTARE TURE SOHA {aum tah-reh too-tah-reh too-reh so-hah} (Calling upon compassion and divine love)

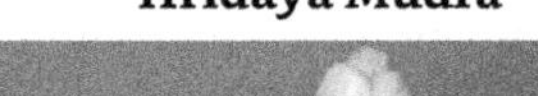

Hridaya Mudra

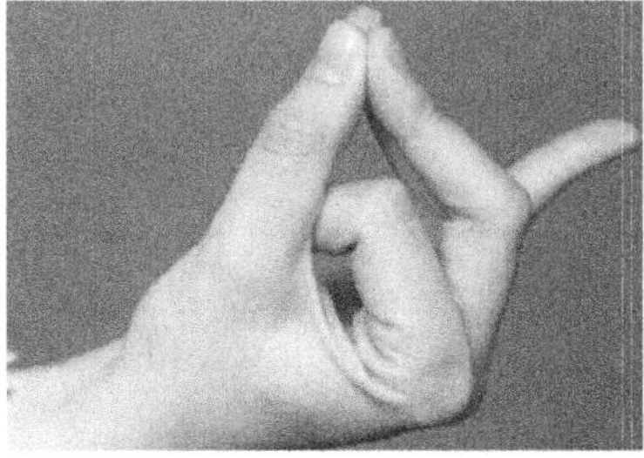

Curl your index finger toward the base of your thumb and bring your ring and middle fingers together with the tip of your thumb.

You can practice this mudra anytime during your meditation to more powerfully connect with your heart space. This mudra helps release pent-up emotions and stress and keeps the heart space open.

5-Minute Meditation

Unleashing an open heart has the profound power to transmute fear, separation, and skepticism. Opening yourself up to divine love, connection, knowledge, and trust enables you to uncover the essence and purpose of your soul. By embracing love, we harmonize with grace, peace, and unity. To initiate this process, let us embark on a serene meditation to delve deeper into the heart space. Practice this meditation in a seated, standing, or lying down position.

Begin by making your eyelids heavy, elongating your spine, releasing tension in your shoulders, relaxing your jaw, and dropping your tongue from the roof of your mouth. Notice your current feelings and send a compassionate breath to any part of your body that requires attention. Now, focus on the center of your chest, your ethereal heart space. Place your hands gently on your chest, ensuring that your palms are facing downwards. Merge the soothing warmth of your palms with the comforting warmth of your heart.

Quiet your thoughts and allow them to settle. Envision your heart space expanding towards the vast expanse of the sky. Engage with your heart space, recognizing it as a distinct part of yourself, and inquire about its feelings. Give your heart space the opportunity to express itself and truly listen to its voice. Make an effort to acknowledge and accept any emotions that arise within you as you attentively listen. Is there any resistance present?

After listening to your heart, allow a broad smile to appear on your face, even if there is no apparent reason to smile. Open your mouth slightly and break into a grin if you feel inclined. Smile at yourself as if you are greeting a dear friend you haven't seen in ages. Observe the warmth that your smile adds to your practice. Set aside your smile for a moment. Do you notice a decrease in your sense of connection? Try meditating with a smile next time and observe the significant difference it can make. This small action has been transformative for me.

I now smile during every meditation, regardless of its length. Take a moment to appreciate the energy flowing in and out of your heart space. Recite a Sanskrit heart mantra to deepen your practice. The Sanskrit language is uniquely beneficial and empowering for the heart space. It enables you to expand your loving consciousness and embrace the new sense of openness you have created. Take one final deep breath and release all tension on your exhale. Open your eyes if they were closed. With a gentle gaze, enter a state of mindful awareness, recognizing what you were able to experience during your meditation.

> **"The fires of the heart control the spinal fires. The fires of the heart control the ascent of the Kundalini. The ascent of the Kundalini happens in accordance with the merits of our heart. In order to get the benefit of only one vertebra in the spinal column, the yogi must submit to numerous trails and terrible purifications. The progress, development, and evolution of the Kundalini is very slow and difficult"** – Samael Aun Weor

15-Minute Meditation

The lotus flower is a representation of purity in body, mind, and speech. Originating from the mud, its tall stalks elevate the flower beyond attachment and desire, beyond separation and fear. Much like the lotus flower, your heart has emerged from the mud to bloom. It can be simple to become lost in the mud, ensnared in pain, suffering, and false narratives, unable to forgive and progress. Understand this is a prison of your own creation. You can choose to remain where you are or bravely let go.

Just make a decision. Extend forgiveness to yourself and to others. The best way to practice this meditation is while seated. Begin by closing your eyes, lengthening your spine, relaxing your shoulders, unclenching your jaw, and letting your tongue rest at the bottom of your mouth.Take note of your emotions and send a loving breath to any area that requires your attention. Concentrate on the center of your chest, your spiritual heart space. Position your hands with palms facing up on your lap or knees. If it resonates with you, incorporate a heart mudra for your hands as you intentionally open your heart space.

Calm your mind to connect with the vastness of openness. Visualize yourself resting on a massive, radiant lotus throne. Choose a pink, green, or alternative color. Allow the throne's light to fill your heart with joy; feel its resonance. Imagine the lotus as a grounding presence encircling you. Picture yourself at the center of the giant, glistening petals and glowing light. Reflect on Buddha's words, "Compassion that neglects oneself is not whole."

Reflect on all the challenges you have endured up until this point. If you find yourself in a difficult situation, it's important to acknowledge the struggles of others involved as well. This practice of compassion extends to everyone, even those who may not appear deserving of it at the moment, but most importantly, it extends to yourself. Whether you seek forgiveness or wish to offer it, recognizing another person's suffering and extending forgiveness does not mean you have to compromise your own beliefs. Instead, it calms inner turmoil by providing you with peace.

Extend forgiveness to yourself and all individuals in your story, and if you're unable to do so at this moment, simply intend to forgive. Forgiveness will come to you when the time is right. Affirm "I possess the courage to forgive," while seeking guidance from your Higher Self. See if you can accept all that has taken place. Let go of the need to control or alter a situation. Trust in divine grace and believe that you are being looked after, even if it's not evident at the moment. Show appreciation to every aspect of yourself, particularly the difficult parts that carry shame, guilt, anger, discord, fear, and suffering.

Each of these emotions serves as a valuable teacher, and the lesson will continue until learned. Follow Buddha's example to break the cycle and prevent it from recurring. Thank yourself for being here today with love. Use your chosen mantra to signify the end of your practice.Take a moment to assess your current emotions compared to the start of your meditation. Write down any new revelations if you feel inclined.

> "When love appears in the heart, it removes all causes of excitation from the system and cools it down to a perfectly normal state; and, invigorating the vital powers, expels all foreign matters – the germs of disease – by natural ways (perspiration and so forth). It thereby makes man perfectly healthy in body and mind." – **Yukteswar Giri**

30-Minute Meditation

The beauty of joy lies in its fleeting nature, which is why it is important to string together these moments of bliss to create a life that brings you immense happiness. However, joy is not the sole requirement for living a life filled with gratitude and love. Often, life presents us with challenges that awaken us to the significance of these precious gifts, which can only be uncovered when we open ourselves up to truth and vulnerability. Today, you have the opportunity to cultivate gratitude. You may choose to focus on one or all three qualities.

This meditation can be done either seated or lying down, depending on your preference. Start by inhaling deeply, allowing your breath to fill your lungs and flow down your spine towards the center of your ethereal heart space. As you exhale, release your breath through your arms, palms, and fingertips. After a few deep breaths, you will begin to feel a sense of centeredness. Take a moment to acknowledge and embrace this sensation. Are you sensing any resistance within your being?

Take a moment to identify its presence. Take a deep breath and intentionally breathe into those areas to promote relaxation. Rest your hands on your lap or beside you, with your palms facing upwards. Imagine a gentle pink or green light and let it flow into your chest, gradually encompassing your lungs, rib cage, heart, and the space between your shoulder blades. With each breath, visualize this light expanding through your heart, forming a soothing circular ring around your chest and extending into your aura.

Whether the light is gleaming, transparent, or murky, simply observe and go with the flow of the energy. Fill each organ with the light one by one. Feel the energy spreading throughout your body. Allow the light to dissolve any closed-off or sorrowful feelings. Release with each breath out. Focus on taking three additional deep breaths to center your energy on any areas in need of healing. If visualizing light colors is challenging, concentrate more on the sensation rather than specific hues.

If you're struggling with this, simply breathe deeply into your heart space. Once you feel ready, transition to the main focus of your meditation.

Joy

Contemplate your most treasured sensations and beloved memories. Indulge in these feelings; evoke the images that evoke joy within you. They might be the familiar sounds of loved ones. It could be a gentle touch, a soothing breeze, warm sunshine, ocean waves, or a verdant forest. What brings you comfort and a sense of well-being? Once you have identified what brings you peace, allow the tranquility and joy to permeate your heart. Acknowledge that everything you desire and require is enroute to you.

Love

Love is often described as a vibrant vibration of beauty, existing beyond the confines of physicality. This energetic frequency possesses the remarkable ability to transmute sorrow, despair, and isolation into moments of profound splendor. It serves as a unifying energy that connects all beings across the expanse of time and space. Embracing love as a way of life guarantees that you will always prioritize your own well-being and growth.

Today, take a moment to observe yourself exactly as you are – an ever-evolving tapestry of beauty and consciousness in its most authentic form. Regardless of the difficulties you encounter, remember to approach yourself with kindness and immerse yourself in loving vibes. It might involve leaving a toxic job, bouncing back from a setback, or breaking free from unhealthy habits like overindulging in junk food, spending too much time on social media, or watching reality TV excessively. Take a moment to pinpoint any areas in your life that are causing stress or discomfort.

Once you've identified them, infuse them with your loving energy. Allow this loving energy to gently release any burdens, using qualities such as acceptance, patience, kindness, or generosity.Today, consider how you can show more love and compassion towards yourself. Do you need to carve out more time and space for self-care? Reflect on the most effective way to accomplish this and take the necessary steps.

Gratitude

Think of five elements in your life that you are thankful for right now. Focus on each one separately, whether it's a person, place, thing, or event. As you exhale, send your gratitude for the positive impact they have had on you. Let your appreciation extend to everything in existence and beyond. Capture your current emotions in a mental image. Reflect on what you hope to gain from this exercise and if there is anything you need to release.

Breathe in deeply for the last time, then let it all out. Repeat a heart mantra three times. Your session is now over. Reflect on any emotions that arose or make note of feelings that may need further exploration.

> "Riding on the golden flames of our power center, we now arrive at the very heart of the chakra system. Here, in a band of green, lies the center of the Rainbow Bridge, the midpoint of our journey. Like the green, growing plants, which push toward the heavens from their roots in the earth, we, too, reach outward in two directions – anchoring the manifesting current deep in our bodies and expanding the liberating current as we reach beyond ourselves. In the heart chakra, these currents come to perfect balance in the center of our being. From the sacred center – the heart of the system – we enter the mystery love" – **Anodea Judith**

"Self-expression is the gateway between the inner world and the outer. Only through Self-expression does the outer world get to know what's inside of us" – Anodea Judith

Positioned at the center of your neck, the **throat chakra** is essential for facilitating clear communication and authentic self-expression. It has a significant impact on the endocrine system, thyroid, parathyroid, as well as the organs responsible for speech and maintaining balance. The throat chakra holds immense significance in maintaining the harmony of your chakra system as a whole. It is crucial to consistently express your truth in order to ensure its equilibrium.

Serving as the primary center for communication, this chakra encompasses both verbal and nonverbal forms of expression, both internally and externally. When the throat chakra is in balance, you possess the power to transform your blueprints and concepts into tangible realities. If you are not honest with yourself and others, you live in chaos, you live in darkness, you suffer from within.

Your voice must be the voice of truth and not that of deception and destruction. When we are honest with our words (and thought) we live in peace and not in anger. Countless of couples break up, or live in chaos because their mind is possessed by the stories (lies/made up) they tell themselves. Made up stories as a result of external conditioning through social media, movies and/or people they hang around with. Many couples yell and scream at each other because their throat energy center is imbalanced.

Therefore, anger will explode like a bomb that will destroy their mindfulness, relationship, children etc. Meditate, clear your mind and see others as people that need healing, just as you need healing. When you see others as beings that need help, your heart will open, when your heart opens, your throat will open.

Recognized as the church of Sardis in the book of revelation, this chakra features sixteen beautiful petals that shimmer with the radiant Pentecostal fire.

Element – Akasha, Ether, Sound

Throat Mantras

I am free to express my truth

I deserve to be heard and understood

I speak with authenticity

Sanskrit Throat Mantras

OM JANAHA {aum jahn-ah-hah} (Om and salutations to the second spiritual region beyond the sun/fifth chakra).

OM MANI PADME HUM {aum mah-nee pad-meh hoom} (Opening up the abilities of expression, developing an attunement with the throat chakra).

Dhyana Mudra

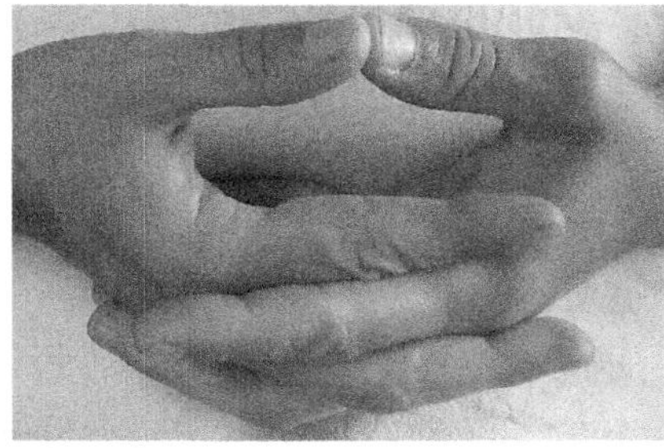

Connect the tips of your thumbs and then interlace your fingers on the inside of your hands.

You can practice this mudra anytime during the meditation to more powerfully connect with throat chakra energy. This mudra enhances communication and balance.

5-Minute Meditation

Your word holds immense power, akin to a magical wand, capable of bringing healing and transformation to the world. Understanding the potency of spoken language is crucial for your personal growth and the manifestation of your desires. Today, surrender to the healing potential of your own words by acknowledging what needs to be spoken. For the most effective experience, practice this meditation while seated and in a space where you can comfortably speak out loud.

Start by closing your eyes and feeling the weight in your eyelids, lengthening your spine, easing the tension in your shoulders, relaxing your jaw, and dropping your tongue from the roof of your mouth. Place your hands with palms facing up in your lap in mudra or resting position. Direct your attention to your breath, quieting any distracting thoughts in your mind. Inhale deeply into your throat a few times. With each exhale, release the tightness in the muscles of your neck that support your head.

Visualize your breath caressing your collarbone, shoulders, and neck from all angles. Relax your muscles. As you exhale, feel your energy streaming down your arms, through your hands, and out of your fingertips. Contemplate a truth that you are willing to accept today. Travel back in time to unlock profound truths waiting to be unleashed. Whisper, converse, sing, yell, or even scream. Speak aloud to validate your own existence. Inhale deeply one last time, and as you exhale, release your breath to the world. Optionally, seal your practice with a potent mantra like, "I am empowered!"

Open your eyes in case they were shut and, with a gentle gaze, step into a reflective state of mindfulness. Acknowledge what you observed during your meditation. Now is the right time to assess your emotions after sharing your truths with the world. Take a few moments to absorb that energy before starting your day.

> **"The throat is the uterus where the word is created. The gods create with the power of the Word. The Kundalini creates with the Word. The Kundalini creates in the larynx. The sexual organ of the gods is the creative larynx"** – Samael Aun Weor

15-Minute Meditation

The equilibrium of your throat chakra holds great significance, as it acts as the intermediary connecting your mind and heart. In Western cultures, individuals often struggle with finding a balance between action and stillness. By focusing on the essence of "being" in this meditation, you will harmonize your energy flow and unlock the pathways to your other chakras. While it is recommended to practice this meditation in a seated position, it can also be done lying down.

Start by taking deep breaths, filling your lungs and guiding the air down to the center of your neck. With each exhale, release your breath down through your shoulders, arms, and out through your palms and fingertips. Imagine a vivid cerulean blue wheel of light starting to form in the center of your throat. See the circle of light expanding outward as it rotates, spinning slowly at first and then gaining momentum.

As you exhale, allow the vibrant blue healing light to expand and extend further into your aura and energetic field. Continue this process until it reaches a width of approximately six feet. Visualize this swirling portal as a powerful megaphone, amplifying your energy as you whisper into it. To enhance this visualization, try chanting your mantra, aiding in the opening of this aspect of your visualization.

After unlocking your vibrant throat center, reflect on three instances where you sense an imbalance. Observe your daily routines and life circumstances by briefly assessing them. Are you exerting more masculine (yang) or feminine (yin) energy in these scenarios? Maybe there's a specific domain where you should assert yourself, express your thoughts, and assume control. Embrace the infusion of yang energy to assist you in this endeavor. Consider the possibility of relinquishing some control and welcoming more yin energy to counteract an excess of yang energy.

Reflect on any aspects of your life that have felt imbalanced for more than three years, whether it be work, finances, relationships, family, spirituality, or creativity. Identify a solution that has the potential to bring contentment, joy, and stability to a particular area of your life. Take the time to connect with the deeper meaning and purpose behind your chosen solution. Your intention and resolution might transform as additional aspects become clear.

When you feel yourself shifting towards a problem-solving mindset or expanding your ability to create room for solutions, welcome positive vibes into your throat area. This healing energy has the power to provide nourishment. Let go of everything that no longer benefits you as you exhale. To conclude your session, vocalize, resonate, or hum towards your blue chakra point. Guide the energy of the chakra downwards and slowly condense it into the center of your throat space.

Pay attention as the light gradually diminishes, eventually causing the swirling wheel to come to a stop, leaving your throat space aglow with a soothing cerulean blue light at its core. Take a few moments to fully embrace this experience and find joy in the present moment. Consider making a personal commitment to continue nurturing your mind and body long after your meditation session. Finally, acknowledge and appreciate yourself for restoring harmony to your throat space.

If you feel inclined, take a few moments to reflect on your current emotional state compared to how you felt at the beginning of your meditation. If you feel compelled, jot down any fresh insights or revelations that may have arisen.

> **"To speak and to speak well are two things. A fool may talk, but a wise man speaks" – Ben Jonson**

30-Minute Meditation

Your true self is ready to speak out. When you are listened to and comprehended, your communication and expression are liberated from any constraints. Speaking with purpose, transparency, and honesty are signs of a harmonious and linked throat chakra. You can do this meditation while sitting or lying down. Start by taking deep breaths. Visualize inhaling a revitalizing breath from your crown area and allowing it to flow down the back of your head to your throat.

With every exhale, release the breath through your arms and out through your hands and fingertips. Take a couple of deep breaths to find your center. Pay attention to how you feel. Are you experiencing any resistance? If so, focus on those areas as you breathe to promote relaxation. Imagine a bright, revitalizing blue light entering your mouth, neck, and esophagus. Inhale deeply to draw the light into your throat, then let it expand as you exhale. Visualize it, sense it, and let it extend beyond your physical form.

Allow the radiance to permeate your surroundings and extend beyond the confines of the room, reaching out into the vast expanse of the cosmos and caressing the sky. Sequentially, infuse each focal point within the throat chakra with the awe-inspiring frequencies of soothing blue healing light. Permit this luminous energy to emanate through your mouth, tongue, throat, clavicle, and upper chest. Envision its graceful journey as it flows into your upper back, merging with the point where your spinal cord meets the base of your skull.

Observe the radiant light effortlessly piercing through any

obstacles that have held you captive. Imagine all the unexpressed fears, disappointments, imbalances, and unresolved soul agreements from past incarnations dissolving in the luminous glow of your throat chakra. Release something with every exhale. Remember, the essence of this exercise lies in the feeling it evokes rather than the specific colors of light. Harness the transformative energy of light and elevate your consciousness to its highest potential.

As you delve deeper into your meditation, invite thoughts that resonate with your greatest aspirations, while releasing any other distractions. Today, dedicate yourself to uncovering and nurturing your deepest innermost value. Begin this journey by choosing one of the prompts provided.

Communication

Assess how you communicate. Does it mirror your true essence? Locate any discrepancies in your communication patterns. To mend these rifts, focus on the people involved, the specific circumstances, and the actions you can implement to amplify the voice of your Highest Self. When confusion arises in a relationship, seek insight from your Higher Self to understand the cause and discover a path to clarity. Pledge to communicate openly and honestly with the individual involved, whether it's your inner child, past partner, parent, or friend.

If face-to-face interaction is not possible, invite their energy into your meditation and engage with their soul essence. Trust your instincts to recognize when it's time to move forward.

Expression

Your external environment mirrors your internal state. When you feel a deep sense of fulfillment in expressing yourself, it creates a space for greater opportunities to manifest what you truly desire. How are you presently embodying your highest truths? In what ways do you feel limited? What behaviors, attitudes, beliefs, and words do you project outwardly? And which ones do you keep hidden within? Take a moment to examine why you choose to keep certain aspects of your expression to yourself. Remember, there is a suitable time and place for everything.

The timing might not be perfect yet, but it could be overdue to share your expression. If something strikes a chord with you as you meditate, go deeper. Think of a way to express yourself today that feels safe and liberating. Close your session with an empowering throat mantra or mudra. Repeat your mantra three times aloud for a full activation of your throat chakra. Feel the fresh energy in your clear throat. Your session is now done.

> "Communication is the essential function of the fifth chakra. As self-expression, it is a gateway between the inner world and the outer. Only through self-expression does the outer world get to know what's inside of us. We only know what's inside someone when they choose to tell us. Self-expression in the fifth chakra is a counterpart to the sensate reception coming in through the second chakra. In the second chakra, we opened a gate that allowed the world in through our senses. In the fifth chakra, we open a gate that allows our inner self to get out into the world. The throat chakra is also the internal gateway between the mind and body. The narrowest passage within the whole chakra system, the throat is literally a bottleneck for the passage of energy" – **Anodea Judith**

THIRD EYE

"When your mind is clear and your third eye is open, you can see and know things that are taking place thousands of miles away from you" – Frederick Lenz

Located between the eyebrows on the forehead, the **third eye** is the core of intuition and the ability to see beyond obstacles. Opening up to imagination and embracing new perspectives is key to unlocking its potential. This center allows us to break free from limited consciousness of time and is associated with light, representing the essence of all material forms. In the book of revelation, the third eye chakra is known as the church of Philadelphia and is said to have eight primary powers and thirty-six secondary powers, enabling clairvoyance.

The third eye chakra is aligned with clear vision, intuition, and a direct ethereal connection to universal energy. When this chakra is unblocked, you embody openness and creativity. You possess the capacity to look beyond obstacles that may hinder your progress. Your third eye will not fully open if you are a prisoner of your own thoughts. If you live in your mind (by overthinking people and situations) you become a prisoner, you will not fully connect with the great MIND.

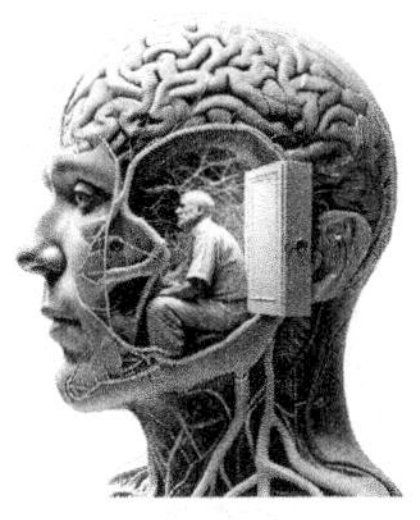

The third eye is associated with dreams and aspirations for the future, a creative state of mind, openness in the present, and an understanding of your spiritual purpose. If you have not realized your purpose yet, it is because your third eye is not opened. There is a difference between an opened and a fully opened third eye. Just as there is a big difference in the rising when you wake up and later on in the day when you are fully awake to analyze, exercise etc. Don't be content with just existing, you must live your life to the fullest. Nobody can take happiness away from you, it is your right. If others cause you suffering, it's because you give them permission to hurt you. That's what happens when you don't know your power or your purpose in this life. It is time that you become the leader of your life.

Element – Light

Third Eye Mantras

I am guided by my own intuition

My third eye connects me to my flow

I see all that is with perfect clarity

Sanskrit Third Eye Mantras

OM TAPAHA {aum top-ah-hah} (Om and salutations to the fourth spiritual region beyond the sun/sixth chakra).

OM CHANDRAYA NAMAHA {aum chahn-drayah nah-mah-hah} (Increases mental health and peace of mind, nervous system; ode to lunar energies).

Kalesvara Mudra

Curl your fingers together, leaving out the middle fingers. Your middle fingers come into a steeple shape, and your thumbs touch.

This mudra enhances intuition and clarity of mind. You can practice any time during meditation to more powerfully connect with your third eye energy.

5-Minute Meditation

The pineal gland acts as a link between our physical and spiritual functions. It serves as our internal compass and plays a vital role in the proper functioning of the endocrine system. Due to its sensitivity to magnets and vibration, playing soft background music can activate the pineal gland. Opt for tones or binaural beats that have a rhythmic quality and no lyrics. For optimal effectiveness, practice this meditation in a dark environment, as the pineal gland functions as a light receptor. Whether you prefer to be seated or lying down, both positions are suitable for this meditation.

Start by closing your eyes and feeling the weight of your eyelids, lengthening your spine, relaxing your shoulders, unclenching your jaw, and dropping your tongue from the roof of your mouth. Keep your hands with palms facing up in your lap or in your third eye mudra. Clear your mind of any busy thoughts. Bring your attention back to your breath if you get sidetracked. Picture a small violet flame surrounded by a deep indigo glowing halo in your third eye center.

Feel the comforting light radiate beyond your closed eyelids and towards the sides of your face and the back of your head. Visualize the light illuminating your head, see the flame moving behind your eyeballs at the center of your brain. Focus on guiding the flame towards your pineal gland, even if you're uncertain of where it is. Imagine the flame, noticing any changes in color, size, shape, or its unwavering presence. Envision this transformative flame igniting your cognitive abilities.

Let go of old memories or false beliefs in the violet flame to make room for higher vibrations. Sync your breath with the tones for added impact. After you've allowed the flame to burn for a few minutes, bring your hands together in front of you and gently touch your closed palms to your forehead. This signals your activation is complete. Take a few moments to thank yourself and notice how you are feeling. Open your eyes if they were closed and, with a soft gaze, come into a reflective space of awareness, acknowledging what you were able to perceive during your meditation.

> **"The kundalini energy rests in potential at the base of the spine. It is possible to take that energy and allow it to move, to unleash it, from the base of the spine up to the third eye"** – Frederick Lenz

15-Minute Meditation

Your Higher Self is an extraordinary being, unrestricted by the limitations of time, resources, or constraints. By summoning your Higher Self, you can seek guidance in creating a roadmap for your journey and understanding the rationale behind your choices. Rather than second-guessing your decisions, focus on embracing your intentions. To bolster your confidence, remain present with your inner vision. This meditation invites you to embark on a quest to connect with your visionary state and receive navigational direction.

You have the option to practice while seated or lying down. Start by taking deep breaths, filling your lungs and guiding your breath from the top of your head to your third eye. Exhale, releasing your breath through your eyelids and the sides of your face, extending it out to your aura. Connect with your inner wisdom and seek guidance on a current situation or challenge. Pick a past event that could impact a future scenario. This could involve altering the outcome of a problematic work situation or resolving an ongoing relationship conflict. Clearly define your desired objective, whether it's resolution, reconciliation, understanding, or closure.

Take into consideration all relevant details, including the individuals involved, timelines, your efforts, focus, intentions, external factors, and the specific outcome you are striving for. Once you have brought these details into focus, take three deep breaths into your third eye, exhaling and releasing all that no longer serves you. Allow yourself to relax into the resulting stillness. Have you observed any messages from your Higher Self? These messages can manifest as visions, emotions, or thoughts. Remember to seek clarity if necessary. Concentrate on gathering the details and don't concern yourself with explanations. The aim is to view these visions as valuable resources to assist you on your journey.

Make sure to remember everything that comes to mind. Jot down any thoughts or images after your meditation so you can stay focused. Once you're finished, end your meditation by chanting three times. Thank your Higher Self for being present and sharing insights. If you didn't receive any messages, try again later and imagine disconnecting your analytical mind before starting. Although you may not be able to perceive your Higher Self audibly, you might still experience sensations of colors or an overall emotion.

Have faith that things are being resolved on a quantum level during this period. If you desire, take a brief moment to compare your current feelings with those you had at the start of your meditation. If you feel compelled, jot down any fresh realizations.

"While our physical eyes are the organs of outer perception, the sixth chakra relates to the mystical third eye – the organ of inner perception. The third eye witnesses the internal screen where memory and fantasy, images and archetypes, intuition and imagination intertwine on endless display. By watching the contents on this screen, we create meaning and bring it to consciousness. The purpose of the sixth chakra is to see the way, and bring the light of consciousness to all that exists within and around us" – **Anodea Judith**

30-Minute Meditation

Your third eye is a center that bypasses your "I" consciousness and moves into your "super" consciousness. The "I" consciousness includes an awareness of oneself. "Super" consciousness is a state that rests above the conscious and subconscious mind states. From this framework, you can begin to view yourself through an observational lens. You may practice this meditation seated or lying down. Start by deeply breathing in, filling your lungs and guiding the breath up to your third eye.

Exhale, releasing the breath past your eyelids and face, extending out to your aura. After a few deep breaths, you will feel centered. Take note of any resistance you may feel. Inhale into those areas to help relax. Introduce a vibrant violet light into your third eye. Inhale the light into your brow line with your next breath, allowing it to expand through your exhale, radiating throughout your head. Visualize pushing this violet light in and out through your third eye, filling the chakra vortex and completely cleansing this energetic center. See it, feel it.

Allow it to grow beyond your body, the surrounding space, and the walls of the room as it travels back out into the cosmos. Gently fill your sinuses, the space behind your eyes, and your brain as you prepare to dispel any discordant energies (unhealthy thoughts or patterns or anything weighing you down mentally). Allow the violet light frequency to soak up any imbalanced energies. Release with every exhale. If visualizing the color proves challenging, concentrate on the emotion rather than the specific hue.

Once you've absorbed the healing light energy, envision it expanding to form a violet bubble surrounding your entire auric field, reaching out six feet around you. Inside your radiant bubble, delicate strands of violet light particles sparkle and mirror the glow of the see-through walls. Consider this area a sanctuary where you can focus without interruption. Embrace any ideas that resonate with your ultimate potential and creativity. Let all other distractions simply flow past your consciousness.

Today, you will surpass the limitations of the self and enter a deeper comprehension that links you to the universal consciousness. Through your third eye, you gain a higher perspective. By honing your skills, you have the ability to broaden your view to encompass not only humanity but also the universe. The power of the third eye is centered on intuition and gaining access to profound understanding. What do you need to perceive clearly at this moment? Envision it right in front of you, and envelop this individual or object with a violet bubble.

Then, tune in to your intuition or higher consciousness. What message does your intuition wish to convey regarding what lies before you? What knowledge can you acquire? Keep breathing steadily as you calm your mind and simply listen. After achieving a sense of wholeness, transition to the next subject by placing it in the violet bubble before you. Be receptive to any messages or information that you are able to perceive. You can repeat this process with up to five subjects in one sitting.

Consider keeping a journal or paper nearby to record your experiences and any action items that come to mind during your session. Conclude your session with an empowering mantra or mudra. To fully activate its potential, repeat your mantra three times. Your session is now finished.

> **"The pineal gland is a link between the consciousness of man and the invisible worlds of Nature. Whenever the arc of the pituitary body contacts this gland there are flashes of temporary clairvoyance, but the process of making these two work together consistently is one requiring not only years but lives of consecration and special physiological and biological training. This third eye is the Cyclopean eye of the ancients, for it was an organ of conscious vision long before the physical eyes were formed, although vision was a sense of cognition rather than sight in those ancient days"** – Manly P. Hall

Whatever you do, keep your wisdom teeth. The so-called mainstream doctors say they grow into the other teeth, pushes them, and cause pain. That is true, but it pushes on them as they grow in, sending signals to the pineal gland (Cosmic antenna to higher realms). Then straighten back out after they fully grow in. These signals are a connection to the divine and ancient wisdom. Which is why they call them "Wisdom" teeth. They knows this, which is why they want you to pull them out.

They want you to stay blocked from that kind of power. With an opened third eye they cannot control you because you see reality for what it is, and you also see the reality that you want yourself to be in.

HOW TO SEE YOUR AURA?

Test your third eye with this technique, on how to know if your third eye is blocked or not. If your pineal gland is totally blocked you can't see your own or other people's auric field. Don't panic if you can't see it. It doesn't mean that is totally blocked. You just need to practice this technique every day, in combination with sungazing. Hold the thumb and the pointer finger together (25-30cm or 10-12 inches) away from your eyes/face, just like in the image below. Look in the space between the fingers.

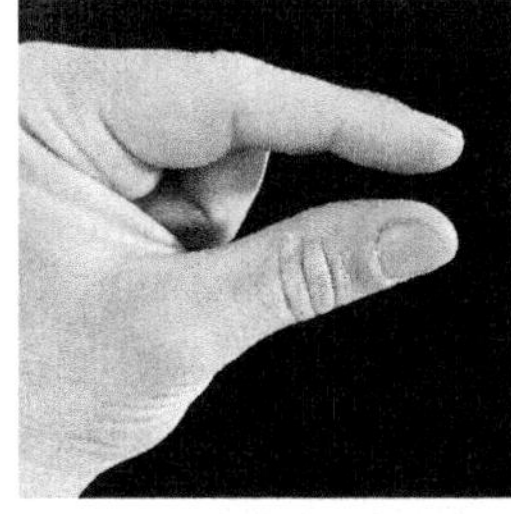

Keep looking and at the same time anticipate seeing a white line along the outline of your fingers. Move a little bit your fingers back and forth (left to right and vice versa) and you should be able to see the auric field of energy around your fingers. You can easily see also the aura of the trees outside, especially after you sun gaze for a little bit. Practice this technique while the background's colour behind the fingers is in contrast with the colour of your fingers, preferably dark colour background. You can also see the aura of other people, other than your own.

But first, practice on yourself, on your fingers and eventually in front of your mirror after you close your eyes for a few second while you are imagining the aura (energy field) sheltering you as if you are (which you are) inside a cocoon. After opening your eyes, look at the outline of your head (*before you're ready to see the whole body's aura*). With practice you should be able to see it with no problem. This is one of the ways. If this doesn't work for you, maybe another technique will.

Have in mind that to see your own aura and others' (animals, plants, people etc.), you must take sunbaths, fluoride free water, grounding etc. Being able to look at your own or other people's aura is a psychic ability. Psychic abilities are dormant if your third eye is asleep or suppressed or calcified. The aura color can vary from white, to pink, blue, purple etc.

I tried many times to capture on the picture the aura outline of my fingers but I couldn't. I was going to say that perhaps the aura cannot be photographed with a simple camera (using my cellphone) but then I remembered that I took a picture of my friend's cat that had his aura around his head all glowing. If you manage to see the aura, then instead of just moving the fingers left and right and vice versa, try also to move them away (about 1-2 inches) and to each other, creating a bigger gap between your fingerers. And you will be able to see a thicker aura. This works for me every time I concentrate on doing this for 5-10 seconds. - Update, I can see my aura within 1-2 seconds of trying this because I have been practicing every day.

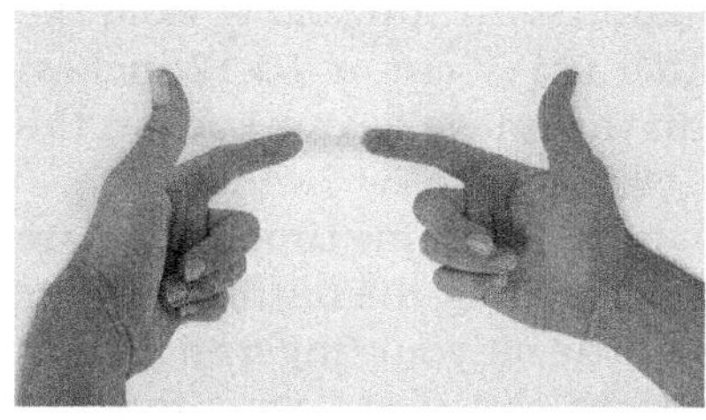

Take all the time you need. Do not become frustrated. At the right time it will happen. You can also try and practice by holding your fingers this way (image on the left). All of us must practice daily our psychic abilities. Do no feel defeated if you can't see your aura now. You too, like every single person that is born with a pineal gland , has psychic abilities. But it takes practice. A great painter, musician, cook etc., practiced a lot before they became great. Technically, we do not gain abilities, we already have them built in us. We just have to expose/realize them, practice them and use our super natural abilities as easy as we breathe. The only people responsible for the opening or the closing of our pineal gland is us. We are both the poison and the remedy.

"Enlightenment is blossoming the thousand petaled lotus flower on the top of the head" – Amit Ray

The **crown chakra**, located at the top of your head and extending a few inches above, governs the top of your head, your nervous and lymphatic systems, and your brain. It is considered the gateway to divine oneness, the universe, and cosmic consciousness, as it receives and transmits universal energy to your entire chakra system. An open crown chakra indicates a strong connection with your Higher Self and spiritual progress. Your crown is responsible for your metaphysical energy, while your root is responsible for your physical energy.

The crown chakra, referred to as the church of Laodicea in the book of revelation, is activated upon the Kundalini energy reaching the pineal gland located in the brain. A subtle and small canal exists between the pituitary gland and the pineal gland, but it disappears in cadavers. The flame must travel through this narrow canal towards the base of the nose. According to Samael Aun Weor, the root of the nose is home to a distinct magnetic field, where the atom of the Father is believed to reside.

As we strive for the radiant light, we breathe in countless atoms of aspiration that journey through our nasal passages towards the magnetic field at the base of our nose, where the Father's atom resides.

The sexual glands and the pineal gland are intricately linked. The potency of the pineal gland is reliant on the potency of the sexual glands.

Within the pineal gland lies the atom of the Holy Spirit. The pituitary gland houses the atom of the Son (Christ). The magnetic field of the root of the nose is where the atom of the Father resides.

Element – Thought/Consciousness

Crown Mantras

I honor the divine aspects of myself

I am connected to infinite wisdom

I am peaceful, whole and balanced

Sanskrit Crown Mantras

OM SATYAM {aum saht-yahm} (Om and salutations to the abode of supreme truth/7th chakra)

SAHASRARA IM {sah-has-rah-rah eem} (Invokes the power and consciousness of the crown chakra to descend)

Mahamayuri Mudra

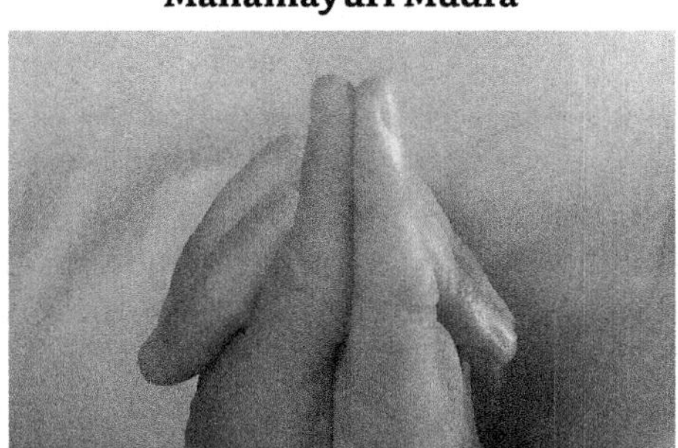

Interlace all your fingers except your pinky fingers. Press your pinkies together, upward in a steeple shape.

You can practice this mudra anytime during your meditation to more powerfully connect with your crown energy. This mudra enhances higher wisdom.

5-Minute Meditation

Your crown space embodies the vibration of your Highest Self. To open up to higher guidance, clear any mental chaos. Sit in meditation with a straight spine for optimal energy flow from your crown to other energy centers. Keep your hands palms up in your lap or in mudra. Prepare for your meditation by manually opening your crown chakra with your hands, visualizing it like opening a book above your head. Slowly move your hands towards each other to feel the boundaries of your crown space.

Acknowledge the resistance you encounter – that is your crown chakra. Quiet your mind from any distractions. Recenter your attention on your breath whenever you find yourself becoming distracted. Inhale deeply, drawing in a fresh breath through the crown of your head. As you exhale, feel your energy spreading outwards, reaching in all directions. Take a few breaths to expand your awareness to your expanded crown. This practice is referred to as clearing your mental energy. With each exhale, envision your thoughts departing from your mind and drifting away on the breeze.

Visualize your worries, cynicism, judgments, and mental stress dissipating like a passing cloud. See if you can simply exist in the present moment. Avoid attempting to "correct" anything. As you breathe in, absorb the immense beauty of unity, receptiveness, interconnectedness, and enlightenment that is accessible to you through this sacred pathway. Embrace the rejuvenating energy arriving in tranquil waves of happiness.

Submit to the delight and elegance streaming towards you at this moment. Inhale deeply through your crown one final time, then exhale your breath back to the Earth. Sense the unobstructed flow of energy from your crown down your spine. Uphold your vibrancy by concluding your practice with a potent crown mantra. If your eyes were shut, softly open them and enter a reflective state of awareness, acknowledging what you were able to perceive during your meditation.

Now is the perfect moment to evaluate how you are presently feeling. Throughout the day, be mindful of the universal connection you have established and your ability to tap into the qualities of peace you cultivated during your sit.

"When the sacred serpent passes through the cerebral center, which is situated where the frontal fontanel of a newborn is found, part of the fire escapes and enters the exterior world. The entire aura shines with fire in those instances, and the immaculate white dove of the Holy Spirit enters within us. All of the vehicles of the initiate must be crucified and stigmatized in the Golgotha of supreme sacrifice. The Golgotha of the Father is the brain. We must rise to the Golgotha with the cross on our back" – **Samael Aun Weor**

15-Minute Meditation

The moment has arrived for you to embrace your destiny and transform into the embodiment of everything you have ever aspired to be – the true manifestation of your soul's mission. Each and every one of us possesses infinite potential, and within us lies a unique gift that holds the power to positively impact humanity. Despite the many individuals who find themselves trapped in fear, limited consciousness, and altered vibrations, by actively seeking enlightenment and expanding our awakened consciousness, we can successfully construct our dreams and transform our visions into reality.

The Merkaba, a sacred symbol, represents duality – encompassing the positive, active, electric, and masculine aspects, as well as the negative, passive, magnetic, and feminine aspects. In the grand tapestry of creation, the Merkaba embodies both the law of spirit and the law of matter. The meditation technique resembles the shape of two intersecting tetrahedrons, which are three-dimensional triangles. You have the option to practice this meditation either seated or standing, ensuring that your spine remains straight and aligned vertically.

To begin, take deep breaths, allowing your lungs to fill up, and guide your breath down your spine towards your belly. As you exhale, imagine releasing your breath through your legs, allowing the prana (the life-force energy carried by your breath) to return to the Earth through the soles of your feet.

Visualize two radiant white tetrahedrons intertwined, with one pointing downwards and the other pointing upwards. From an external perspective, a white, six-sided, three-dimensional star surrounds your body. You are seated at the center, creating a point of equilibrium. The intersecting points gleam in a golden light, with interconnected bands of luminous light. The tetrahedrons symbolize pure divine energy, spinning continuously – initially at a slow pace, then increasing in speed.

As you reside within this Lightbody vehicle, the energy of the Merkaba shifts and flows, harmonizing with you, providing support, and balancing your energy. While engaging with the Merkaba, focus on cultivating positive thoughts and visualize the multidimensional star spinning and expanding. What unfolds when a negative thought arises during this experience? How does it impact your Lightbody?

This exercise strengthens your aura and enhances your connection to your inner light. With a fortified aura, you navigate life with unwavering faith and remain unaffected by others' opinions.

The Merkaba represents a perfect fusion of energies, with you as its core, empowering you to transform thoughts and actions spanning the past, present, and future. As the bridge connecting spirit and matter, you harmonize your Lightbody. Any negative words or restrictive beliefs absorbed from others will fade away, resembling sparks or bursts of light. Observe as thought paradoxes, conflicts, and limitations are expelled from your orbit. Gradually, you will experience a sense of liberation, both in your mind and soul. Visualize yourself emanating radiant light, boundless love, and selflessness to the world. Capture a mental image of the energy you currently feel, and revisit it whenever you seek to reconnect with your authentic, limitless, and divine essence.

The Merkaba serves as a vehicle designed to cleanse your energy, and it operates effortlessly without any action required from you. It remains energetically present in your daily life. To summon it, simply visualize it in your mind's eye. Show gratitude towards yourself for being present today.

To signal the completion of your practice, you may choose to chant or say aloud your crown mantra. Take three deep breaths to clear your mind before returning to your surroundings. If you wish, take a few moments to compare your current feelings to how you felt at the beginning of your meditation.

If you feel compelled, write down any new insights that may have emerged.

"We can be Knowledgeable with other men's knowledge, but we cannot be wise with other men's wisdom" – **Michel de Montaigne**

30-Minute Meditation

The purpose of your soul's incarnation in this lifetime is to experience personal growth. Some individuals encounter hardship, struggle, and density throughout their life, while others embark on a journey filled with light, peace, and joyful circumstances.

Your soul has intricately planned its path back to its true essence, perfectly tailored for your unique journey. You are arriving at the precise moment and you are exactly where you need to be in the present moment.

Regardless of the choices you make, always remember that you are unconditionally loved and supported by your Higher Self. If possible, find a comfortable seated position, such as lotus or cross-legged, for this meditation. Allow your hands to rest gently in your lap, palms facing upwards.

Take a moment to begin by taking deep breaths, allowing your lungs to fill completely. As you exhale, imagine your breath flowing down your spine and leaving your body. With each breath out, visualize the energy within your breath returning to the Earth through the soles of your feet.

After a few breaths, you will start to feel a sense of calm and centeredness. Take note of this feeling. Are there any areas of resistance? If so, focus your breath on those areas to help release tension and promote relaxation. Now, picture yourself seated on a magnificent lotus throne, surrounded by soft petals. You are at the very center of this beautiful flower. Notice the light around you glowing so brightly that your whole body begins to radiate with this white light frequency.

A space opens above you, and you recognize this as a portal to the cosmos. Visualize a golden thread dropping down from the sky, running into your head, down the back of your spinal column, and out below you to Earth, anchoring you. You may feel tingles, pulsating energy, or electricity as the thread aligns all your other chakras with your crown space. Notice how this feels and any other sensations. Receive the balancing and healing energy coming to you from your Higher Self. Today, make a choice to elevate your decision-making.

Your individual life choices will resonate with you in a meaningful way. This is because you are drawing in the energy of each potential outcome into your reality. To align yourself with your Highest Self, it is important to consistently pursue your passions.

By doing so, you will remain in a state of constant growth and expansion, flowing with perfect timing and grace. As you visualize yourself on your lotus throne, begin to manifest your greatest joys. Whether it's a recent pursuit or an upcoming experience, take the time to explore if there are deeper layers for you to uncover. For example, if you are planning a weekend getaway, consider what other exciting possibilities may await you.

Think of all the details; who else is going, what places you would like to see there, an extra stop on your trip. This exercise is not a master to-do list. Rather, it's a download from your Highest Self, a transmission of what lights you up, because what excites you is a key to your revelatory soul-journey.

Gather any insights you can. Continue to breathe in and out, peacefully enjoying the ecstatic communion of this intersection of joy, creativity, spirituality, and divine exchange. You may close your sit with an empowering mantra or mudra.

Chant your mantra three times for maximum expression and activation. Take three deep breaths, letting the white light energy from your crown cleanse and flow through you, releasing any vibrations that need to be released. Show appreciation to your Higher Self for being present with you today, and request for this version of yourself to merge into your consciousness even after your meditation session has ended. Your session is officially over.

> "Consciousness, the final frontier. That vast and indispensable key to the ultimate mystery, endless and unfathomable. The very thing that allows us to look into the mirror of the soul and perceive our own experience. Consciousness is both our final destination and the means of travel. We think of consciousness as our thoughts, but thoughts are what consciousness creates, not what it is. We think of consciousness as our perceptions, but there is a faculty that not only perceives, but also remembers, discriminates, and integrates our perceptions. Who or what does this? We feel the pull of consciousness on our emotions, but who or what feels those emotions, and how do we experience feeling? This is the mystery that we embrace in the crown chakra – a mystery that can only be experienced, not explained" – **Anodea Judith**

The crown chakra is above the head. Unfortunately, some think that hair is the crown chakra. Don't let anyone do/cut your hair unless it's your mother, a priestess, or any awakened spiritual person who has an opened heart. Don't put any man-made unhealthy products on your hair. Your mind is your conscious awareness. This awareness is everywhere in your body and anywhere else, in other people, animals, birds, plants oceans, air etc. Your crown chakra (and the 3rd eye) is what connects you to the great spirit and your higher self which is a sense of universal consciousness, wisdom and unity with all sentient beings on a divine/source level. Native Americans were firm believers that hair was sacred. Why in the modern world many women have short hair? Is it their choice or a taught choice by those that wanted women to lose connection with their Goddess selves/ source?

> **Whether you have hair or not, anyone can tap to that inner magickal power from the Source/All That Is, but one has to really be a very powerful person mentally. If you are not yet at that level, at least your hair is extra help.**

And if you are bald, well, one could say that your antenna is cut off, but I strongly disagree. Bold people too, can equally tap and experience spiritual connection with their divine selves and the Supreme Divine the Great Mind. The energy of the crown chakra is about our connection to the Infinite, to the universal consciousness that flows through every being. Your hair can regrow. If you liver can regenerate, anything else in the body can. Seek, and you shall find. Even the movie Avatar showed us that we can connect to nature through our hair. Our hair acts as an antenna that channels energy. Technically, hair is an extension of the crown chakra and not the chakra itself.

Chakras are not in our physical body, they are in our 4th body known as mental body. Their connecting points in physical bodies and crown happens to be on the top of our head.

> **Witchcraft, telepathy, clairvoyance, meditation, orgasm, chakra, kundalini energy all happens in our 4th body which is the bridge between earth and sky, mind and above mind, survival and liberation.**

While the mental body certainly influences and interacts with our chakras, especially through our thoughts and consciousness, the chakras themselves are anchored in our 2nd body known as the etheric body. This layer is like a bridge between our physical reality and higher spiritual realms, facilitating the flow of energy and insights between them.

I do find the idea that mystical practices operate within the 4th body, the mental body, to be intriguing. Second body etheric body or sky body is emotional body mostly developed from 7-14 years of age. Most of our trauma that needs to be healed, is from this age group. Etheric body is just an expression of energy that is conditioned by our third body known as astral or logical thinking body which decides good or bad depending on our conditioned mind. Accordingly, our second body reacts and responds and our first body physical body reflect. Chakras in 4th body is where energy blockages happens, vibration blockages and we can align, balance, ground ourselves and move the energy towards higher chakras.

After the awakening, some people's hair became curly. Some have unexplained hair loss, could this be a crown chakra issue? Some people have lost hair when they were experiencing a lot of stress, when they began to feel much better and relaxed, their hair began growing back again. Depends on anyone's personal situation, to some, the crown chakra may be blocked and that's why they started losing hair, when they feel connected again their hair were coming back. I am speaking of hair loss in relation to the one's awakening and not as a result of chemotherapy (actually *death inducing therapy*) or any other issues caused by people who neglect their personal health through bad lifestyle and carelessness.

All chakras are etheric and not physical. All chakras have energy points manifested in physical form. They have physical correspondences yes, but those are not the actual chakras. Hair is not the crown-chakra correspondence. Hair is your body's crown, not your being's. We should not restrict ourselves to our body or confuse the two. That will limit us if we believe it. We are far bigger than our body. We can perceive space outside of our body because we exist and take up more space than our body ever could. We might feel it in our hair but we must not stop there unless we want to retard our growth. Body consciousness is important, but we're way more than that, and it is time we realize that we are not our body. We have a body but we are not it.

Chapter 14

THE HEALING POWER OF THE SERPENT

"It is possible that the product of the serpent may be everything needed for the healing of man" – James Taylor Kent, Physician and Homeopathist

It is important for mainstream Christians (*the ones blindly believing that medicine/savior/remedy is external*) to recognize the presence of a serpent within themselves. The serpent is associated with the kundalini energy. Without a doubt, the serpent reigns supreme as the most potent and enduring symbol in the tapestry of human history, its presence resonating across countless civilizations and epochs. The serpent has been a recurring symbol in every spiritual teaching, mystical knowledge, and religion throughout history. From ancient civilizations to mystery schools and philosophies, the presence of the serpent or dragon can be found in various forms.

In the pursuit of healing, transformation, self-mastery, or the transcendence of man's lower nature, the serpent assumes the role of a vigilant guardian, protecting a hidden treasure. Conquering this serpent becomes essential to unlock the desired rewards.

Despite its various forms, such as a regular corn snake, a large green emerald tree python, or a fire-breathing dragon, this mystical being instills a significant amount of fear in the average person. The serpent is often associated with evil, leading many to avoid anything related to it, including our blog named The Serpents Way. With a comprehensive understanding of diverse religions, philosophies, and the ancient wisdom bestowed by mystery schools, it raises the question whether the spiritual teachings and profound knowledge associated with the serpent are viewed as hazardous and a challenge to those desiring to govern humanity. Might the doctrines revolving around the serpent pose a danger to the existing power dynamics on Earth?

This is precisely what occurred, as revealed in different locations throughout our blog (www.theserpentsway.com) and our books. The official religion of black sorcerers hindered the mental and spiritual advancement of the people of ancient Atlantis and Egypt. It was revealed that the Pharaohs were manipulated like puppets by the Scarlet Council. This group of sinister arch-sorcerers was elevated to authority by the corrupt priesthood. Within today's globalized economy, the bloodlines of sinister dark arch-sorcerers, known as the Order of Illuminati or International Bankers, have skillfully placed government leaders, corporate CEOs, and Popes in positions of authority. The present condition of the world makes it evident that the ancient power structure is still controlling humanity today.

These archaic arch-sorcerers were the ones who tainted and distorted all religious doctrines to advance their sinister agenda. Orthodox Christianity serves as a prime exemplification of this dark plot. The emergence of Christianity resulted in the eradication of numerous spiritually revered beings such as the serpent, goddess, pagan religions, Gnostics, philosophy, knowledge from mystery schools, druids, and Cathars to name a few. The serpent and its spiritual teachings were unjustly condemned by the dark sorcerers who controlled the Christian Religion in Rome. They portrayed these teachings as evil, attributing them to a fictional being named Satan, residing in a mythical place called hell.

John Lamb Lash, in his book "Not In His Image," points out a rising awareness that mainstream religious values may be flawed. The Christian faith, according to Lash, centers morality around a master-slave dynamic, fueled by a deep-seated resentment towards the vitality and strength of the life force.

What caused the serpent to be stigmatized and depicted as a villain? The serpent imparts wisdom rooted in elevated awareness, personal enlightenment through the awakening of one's inner serpent, and the exploration of one's spiritual capabilities. In essence, these teachings offer a path to spiritual liberation for humanity, empowering us to evolve into divine beings, completely opposite to any agenda seeking to enslave through religion.

> "The Bible must be shaken upside down before it will yield all its secrets. The priests have censored and clipped and mangled: they give us a celibate Jesus born of a virgin without the slightest "stain" of sexual contact, which is blasphemous nonsense" – **William Blake**

Healing Power of The Serpent

The serpent and its teachings encompass a broad subject that can be extensively covered in many books. Snakes have always captivated and terrified mankind ever since our connection with the serpent began. It's truly ironic that a creature capable of instilling fear, repulsion, and even hatred in humans is also widely regarded as a symbol of medicine, and has provided us with powerful healing remedies.

The Serpent's initial link to healing probably started with simple observations and ponderings. It could have unfolded like this: witness how snakes routinely shed their skin, revealing a shiny and renewed state? Maybe humans can also tap into their regenerative abilities. Snake blood, bile, and venom were commonly used for medicinal purposes in ancient times. The earliest documentation of snake medicine dates back to China in the first century, where shed snakeskin was utilized to heal sore throats, rashes, and skin ailments, such as cloudy corneas.

Historical Chinese medical texts also recommend consuming roasted snake slough or using it externally to address tumors, boils, and abscesses. Early physicians thought that the speed and agility of snakes could be beneficial in treating conditions such as sore muscles and stiff, arthritic joints. Due to their exceptional speed and flexibility, snakes were believed to possess a 'chi' or vital energy that could flow rapidly and beneficially through the human body. This belief has been deeply rooted in traditional Chinese medicine for ages, leading to the utilization of snakes as a fast-acting solution to relieve pain, promote body relaxation, and alleviate tension.

The ancient Egyptians possessed extensive knowledge about snakes and the effects of snake bites. Their medical papyrus contained elaborate accounts of different snake species, the symptoms caused by their venom, a range of antidotes, the deities associated with each snake manifestation, and prayers or incantations to neutralize the venom. The understanding of both Egyptians and Greeks was that snake venom does not pose a threat when ingested, but only when it

enters the bloodstream.

During the 16th century, Paracelsus, a physician and philosopher from Switzerland and Germany, declared that everything can be considered a poison – whether it leads to illness or death depends on the quantity we consume. In simpler terms, the harm caused is determined by the dosage that triggers a toxic reaction. While both poison and venom are toxic, they differ in their modes of toxicity. Poison becomes toxic when inhaled, absorbed, or swallowed, whereas venom is only toxic when injected. Hence, it is accurate to say that there are no poisonous snakes, but rather venomous ones.

Known as the ultimate cure, snake healing has the ability to deeply affect the body on multiple levels – physical, energetic, and cellular. Its profound transformative nature cannot be underestimated. By overseeing the energy flow within the body, snake medicine can bring about rapid changes, akin to the swift strike of a snake or the intense rise of kundalini energy. It is crucial to understand that this process may not always be easy or comfortable.

It is truly captivating how the serpent has consistently served as a symbol of medicine across various cultures and throughout countless ages. By tracing the serpent's role as a healer throughout human history, one can observe instances where its influence waned significantly (seemingly losing its significance multiple times). However, just like a snake shedding its skin, the serpent continuously rejuvenates itself, adapting its essence through various forms, symbols, and narratives. Similar to life itself, the serpent persistently discovers a path forward.

"The serpent is the earthly essence of man of which he is not conscious. Its character changes according to peoples and lands, since it is the mystery that flows to him from the nourishing earth-mother" – Carl Jung

The Serpents of Asclepius and Hermes

Asclepius, a highly respected healer, resided in Greece three millennia ago. His remarkable ability to heal was so renowned that he was praised by Homer in The Iliad, along with other poets and storytellers of that era. Over time, Asclepius became a deity, recognized as the son of Apollo, the guardian of doctors, and the

Greek god of medicine.

Legend has it that Asclepius was seen bent over a man who had just passed away, examining him closely. A snake happened to slither past, startling Asclepius, who promptly killed it with his staff. Another snake then approached, fed the first snake some herbs, and brought it back to life. Witnessing this, Asclepius followed suit and managed to revive the deceased man. This act resulted in the snake coiled around a rod becoming the enduring symbol of healing linked to Asclepius – a symbol that would eventually signify medicine.

As a homage to the renowned abilities of Asclepius, numerous healing temples known as Asclepions were constructed across the Greco-Roman realm. These establishments served as both sanctuaries and educational institutions, attracting individuals from various parts of the Mediterranean seeking remedies.

Certain individuals seeking healing rested in chambers designed for dreaming, where serpents roamed without constraint. Acting as messengers of Asclepius, these snakes bestowed blessings and guided the ill towards receiving therapeutic visions during slumber. Different travelers arrived as pupils, eager to acquire knowledge in the revered practice of healing. Legend has it that Hippocrates, the renowned father of medicine, initiated his journey at the Asclepion on the island of Kos.

In the Middle Ages, the Catholic Church prohibited the use of the "pagan" Rod of Asclepius. Nevertheless, during the Protestant Reformation, these ancient healing symbols experienced a resurgence in popularity and reappeared in Renaissance artwork. By the seventeenth century, physicians widely embraced the snake-twined rod of Asclepius. Eventually, in 1910, the so-called American Medical Association adopted this staff as its official symbol.

The Rod of Asclepius is commonly recognized as a symbol of healing, but it is often mistaken for the caduceus. The caduceus, which features two serpents entwined around a winged staff, was originally presented to the Greek god Hermes by Apollo, the god of healing. Hermes, or Mercury in Roman mythology, possessed a paradoxical nature as a god. While he safeguarded and guided travelers and merchants, he also extended his protection to thieves. Furthermore, he played a pivotal role in escorting the departed souls to the underworld of Hades and acted as a conduit for communication between humans and gods.

Portrayed at times as a hermaphrodite, Hermes symbolizes the fusion of masculine and feminine qualities, as well as the balance between yin and yang. As a messenger deity and psychopomp, he adeptly navigates between worlds, facilitating communication between humans and supernatural realms. It is common for the symbols of one snake winding around a rod and two snakes twirling upon a staff to be mistaken for each other. The resemblance between these symbols can lead to confusion. Furthermore, Asclepius and Apollo have a significant association within the healing tradition, as evidenced by the original Hippocratic Oath, which begins:

"I swear by Apollo the physician, and by Asclepius, Hygeia, Panacea, and all the gods and goddesses as my witnesses, that I will fulfill according to my ability and judgment this oath and covenant..."

Hermes, the god of dualities, symbolizes balance in healing through his caduceus, a double-snaked symbol. The authors of this book believe the caduceus staff represents the spine, the central channel through which nerves and vessels animate the organs of our body. The dual serpents symbolize not just the DNA, but also the activation of the kundalini rising along the spinal cord, awakening all the chakras, the energy centers. The wings of the caduceus represent the transformation that occurs when the kundalini energy is absorbed by the pineal gland, depicted as an eagle consuming the serpent. These wings signify a person who is spiritually enlightened, which is the main focus of our books.

C.G. Jung observed, "The way of life writhes like the serpent from right to left and from left to right, from thinking to pleasure and from pleasure to thinking. Thus, the serpent is an adversary and a symbol of enmity, but also a wise bridge that connects right and left through longing, much needed by our life." From the tips of its forked tongue to the tender endpoints of its hemi Penes, the serpent is a master of duality. Both harmer and healer, it brings together that which is contradictory, ambiguous, and opposed. By opening to the serpent's medicine and exploring the deeper mystery of two-in-one, we may access larger perspectives and expanded consciousness.

This statement applies not only to individuals but also to the world we inhabit. The serpent serves as a representation of the internal struggle between conflicting aspects of the collective human psyche. Whenever and wherever the serpent is degraded, an imbalance arises, often resulting in societal inequality, corruption, and chaos. Conversely, when the serpent is revered, a state of equilibrium and homeostasis is achieved, enabling us to acknowledge both the dangers and the transformative potential embodied by the serpent.

> "It is urgent to first awaken the Kundalini and then to be devoured by the Kundalini. We need to be swallowed by the snake. We need the Kundalini to swallow us. We need to be devoured by the serpent. When one is devoured by the serpent, one also becomes a serpent. Only the human serpent can incarnate the Christ. Christ can do nothing without the snake" – **Samael Aun Weor**

The Value of Venom

Snake venom has been utilized as a potent biological weapon since ancient times. In the past, Greek warriors would coat their arrows with snake venom, resulting in deadly consequences for their enemies. Alexander the Great himself witnessed the devastating effects of these venomous arrows in India, where many soldiers fell victim to their lethal power. Remarkably, even today, indigenous tribes in Brazil continue to employ the venom of the Brazilian lancehead snake as a toxic arrowhead. The cure for venom was not a mystery to the ancients. They possessed extensive knowledge of this remedy, as evidenced by the countless narratives of early healers skillfully extracting snake venom and utilizing it to concoct antidotes and medicines.

Over 2,000 years ago, King Mithridates VI of Pontus, famously known as the Poison King, explored the realm of toxicology. His motive was self-preservation, leading him to experiment with consuming minute quantities of poisons and venoms, with the aim of developing immunity. Mithridates was also saved by venom. While on the battlefield, he once suffered a near fatal sword cut. When the viper venom was applied to the wound, it coagulated the blood, staving off the severe hemorrhage that would have ended his life. The same principle is used in modern medicine, as a synthetic form of *Vipera ursinii* is utilized in many emergency rooms around the world today.

Hygeia, the daughter of Asclepius, played a crucial role as a healing partner to her father. She was known as the goddess of good health and hygiene, represented by a snake wrapped around a chalice stem with its head raised. This simple yet powerful symbol illustrates the paradox of snake venom, which can possess both harmful and healing properties, similar to the dual nature of certain drugs. The serpent's evolutionary strategy was greatly enhanced by the development of venom, which proved to be one of its most intelligent adaptations. By utilizing venom, snakes that don't rely on constriction methods can effortlessly capture and digest their prey, while also effectively protecting themselves against potential predators.

Comprised of diverse proteins, peptides, and sugars, venom is a specialized saliva produced by snakes through digestive enzymes. This precious substance demands significant effort and time to create, serving as a vital resource that may be needed at any moment. Venomous snake bites can result in a diverse range of symptoms. These can include tingling and numbness, vertigo and vomiting, as well as cold, clammy skin, fainting, and lethargy. Some individuals may experience severe, stabbing pain, while others may not feel any pain at all.

Swelling can vary from extreme heat and outrageous swelling to a chilling sensation followed by complete loss of sensation. In summary, the effects of venomous snake bites can range from panic to paralysis, and from a quick and sudden death to a slow and agonizing one. Venom differs not only among species but also within the same species. Furthermore, the composition of venom can vary depending on the life stage of each snake, as the venom of a young snake may be distinct from that of the same snake as an adult.

Scientists have uncovered that snake venom is packed with numerous toxins – with some snakes possessing as many as one hundred toxins in their venom – and each toxin has a distinct mode of action. Some toxins induce blood clotting, while others result in hemorrhaging. Moreover, certain snake venom can cause cellular necrosis, while others can paralyze the muscles or heart.

To harness the power of snake venom as a cure, it is crucial to align the advantageous properties of the toxin with the requirements of the human body.

Among the 3,000-plus snake species found on our planet today, just over 600 species are venomous. These are the ones most likely to be fatal to humans – and are commonly used in the creation of therapeutic snake treatments. It is remarkable, but not surprising given the nature of snakes, that the same substance that can be deadly to us can also possess healing abilities. For centuries, venom has played a significant role in Eastern healing practices, yet its application in the Western context is a more recent phenomenon. The integration of snake venom into modern Western medicine was introduced from Europe, in conjunction with the specialized field of Homeopathy.

> "In the transference of the fire from the base of the spine...lies the redemption of man. With the raising of Kundalini, with the uncoiling of the serpent fire, comes the advancement of the race to superhuman glory. This is what nature's law of evolution has intended for mankind, for man and woman alike" - **C.J. Van Vliet**

Serpent and Homeopathy

Over an extended period, German physician and pharmacologist Samuel C. Hahnemann dedicated himself to exploring holistic treatments for his patients. By the late 1700s, he achieved significant success with his innovative approach known as homeopathy. Allopathy, also known as conventional Western medicine, employs drugs that counteract the symptoms of a disease. On the other hand, homeopathy utilizes minuscule amounts of substances that would cause similar symptoms in larger quantities to treat illnesses. Essentially, homeopathy follows the principle of "like cures like.

The news of Hahnemann's exceptional outcomes in curing cholera and scarlet fever in Europe swiftly reached the United States, sparking widespread interest in his treatment. Homeopathy is based on matching the individual's needs with the appropriate remedy. In order to identify the right remedy, the homeopath carefully considers the patient's personality, behavior, and symptoms. The remedies used encompass extracts from animals, plants, and minerals, including snake venom which has been utilized since the mid-1800s.

A German physician named Constantine Hering, known for his contributions to homeopathy, was the pioneer in utilizing venom for medicinal purposes in the Western world. In 1835, Hering organized an expedition to the upper Amazon, accompanied by his wife and a group of collectors focusing on botanical and zoological specimens. Upon learning about a dangerous viper from native assistants, Hering incentivized the capture of a live specimen.

During the titration of the snake's venom, Hering experienced heightened mental activity, a rapid stream of ideas, and an increased inclination to talk. It was thanks to Hering's wife diligently documenting his symptoms throughout the night that the first homeopathic proving of *Lachesis*, one of the leading homeopathic remedies today, came into existence.

Hering went on to co-found the North American Academy of Homeopathic Medicine in Pennsylvania and shared numerous accounts of his experiences with snakes. Today, nearly two centuries later, Hering's contributions remain a vital resource for understanding the therapeutic potential of snake venoms.

In homeopathy, remedies are made from venomous snakes such as vipers, cobras, kraits, and sea snakes. Homeopaths determine which snake can cure a particular ailment by observing the habits, behaviors, and venom effects of the snakes, and then correlating them with human symptoms. This approach relies on precise observation and pattern recognition.

By observing the physical attributes, capabilities, and symbolic significance of a snake, we can enhance our comprehension of the connections between snakes and humans. Take, for instance, the initial homeopathic snake remedy called *Lachesis mutus*, derived from the bushmaster snake. Within the realm of homeopathy, *Lachesis* is commonly regarded as the quintessential snake remedy, widely recognized and frequently recommended.

Those who require *Lachesis* share similarities with the agile and expertly concealed bushmaster, often displaying quick thinking and resourcefulness that may not be immediately evident. Just as the bushmaster is renowned for its swift and accurate strikes, *Lachesis* personalities also react promptly. With their sharp intellect and astute perception, these individuals effortlessly comprehend new ideas with precision and efficiency. The potency of the bushmaster's venom is truly remarkable, just like the individuals who resonate with *Lachesis*, who often display an overwhelming passion and express themselves with great intensity, sometimes even impulsively. Despite possessing fangs, the bushmaster prefers to coil and constrict, mirroring the tightly strung nature of those who require Lachesis, who find solace in movement and seek release through physical activity.

While the majority of snakes are typically associated with movement, *Lachesis* distinguishes itself by embodying the very essence of fluid motion. Those who require *Lachesis* often find themselves facing obstacles that impede their ability to move forward. They possess a deep longing to flow seamlessly on all fronts – physically, emotionally, sexually, creatively, and spiritually – and they pursue this yearning with an intense passion, as it is vital for them to experience a sense of wholeness.

Lachesis's bite, characterized by its elongated fangs, delivers an immediate and intense stabbing pain, followed by the rapid dissemination of venom. This results in the prompt onset of symptoms such as pain, nausea, vomiting, and a weakened pulse. As time passes, blurred vision, clamminess, unconsciousness, or even coma may ensue. The venom's anticoagulants can thin the blood to the extent that it may cause hemorrhages to ooze. *Lachesis'* hemotoxic venom is primarily utilized in homeopathy to address various blood and circulatory issues, such as varicose veins, inadequate blood circulation, irregular heartbeat, and breathing challenges. Additionally, it is frequently employed to alleviate menopausal flow disruptions and menstrual obstructions.

Homeopathic remedies are formulated using fresh venom, which then undergoes an extensive process of dilution. As a result, only an incredibly small quantity of the initial toxin is present in the final remedies. How can such tiny quantities bring about any significant change? Despite its counterintuitive nature, homeopathy proves that high dilution results in high potency. A competent homeopath possesses the knowledge to identify the appropriate remedy and dosage that will yield the desired effects. It is fascinating to note that many remedies have remained unaltered since their original discovery. For instance, the dilution range for cobra venom in homeopathy papers from the 1870s remains unchanged.

"In the mid-1800s thousands of Chinese laborers migrated to the West to work on the Transcontinental Railroad, bringing with them traditional medicines. After a long day's work, the Chinese would rub snake oil into their sore muscles and aching joints. Because the oil was so effective in relieving pain, the Chinese shared it with their American coworkers" – **Dawn Brunke**

Serpent's Healing Power In The Psyche

The serpent was revered by the ancients for its ability to bring forth clarity and profound insight. With its ever-attentive eyes, the serpent remained watchful not only in the realm of wakefulness but also in other realms beyond. This constant vigilance bestowed upon the serpent the esteemed title of being wise. Additionally, the ancients believed that the serpent, with its keen perception and intimate understanding of the cycles of existence, possessed an uncanny knack for catalyzing change precisely when it would be most advantageous.

As a master of transformation, the serpent is attuned to the larger cycles and rhythms, guiding the shedding of the old to make way for renewal. Despite the conscious self's ignorance, a stirring from within signals the necessity for change. Transformation is on the horizon, and the serpent anticipates a profound shift beyond what meets the eye. Throughout history, the serpent occasionally took on the form of the Dragon archetype. It is fascinating to note that the term "dragon" originates from the Greek word *dracon*, which translates to "giant serpent" or "water snake," and is linked to the ancient Greek word *drakein*, meaning "to see clearly." Dragons, legendary beings with snake-like characteristics, are found in myths from various cultures, each with their own unique interpretations.

Some dragons are known for their wings, fire-breathing capabilities, water-dwelling tendencies, and oversized eyes for protecting valuable treasures. Throughout many mythologies, Dragons symbolize wisdom and change, especially in navigating challenges to personal development. With their connection to ancient magic, Dragons tap into a deep part of our psyche. Assertive and practical, Dragons push us to evolve by uncovering essential insights for progress.

Joseph Campbell pointed out that in the hero's journey, facing the dragon is crucial, but the true revelation comes when we realize that the dragon is actually a reflection of ourselves. The real question is: Are we ready to confront the dragon – and ourselves – with clarity?

In his book The Power of Myth, Campbell highlights the significance of the dragon as a representation of one's psychological bondage to their ego. He emphasizes that we are confined within our own dragon cage, and the true dragon lies within us, symbolizing the grip of our ego.

As the embodiment of both Serpent and Dragon, this powerful entity urges us to confront our fears without hesitation, allowing us to tap into our untapped potential that we have kept locked away. By bravely facing the Serpent-Dragon, we gain entry into the hidden recesses of our psyche, embarking on a transformative quest of self-discovery. Although a serpent residing within our psyche can provide us with clarity and wisdom, it does not necessarily guarantee that we will find satisfaction in what we uncover. Hence, the presence of serpent and its treasures may initially seem overwhelming. From the perspective of someone commencing their journey, shedding one's skin signifies a process of rebirth, a profound release from their previous life.

The serpent urges us to discard outgrown aspects of ourselves, to relinquish anything that confines or limits us. This can be challenging, and at times even traumatic, as we bid farewell to our former selves. However, ultimately, we come to realize that this is precisely what we require. Breaking out of our self-imposed restrictions requires us to let go of what no longer serves us. The serpent serves as a powerful symbol of transformation and renewal, leading us towards a deeper understanding of our own potential and limitations.

Amidst profound shifts, we liberate ourselves from the societal expectations and judgments imposed by others. This liberation enables us to embark on a profound journey of self-discovery, reconnecting with our true essence. This journey often entails embracing vulnerability and delving into the depths of our shadow self – the aspects of ourselves that we have disowned or neglected. However, it also presents an opportunity to reclaim the wisdom and insights that our inner self has safeguarded for an extensive period.

Through self-discovery, we empower ourselves; we begin to experience the transformative impact of sharing our authentic light with the world. The serpent acts as the protector of our psyche, preserving our inner treasures. However, before we can unlock those treasures, we must find the courage to confront our psyche's serpent or dragon and venture into the depths of our inner world. Just as a serpent sheds its skin, we too must discard anything that impedes our progress – such as close-minded attitudes, self-destructive tendencies, or antiquated views – to advance towards a more enriched and expanded version of who we are.

Alchemy, the main focus of our blog and books, is an age-old discipline that emerged in China, India, and Egypt. Over time, it expanded and transformed in various regions, including classical Greece and Rome, the Middle East, and Europe. Alchemists embarked on a multifaceted journey, exploring both the tangible and intangible aspects of their craft. Their endeavors involved the transmutation of ordinary metals, like lead, into the precious metal, gold. The alchemical process of turning metals into gold was a symbolic representation of the inner transformation one undergoes on a spiritual level, moving from a lower state to a higher state by awakening the inner serpent/kundalini.

Yet, their aspirations extended beyond the physical realm, as they sought to unravel the enigmatic nature of life, driven by the pursuit of eternal freedom from death. The serpent, a symbol of transformation, immortality, and enlightenment, aptly represented the alchemist's emblematic quest. Throughout history, alchemists tirelessly sought after the fabled "*philosopher's stone*," a mystical elixir thought to unlock the power of transformation.

The yogis of India have claimed that the Tree of the Knowledge of Good and Evil with its trunk and divergent branches represents the human spine and the nerves which branch from it. This inner "tree" bestows intellectual wisdom by allowing humans to interact with and learn from the phenomenal world. The serpent at the tree's base is the body's root life force which, at some point during the evolution of the dense, physical body, descended to the Root or Earth Chakra at the base of the spine and perpetually fuels the body from that distal location.

> Eventually, however, the serpent life force will once again ascend the spine. This event, claims the yogis, is depicted in the Eden allegory as the Tree of Life. The flaming sword-wielding cherub which guards the base of the tree, they say, is the fiery Kundalini Serpent which resides at the base of the human spine. When a person can move this TRANSFORMATIVE SERPENT up the Tree of Life or spine and merge it in the top of the head, he or she will achieve eternal life and potentially live forever" – **Mark A. Pinkham**

Conclusion

There is something raw and honest about working with the Serpent. We could be required to be brutally honest with ourselves, be open to broader perspectives, or live life in a new and unique manner. The shadow aspect of the serpent may signify the power to overcome our fears, confront our hidden desires, and inspire us to fully embrace our true identities. The serpent symbolizes the need for transformation, prompting us to shed our skin when it no longer accommodates our expanding selves, restricting our potential for growth and evolution.

The comprehension of this phenomenon may elude us in a purely rational sense, but its effects are undeniably felt. Whether physically bitten by a snake or not, those who willingly follow the serpent's path of healing now possess an unwavering certainty that they have undergone a remarkable transformation.

Energetically, the serpent embodies the sexual fire that rests coiled three and a half times within the Muladhara chakra. When we preserve, transmute, and awaken this passionate flame, the dormant fire within us comes alive. The powerful Kundalini force, once awakened, aligns the molecules of our body in perfect harmony, creating a profound transformation. Then the human body begins to vibrate with health, grows strong in wisdom, and gains the ability to perceive all things. The authors of this book can attest, based on their own experiences, that preserving and transmuting sexual energy leads to a heightened vibration that provides immunity against sickness and disease. When sexual energy, referred to as the serpentine fire, is harnessed and awakened, it becomes the most effective form of medicine.

Every human being harbors a collection of "I"s within them – one for desire, one for anger, one for jealousy, one for envy, one for manipulation, and so on. These numerous "I"s together form the ego, or the demon of multiple personalities. With the awakening of the Kundalini serpentine fire, the various "I"s are disintegrated, leaving no trace of the ego personality. In essence, on a metaphysical, spiritual, physical, mental, energetic, and emotional level, the serpent in any form embodies the supreme healing energy that can elevate us to divine beings. The activation of Christ Consciousness can only be initiated by the serpent.

"If the account given in Genesis is really true, ought we not, after all, to thank this serpent? He was the first schoolmaster, the first advocate of learning, the first enemy of ignorance, the first to whisper in human ears the sacred word liberty, the creator of ambition, the author of modesty, of inquiry, of doubt, of investigation, of progress and of civilization" – **Robert Ingersoll**

Chapter 15

REGENERATION & UNCOILING THE SERPENT

> "When you have conquered entirely all sex desires then the regenerate body becomes a vessel to hold spirit" – **Hiram Butler**

In numerous instances within this book, we have stressed the significance of sexual energy as the foundation of mystical and spiritual practices. It was a shared belief among ancient civilizations that in order for individuals to evolve and unlock their hidden potential, they must conquer their desires and lust. Moreover, we have emphasized in our blog and books that there exist influential figures who have practiced black magic since ancient times and oppose the idea of man preserving his seed and uncoiling the serpent. By now, it should be clear that there exists an **A.I.** Agenda with the intention of enslaving humanity through digital means. The individuals in power, who can be likened to dark sorcerers, have a vested interest in suppressing the spiritual evolution of humanity and keeping their hidden potentials locked away.

In our discussion on the shadow dragon consciousness [*which we will most likely put it as a chapter in our next book, not titled yet*], we shed light on the porn industry, revealing disturbing statistics from this morally corrupt and depraved sector. Pornography is associated with dark rituals in black magic. These dark sorcerers are highly conscious of the power held within the seed of man The power structure has a vested interest in keeping you lustfully ignorant, which is why it perpetuates a pornographic culture under the guise of "freedom of expression" and advocates for the health benefits of masturbation. There is a large number of people, including both men and women, who falsely believe that masturbation is good for health.

Masturbation, particularly for men, can result in degeneration, devolution, and ultimately mortality due to the nature of their ejaculation. For further insights into this subject, we recommend reading the chapters 17, 18, 19, 20 and 21 in the book *Rebuild Yourself From Within* by J.J. & TAMO

This insidious culture seeks to enslave individuals to their lowest instincts, draining them of their vitality and transforming them into mindless consumers. Undoubtedly, pornography stands as the most sophisticated weapon ever created in the annals of humanity. Consider this scenario: if you were the one in charge, you would not prefer individuals who possess immense power, creativity, and an unparalleled drive to revolutionize the world. Instead, you would favor individuals who possess only enough strength to barely rise in the morning, fulfill their work duties, and return home.

The aim is to have loyal customers who never challenge your authority. This is why you flood them with pornographic material and normalize sexual immorality. This deceptive tactic gives the appearance of freedom while depleting their life force, which holds the potential for unlocking superhuman capabilities. Through our profound experience, we have come to realize the extraordinary potency of semen retention on the physical, mental, and spiritual levels. It is astonishing how a single human body, when fully harnessed, can bend this entire system according to their own will.

Reflect on Pythagoras, Plato, Beethoven, Newton, Da Vinci, Nietzsche, and Einstein, just to name a few. The idea that a single component can influence the entire entity is a testament to the immense power that lies within each person. Your body and life-force, if preserved and transmuted, act as a channel for energy, capable of accessing unimaginable levels of power.

It is crucial to recognize that when talking about semen retention, the intention is not to diminish the strength of women who are also capable of overcoming their desires and achieving extraordinary abilities by awakening their inner energy. Rather, it is due to the inherent differences between male and female orgasms.

During male ejaculation, the semen-essence is expelled from the man's body. On the other hand, when a woman experiences orgasm, she internally releases various sexual secretions, which, unlike in men, are retained within her body. In French, the term La Petite Mort translates to "the little death" is a term used to refer to the male sexual orgasm.

"Before we can regenerate ourselves we must fix any "leaks" within us that are dissipating our energies. Sexual activity and its subsequent sexual secretions are a major source of this energy loss. Regeneration of your body can occur when you stop this leakage. Over time your body will begin to accumulate proteins, lipoids, and other constituents that are essential to the nourishment of the brain, nervous tissues and organs, down to the very cell and mitochondrial functions of your body" – Edward Green

THE SERPENT

The powerful grip of the giant serpent of Sex has humanity teetering on the brink of destruction. Initially meant to assist in human development, this serpent was naively taken in as a pet and lavished with excessive affection. Through overindulgence and submission to its every desire, the pet has evolved into a monstrous force that now looms over its master, poised to bring about their downfall. Emerging from the suffocating grip of humanity's plight, a desperate plea for help resonates within the inner recesses of our being. It is a cry tinged with fear, rising and falling, beseeching liberation from the unyielding clasp of a malevolent force. Yet, no answer comes, no external assistance arrives.

Man's precarious position is entirely self-inflicted. It is he who bestowed upon this creature its current power by habitually yielding to its escalating demands. Therefore, it is solely up to him to remedy this self-created anguish through unwavering self-exertion. The serpent, representing the formidable foe, can be triumphed over if man so desires. Through sheer willpower, he can weaken its dominance and stand firm against its eerie entanglement. In fact, by resisting its corrupt longings, he can still assert control over the cumbersome and unruly reptile. The serpent also symbolizes the dormant dragon. When the dragon awakens and rises up in the air (spine), he will obtain wings and fly (en**light**enment/in-LIGHT-ment).

By exerting his willpower, he can once again bring it under his control. As a result, its hidden power will greatly assist him in his pursuit of evolution. Indeed, "once conquered, the serpent becomes a source of life. Instead of appropriating man's life force, it will then provide him with the greatest catalyst for attaining a higher level of human existence. The turbulent serpent of Sex will transform into the submissive serpent of Wisdom, guiding the way from the human realm to a state beyond. Various civilizations incorporate the image of a snake as a metaphor for human existence in their myths. In Eastern texts, there is mention of a serpent coiled within a mysterious core of energy within the human body.

While not exactly the same, the release of this serpent within oneself, like a twisting beast, is believed to be humanity's path to evolution. Serpent symbolism has been discovered in various cultures across the Earth/world. One common theme is the legends of heroes triumphing over evil serpents. These legends serve as a powerful symbol of mankind's need to overcome the overpowering influence of sexuality. Throughout history, folklore has consistently associated serpents with the sexual function.

Knowledgeable investigators have arrived at the conclusion that the serpent always carries a phallic connotation. However, what often perplexes students of symbolism is that, despite being portrayed as the embodiment of evil, the serpent is also seen in a contrasting light. However, in cases where the symbolism remains unchanged, there is a noticeable difference between the two depictions.

While the malevolent serpent is coiled, the benevolent serpent is consistently depicted as upright. This transformed serpent, no longer coiled but standing on its tail with a slightly curved body, bears resemblance to the human spine, which plays a crucial role in the actual uncoiling of the serpent. It remains a phallic symbol, albeit one that has been conquered, tamed, and transformed into the most valuable asset for humanity.

Through a reflective exploration of various depictions of serpents, it becomes clear that they encapsulate a principle of paramount importance. This principle asserts that resisting the demands of the sexual urge will progressively unwind the serpent, leading to spiritual liberation and unhindered evolutionary advancement. However, attaining this ultimate outcome necessitates a conscious recognition of the essentiality of purifying oneself. The key to unlocking spirituality lies in its remarkable purity. This often-neglected factor of evolutionary growth is essential and should be pursued after the acquisition of intellect. Unfortunately, mankind has largely overlooked its importance.

> "The serpent represents the sexual fire of the Third Logos. The blood of the serpent represents the waters of Genesis, the great universal sperm, the ens seminis or Christonic semen, in whose waters is the germ of all life. The serpentine fire, the igneous serpent of our magic powers, sleeps coiled three and a half times inside the chakra Muladhara, which is situated in the coccygeal bone" – **Samael Aun Woer**

REGENERATION

Degeneration, generation, and regeneration are closely intertwined, all influenced by the same force. The distinction lies in the way this force is utilized. Misusing it for sexual gratification leads to degeneration, while using it for reproduction results in generation. To achieve regeneration, the very same force needs to be converted into spiritual power within the individual. Regeneration involves redirecting the generative force towards spiritual enlightenment, signifying the awakening of higher consciousness. To be regenerated is to be reborn into spiritual existence.

Individuals who have undergone this transformative experience have attested to the undeniable reality of a new birth that can occur within human beings, enabling the profound development of their spiritual essence. This second birth leads to the harmonization of one's consciousness with the universal and divine. The new birth in all possible ways enhances the potential of both mind and body; it results in immense mental and spiritual power, which when wisely utilized can unlock extraordinary abilities. Even the physical body will undergo purification. The rejuvenating energies dormant within one's inner self, once awakened, will eventually elevate him to a divine state. Anyone can reprogram their own DNA.

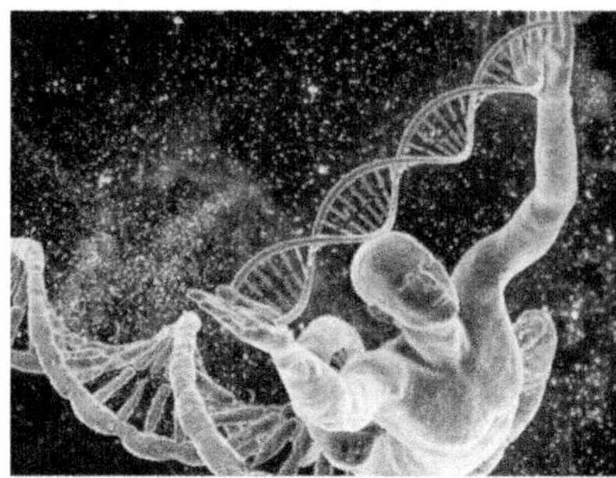

Program your own DNA with conscious thoughts

Through the process of regeneration, a person constructs a brand new body for themselves. Cell by cell, they are revitalized and elevated to a higher vibration by the transmuted life force. The utmost crucial evolutionary feat of mankind is the prioritization of utilizing one's generative energy to perpetually reproduce and maintain their own body, relegating propagation to a subordinate role. Regeneration is like being born again without the need for death. It involves transitioning into a fresh existence in a different realm, governed by new principles and filled with novel encounters, all through an internal transformation while still inhabiting the physical form. The transformation occurs without physical death, but something must still die in order for rebirth to occur. Man's renewal hinges on shedding all that hides his authentic self. None of the old, worldly desires can accompany the spiritual awakening.

The birth process involves purging lower tendencies and replacing them with divine energies. Only after this transformation can a new spiritual being emerge within the earthly body. The physical body then becomes a vessel for the spiritual self, which is recognized as the true identity.

The sage who reaches this spiritual state transcends the ordinary existence of man, just as human life surpasses the foetal stage. In this state, life is lived to its fullest potential, free from mere sensory experiences. However, one must first eliminate all animalistic tendencies to attain this state of being.

Each individual must prepare for their own rebirth. When the life energy is focused on creating new life, it splits into male and female components, which must work together. As evolution progresses, sexual energy redirects itself inward within the organism, resulting in the creation of a new life form with the potential for regeneration.

The force is equal in both women and men in this new form. Not only is the spiritual energy the same in both sexes, but the organs for regeneration are also identical. Thus, each individual must achieve regeneration independently. Not all individuals can successfully and promptly undergo the process of new birth. This can only be achieved by those who have attained a high level of mental and physical purity.

Progress in this endeavor is only possible once one recognizes the necessity of overcoming physical desires and completely ceasing any wastage of energy. In essence, celibacy is the initial and essential prerequisite for the task of self-renewal. The requirement stems from the fact that, as previously mentioned in both generation and regeneration, the powerful force of nature at play is the one related to the sexual organism.

This energy has the ability to be channeled towards the physical generative organs located in the lower regions of the body or towards the spiritual regenerative organs in the head. The functions of regeneration and generation are so different that they are incompatible. Spiritual regeneration can only be achieved if all sexual expression ceases.

The universal emphasis on chastity by great spiritual leaders can be traced back to the core principle of regeneration. A spiritual leader must uphold strict standards of chastity, as it is crucial for the mystical rebirth of individuals. The transmutation of sexual energy is at the heart of regeneration, making it impossible for man to achieve true regeneration without perfect chastity.

> "The force that generates in the human body those elements which, when used in accordance with natural law, serve to perpetuate the race, is the same force, which, when recognized, properly understood and rightly used, will regenerate the body, strengthen the mind, build up character and develop a true and pure manhood and womanhood" – **Arthur Gould**

UNCOILING THE SERPENT

Through the accumulation of evidence, it has been revealed that absolute purity is crucial when one seeks to follow the path of spiritual growth. Each piece of evidence adds to the credibility of the concept of perfect chastity. Based on the extensive evidence provided, this concept could stand on its own without further validation. However, one key reason for the importance of sexual purity in spiritual progress has not yet been discussed. The very basis of our entire blog and books, encompassing its domain name, is firmly grounded in this underlying principle.

All applications of chastity must have a foundation in physiological phenomena. The physiology of the Occident, with its understanding of the internal secretions of the sex glands, provides a close approximation to this ultimate basis. The internal secretions are not only crucial for the body and mind, but they also hold the key to our deepest secrets. There is a growing recognition that the reproductive system is a source of vital energy, which plays a pivotal role in all aspects of life, including spirituality. However, Western **science**'s general neglect of the spiritual element has resulted in a lack of understanding regarding the essential factors of sexuality.

The rationale behind sex purification can be comprehended by exploring the metaphysical aspects of the less materialistic Orient. Throughout thousands of years, the Oriental mind has extensively studied the process of spiritualization. In the realm of spiritual science, it is imperative for our Nordic intellect to show reverence towards the claims and assertions put forth by the Oriental mind. There one can learn of the intricate workings of nature's subtle energies within the human body, uncover the true functions of often misunderstood organs in the head, explore the chakras and psychic nerve centers, delve into the force channels and currents along the spinal column, and unlock the secrets of the Kundalini, the enigmatic serpent fire at the base of the spine.

The existence of psychic centers is not acknowledged by so-called Western scientists due to their invisibility, non-dissectibility, and non-measurability with physical instruments. However, the fact that these centers are made of matter finer than what can be observed by any physical means renders microscope detection inconsequential. The forces and fires of occult physiology can be acknowledged for the same reasons we accept nerve force and mind – they are intangible and known only through their outcomes. Similarly, the existence of secret fires and forces has been demonstrated through the results achieved by those who have mastered their use. It is possible to demonstrate the existence of these forces within oneself. However, the challenge lies in the fact that comprehending "the functioning of the spinal fires" is extremely complex, requiring many years to grasp even the basic principles.

Essentially, in the Far East, it is believed that both men and women possess a power known as Kundalini. This powerful occult force is said to be dormant, coiled like a serpent, at the base of the spinal column. The all-important force known as Kundalini holds both a collective and personal significance. It is not only the creator and sustainer of the universe, but also the universal life principle that manifests in nature. Within the human body, Kundalini represents the most powerful manifestation of creative energy.

Kundalini can be considered as the personalized divine power, residing in the body like a seed from which a flawless human flower is meant to blossom. This sacred seed is often abandoned in the reproductive area, where it may be consumed by the worms of sensuality or wasted due to neglect, never given the opportunity to grow. Nevertheless, a knowledgeable individual should raise it from its original position and bring it to rest at the midpoint of the eyebrows. Diligent care is necessary to facilitate its germination and the emergence of a stem along the spine.

The spinal cord, serving as a crucial conduit for nerve energy, extends from the lower part of the torso to the head for a specific purpose. It is through this pathway that the life force must be redirected from the reproductive system and conveyed to the regenerative organs located near the uppermost part of the skull. Once the serpent power awakens, it ascends through the psychic nerve centers until it reaches the thousand-petalled lotus [3rd eye] in the brain. However, as long as man is dominated by his senses, reviving the dormant center in the head necessary for controlling creative forces remains impossible. When the serpent power reaches this pinnacle, it unlocks the highest spiritual center of man - the thinker, the knower, the creator, finally reflecting the image of God.

The liberation of humanity is in the passing of fire from the base of the spine. Through the elevation of Kundalini, through the release of the serpent fire, humanity advances towards a state of superhuman excellence as ordained by the laws of evolution. Caution must be exercised when it comes to intentionally awakening Kundalini until a thorough purification of one's being is achieved. An in-depth understanding of the intricate ways in which Kundalini manifests is not necessarily essential for advanced evolutionary growth. Regardless of one's knowledge or aspirations for spiritual development, the serpent power becomes active in the body.

Regardless of awareness, nature answers spiritual aspirations by triggering a force when the individual is prepared. The journey to the brain is intertwined with the ongoing evolution. Achieving the uncoiling of the serpent, even with the individual's conscious cooperation, is still a slow and challenging process. Those who aim to perfect it must be prepared to repeat the procedure for years, ensuring no impurity taints them mentally or physically. The purification of thought, will, and morality is essential before they can be intensified by the awakened force. Unleashing the immense power of the higher aspects of this energy should only be done after one has achieved the utmost purity of life and thought. Prior to awakening this potent force, it is crucial to undergo a rigorous process of purification. Failing to do so can result in grave dangers and severe consequences.

As long as the power of Kundalini remains confined to the reproductive organs due to sexual acts or thoughts, it will be incapable of ascending to the higher organs responsible for regeneration and creation. Moreover, if it is forcefully brought down after starting to rise, the disruptive effects on the subtle energy currents will inevitably impact the entire body, particularly the brain, leading to the manifestation of both physical and mental ailments.

When Kundalini energy starts to ascend, it is crucial to remember the strong link between the brain and the reproductive system, requiring a complete preservation of life force. The ultimate and foundational reason why achieving perfect sexual purity is crucial for individuals aiming to accelerate their evolutionary development lies in these physiological, or at least meta-physiological, truths.

It is important for everyone to realize that playing with the sacred serpent fire will result in suffering and the struggles of human existence. Oriental meta-physiology teaches us that true happiness can only be attained by letting go of worldly desires. Indulging in sexual pleasures and seeking self-gratification only hinders the journey towards freedom from suffering.

"Kundalini, the serpent power or mystic fire, is the primordial energy or Sakti that lies dormant or sleeping in the Muladhara Chakra, the center of the body. It is called the serpentine or annular power on the account of serpentine form. It is an electric fiery occult power, the great pristine force which underlies all organic and inorganic matter. Kundalini is the cosmic power in individual bodies. It is not a material force like electricity, magnetism, centripetal or centrifugal force. It is a spiritual potential Sakti or cosmic power" – **Swami Sivananda**

Chapter 16

DEFRAGMENT YOUR SUBCONSCIOUS MIND

Who are you? Are you your name, nationality, social status? Think again. Do you identify yourself with the IDENTITIES mentioned above? Identifying ourselves in anyway, makes us limited beings. Identifications spring comparisons, jealousy, racism, hatred etc., which in turn we end up causing pain to ourselves. Your first major step is when you ask yourself this question "**WHO AM I**". All of us are creators, we create daily, some of us create consciously and others create unconsciously. Creating unconsciously brings mostly suffering and struggle in life. Our subconscious mind is what drives our conscious actions. Our daily habits dictate the path that we take, a path of wisdom and freedom or a path a destruction. The major first step is to defragment our HDD (hard drive). See pain as the weeds that need to be pulled off from the garden.

Subconscious mind – The hard drive holding both pain and joy through memories and habits.

What does ABRACADABRA mean? Abracadabra is a phrase in Hebrew that means, "***I will create as I speak***". Only speak if it's better than your silence. The words you speak are the spells you are casting. That's why it's called "spelling". You can attract anything based on your thinking. If you are someone that complains a lot, you're going to keep complaining and you will attract people of the same mindset. It's an addiction that immobilizes you.

If you are true to yourself and vibrate only in love, then you will live a wonderful life and will attract people of the same mindset. I'm true to myself and when I encounter complainers or negative people, they weed themselves out of my life for me. I don't even need to tell them. To vibrate in love, you first must love yourself. By loving yourself, you know your worth and you don't need anyone else's approval. By not needing anyone's approval, you are truthful to yourself, others and your life will shine.

You become the captain of your ship. You decide the direction that your ship will take, toward calm smooth open waters full of possibilities or toward the direction of the storm that you will be engulfed in and thrown toward a cliff. You are the programmer of your mind. Your life is essentially a printout of your subconscious mind. What are the programs in your mind?

If you want to change and choose a different direction in life you must overcome those limitations that are keeping you a hostage. You can't tell your subconscious mind to record anything, because it is not there. Your subconscious is just a player, unless you catch your subconscious those two times where it changes profession, from player to a recorder. Those two times (profession/function change) are,

1- *Before bed* and

2- *As soon as you open your eyes in the morning/rising*. You must engage in hypnosis/ habituation regularly to the point that you will be in charge of your life and you will be mindful every step of the way. Yes, you have that power.

3 WAYS ON HOW TO REPROGRAM YOUR SUBCONSCIOUS MIND

One-From the age 0-7. That's when the children's brain operate in *"Theta brain wave"* where to them everything is true that's why it is very important on how you speak to your children and what content you let them watch on TV or on the Internet.

Two-In your sleep while the brain is in THETA state (*any age after 10*). For children up to 7 years of age this works automatically anyway. But this step applies to adults that have their brain full of opinions and conditioning from the system to live in a herd mentality lifestyle/mindset.

Three-While conscious/awake, which out of all three is the most difficult one. This is the most difficult one because during the time you are awake, your nervous system (your consciousness) is constantly bombarded with what you see, hear, taste, smell or touch therefore is very difficult to be mindful (and not mindFULL) all day long but it is not impossible. With practice anything is achievable. Look at your daily life, anything that life throws at you and things that you want, come to you because you have programs in your subconscious that encourage them being there.

Anything you struggle with, anything you have to work hard at, anything you put effort into, you are doing is because you are aiming (consciously or unconsciously) to overcome a program of limitation that is stopping you from getting out of that limitation or fragmented hard drive.

We record information into our subconscious mind in the first 6-7 years of our lives. The information can be downloaded straight into the subconscious mind when in theta brain wave or hypnosis state before going to bed and as soon as you wake up. In the first 6-7 years of life, a child's brain is predominantly operating in theta hypnosis and a child's brain records everything he/she hears. It is particularly important that you know this so you can teach your children the right things from the start. I have heard many parents swear or say all kinds of horrible things in front of their children.

They don't realize that after the first 7 years, the child will start showing their parents' personality's traits. When you go to the doctor for a mental or emotional problem, the doctor will ask you about when you were a child and if there was a bad history in the family.

Twice a day your brain goes through a period of Theta vibrational activity. Twice a day your brain is prepared to download information through hypnosis. When you are sleeping, you are at the lowest vibrational frequency called Delta. When you are about to wake up or when you are about to fall asleep, they are two times where your subconscious brain records information. That's when you are in the dream world and you are mixing the two. This period is called Theta, where hypnosis occurs, the recording process.

As you become more awake, Theta goes to a higher vibration called Alpha. That's a calm consciousness. You start doing your morning routine while being calm and maybe getting ready to leave the house. By the time you get to work or anywhere where there are noises or people, your brain ramps up from Alpha (calm consciousness) to Beta brain waves which is the brainwave we operate in when we engage in a busy working environment. Before you get into a hypnosis state before bedtime, listen to affirmation programs and guided meditation. You can choose specifically guided meditation music tracks.

For example, if you want to have prosperity you can play the meditation that is for that desire. You can listen to a guided meditation program that is about peace of mind or any other type of healing music. And leave the music on all night. The hardest method to reprogram subconsciousness is during everyday life while conscious. You must be mindful every step of the way. You must consciously be your own recorder and player. Be careful of what gets recorded in your subconscious while you are not living in the moment. Be careful of what you watch and listen to. Every word you think or say, you are either cursing or blessing yourself.

EPIGENETICS

Science (not $cience) is continuously proving that the ability to heal is influenced by our thoughts, ***beliefs** and intentions. Everything is energy so your thoughts and beliefs have a profound vibrational effect upon our evolving genetic code. But it works in a negative way also. If you strongly believe that aging is normal, then your powerful vibrational thoughts and beliefs dictate how your cells behave. You are the programmer of your own code. You are powerful enough to fully activate your DNA. Question continuously what you believe. You can not get answers without questions. Your thoughts alone [beliefs derive after thoughts] can be healing frequencies. Our soul is composed of harmony. Disease is a form of disharmony.

Every single organ in your body is affected by sound, music and vibration. The people you hang around with, the music you listen to, the frequencies (Tv, tablets, phones, cell towers etc.) you are living in, dictate whether you live in disharmony or harmony. Your actions are based on your thoughts which create beliefs. If you believe you have been hurt by someone, even if they did not hurt you, your nervous system/consciousness believes it to be real therefore, you are living as if you were hurt for real. Others cannot be responsible for how you filter their words.

You are only harming yourself if you put more weight/importance on other people's words than your own words and feelings. This is about when you are fragile and easily to be hurt or offended by others. Reminder – Nobody can hurt or offend you, it is your belief that someone hurt or offended you. Unless we're speaking for when someone actually hurt you physically which in that case it is 100% their fault because it's nobody's right to lift a finger on you, no matter what you said to them and vice versa if you hurt them physically from being triggered by their words.

Pain is needed to a certain extent to learn lessons, but most people self inflict pain by making up stories in their mind about whatever it is that they went through daily. That's why it is very important to spend time alone so that you can face the self-inflicted pain. If you hang out with others while you are unhealed, you will misunderstand their words. Some of them are decently healed, some others are not and you will add more pain on the pile of pain that already exists within you.

"You can become sick or heal just by thought alone".

And if you disagree with this, then you are proving the statement to be accurate, because your own thoughts are denying the healing. Why when you truly like to do something you do it, you have that will and aspiration to do it. Try and remember about anything that you loved to do and did in the past. Then why don't you apply the same empowered state of emotions/mind to achieve other joyful things that you may think are impossible? That's because we tend to be lazy. In laziness you cannot grow. If you truly liked a person (intimately for example) I bet you would even walk for 3 hours to get to that person, assuming there were no cars/trains/buses. Many people are too lazy to exercise.

You don't need to go to the gym to become healthy, you can walk and run daily. Don't got to the gym to escape from whatever it is that you try to escape from. Wherever you go you cannot escape from what is in your mind. You are both the monster and the remedy, clean your mind from darkness so that you become free. People would find excuses anyway, they'd say they live in a city, no were to walk or run, or that they are too busy. You can even exercise without even leaving the house. Just do jumping jack, push ups or anything in the house daily and watch how you'll feel. Blood is your life's river.

> Rivers move, so does your blood needs to move/flow in a clean/clear state. Time is not an issue, the belief we have of anything dictates if we gravitate toward achieving our desires or succumbing in laziness, pain and destruction.

***beliefs** – *I think somewhere in the book I wrote that beLIEf is an illusion and kNOWingness is a fact. "Belief" being an illusion means when you blindly believe someone else's words, research, opinion without crisscrossing information from different sources so that you can draw a self-aware/conscious decision as to what is a fact and what is a lie, even though for the most part, a fact is when something is personally experienced. But in this case [in the "epigenetics" subject] we are talking about the ability to heal, therefore using the word "believe" when it's about something positive as in healing yourself means that you truly resonate and know for a fact that you can heal. You know that you are powerful. Unfortunately, most of us use the word "believe" in a positive or in a negative [unconsciously or unknowingly] way.*

HOW DOES MANIFESTING TAKE LONGER?

Let's make an example. Let's say that you like someone at work but you want to manifest that person to like/love you. During the day or whenever you are not at work you will replay in your mind interactions you had with that person, but also interactions that haven't happened yet. You will imagine the potential scenarios of course. You will spend a lot of time on thinking about what passed and on what hasn't happened yet.

You may imagine flirting or even more than flirting scenarios. Since what you think also creates emotional/physical triggering, you will most likely flirt, or say something way in advance to that person. Now, that person may go on defense mode, he or she will think that you only care about physical interaction. Now you are postponing or even destroying any chance of manifestation. You are causing a ripple effect that will distance that person from you.

Have you ever thrown a stone on a calm sea or a lake? If you have you'd know that the water will create circles/ripples getting away form the spot where the rock was thrown in. In this metaphor the rock is you. But if you do not throw the rock, then the water will remain calm as it was before. The same it should apply in this manifestation example. If you live in the moment and are not

consumed by the past or potential future, then the universe will create the circumstances that are parallel to the energetic frequency that you emit at any given moment.

Do not confuse joy with pleasure. If the person that you like is of a high frequency, but you just want to have sex with that person, then good luck. Even if you become deceptive and manage to be with that person, it won't last because the frequencies will find frequencies of the same wavelength in the long run. This was just one example for when you don't have to do anything. Some manifestations require your actions. If you want to have a painting you have to paint, use your hands, the brush, the canvas and the paints. Well, you can buy a painting but that's not truly *"manifestation"*.

The painting was already manifested by the person that painted it. Going back to manifesting the person that you like/love, even if you live in the moment but you still don't manifest that person, it doesn't mean that you did something wrong. It simply means that she (assuming you are a man, but you can switch situation if you are the opposite gender) was not for your highest purpose, or you were not for her higher purpose.

There are some things that we cannot know, for example someone else's purpose. You can only know your own purpose; this is a FACT. But because you were influenced by her smile, her beauty, her mind or any other reason, you initiated a chain reaction that began from your thoughts. But because you (just like anyone else) think that what you think you want is the right thing, you may be disappointed when you don't get what you want. How do you know what you want is the right thing? You know it by how you feel and not by what you think. What you think is based on unlimited opinions you have heard all life.

What you feel is based on the connection you have with your higher self and the **Source of All** or **All That Is**. I try to avoid the word God because unfortunately, most people think God is a person. The moment you think like that, the manifestation taken on a whole new meaning. You become limited. You know the magnetic North (technically, the magnetic center), where no matter where you are in the world, the compass will always point North/Center. That's on a Macrocosmic level.

On a Microcosmic level, you are the center of everything. Everything point at you. Everything that exists in the world is a manifestation from your own mind. You are a magnet at all times. So, instead of going anywhere to bring what you desire and deserve, how about you allow everything you want to come to you effortlessly, by being in the moment. How that will happen, neither me, nor anyone with a human mind can explain. That's beyond our understanding. All we know is that when we live in the moment, the universe is our servant.

Chapter 17

TIME – BASED ON YOUR PERCEPTION OF TIME, YOUR ACTIONS BEND TIME OR TIME WILL BEND YOU

> Do you want to stop time?-**Kiss.** Do you want to travel in time?-**Read.** Do you want to escape time?-**Listen to the music.** Do you want to feel time?-**Write.** Do you want to release time?-**Breathe consciously.**

The past is just previous present moments and the future is awaiting present moments. Therefore, what matters is that there are only present moments. Don't look at the time if you don't have to do anything based on time. It will make you anxious. There is no point in wasting energy that you will not get back. You were born with a full battery. Every time you spend energy on things that don't benefit your overall well-being, the power of the battery empties. Do you realize how many times throughout life you unnecessarily waste your battery?

Thousands of times. We could live for hundreds of years if we were conscious of every thought and action during our everyday life. We are distracted with memories and imagination of an unknown future outcome. And in the meantime, we lose the present, we lose what we can never, ever get back. Looking at things and enjoying them in the moment is way better than taking pictures or videos of everything for viewing at a later moment.

> **"No matter how much energy you waste in memories and imagination, the only thing that matters is NOW".**

Many people say, "One day I will do that, or eventually I will get into this or that". That is the procrastinator's trait. If you want to do something, start Now. Today is the day. Tomorrow never comes. You are blessed as soon as you were created by and from the Divine Source. Every day is a new beginning.

If the new day doesn't bring you upliftment and peace, then you are living in the past through your memories or in the future through your imagination. Time and space happen all at once. Time doesn't move forward or back. Time is a fixed nature. Time is an interesting subject.

Time can work in your favour or not.

Time can reward or punish you.

Time can be your enemy or friend.

Time can kill you or give you life.

Your perceptions and emotions dictate whether time favours you or not. Time simply reflects your state of mind. Time will keep ticking no matter the choices you make in life. Time does not have any feelings. Time doesn't judge. Time is not racist. By being in the present, time will cease to exist. All you have is "NOW"

"Time is only an illusion produced by the succession of our states of consciousness as we travel through eternal duration, and it does not exist where no consciousness exists in which the illusion can be produced; but "lies asleep" - H. P. Blavatsky

Time doesn't exist, clocks do. Time is just an agreed upon construct. We have taken distance (one rotation of the Earth, and one orbit of the Sun), divided it up into segments and then give those segments labels. While it has it's uses, we have been programmed to live our lives by this construct as if it were real. We have confused our shared construct with something that is tangible and thus have become its slave.

Time is running out, time is non existent, time is fluid, times is the only commodity that exists. All these definitions are simply beliefs that we tell ourselves what time is. We must use time to our benefit and not to be destroyed by it as a result of our ignorance of the powers that we possess. Virtually anything in existence is neutral. We decide if something is used in a negative or in a positive way. Knowledge of self is the ultimate knowledge.

Do not believe anything in this book, because you may fall in the trap of becoming a follower. Read but don't believe. If something rings true where you resonate from the depths of your being, then the information you resonate with is true. Resonating and beliefs are two different things. Now, if you are addicted to something and you talk about that addiction with another person that is also addicted to it, then you resonate with that person therefore, the addiction (videogames, alcohol, pain medications, porn etc.) is true to you because you created the belief based on pleasure, taste, hearing or seeing/ watching something that you become addicted to. Something is true when it resonates from the soul and not from the 5 senses.

Reading books or articles or watching videos that talk about truth-health etc., serve to activate remembrance in you because you already know everything you need to know in this lifetime. Your daily thoughts, words and actions dictate the definitions of time. Time is merely a figment of our limited perception of our reality. Everything that has happened in the past, or that will happen in the future, is technically happening simultaneously right now.

When a hypnosis technique is used to tap into past lives, it's actually tapping into a parallel life. After all, how could it be a version of you in the past if you are still able to communicate with them (beings from the other side of the physical life) now? That is because it's not the past. That version of you, currently still exists in another reality. It exists in a parallel life or alternate timeline.

Do you want to stop time? -Kiss.

Do you want to travel in time?-Read.

Do you want to escape time? Listen to the music.

Do you want to feel time?-Write.

Do you want to release time?-Breathe.

The best thing you can do to be in the moment is to practice GROUNDING (walking barefoot in nature, hug a tree etc.), heal and shift your frequency to that of LOVE and send it to her (GAIA/Earth) core. Some deep planetary healing is taking place right now as we all shift through this experience together. Even though it will manifest for each of us differently (some will awaken faster than others). You just got to roll with it. Like swimming in the ocean, there are swells and currents and the key is to flow with them and not against. If you are losing reference points as in missing a day, there is a reason for it.

On one frame (moment in time) it's a day, on another it's just a dream you feel like you live in between realities. It may feel like the memory of a dream and/or the memory of a memory of a dream. Some people are so affected by the speeding of time that it is causing a complete split in their psyche. We are all being shown to become intuitively led versus mentally or analytically. A linear time is just a construct not the reality.

Time as we know it, will no longer be relevant to this realm. At least not to the extent that we have used it so far. It's all in the head, the perception you have of time will dictate how your actions and feelings will be projected in the world . No matter what you do, eventually you will be faced with the inevitable which is to flow in time as opposed to be condemned by it. Time doesn't condemn us; it is us that condemn ourselves by living in the past or in the future that doesn't exist.

TIME, THE FEELINGS' TRIGGER

Time is a strong tester. It will test your limits. Time can be your master if you give yourself in. Time can be considered to be the 4th dimension of reality, used to describe events in three-dimensional space which is Earth. Time becomes evident through motion; sunrise, sunset, night and day, the changing seasons. The movement of the celestial bodies are all indicative of continuous change. Time is a measure of non-stop, consistent, change in our surroundings, usually from a specific viewpoint. While the concept of time is self-evident and intuitive, the steady passing of events before our eyes is much harder to explain or innerstand. Maybe because time is an illusion?

Time is **slow** when you wait

Time is **long** when you feel bored

Time is **fast** when you are late

Time is **deadly** when you are sad

Time is **short** when you are happy

Time is **endless** when you are in pain

Time is **beautiful** when you are in Love

Time **stops** when you meditate

Every time, TIME is determined by your feelings and your physiological conditions and not by the clock. Although it seems like it's the clock that causes your feelings, it is your reaction to it that triggers you. So, you trigger YOU. You are more powerful than you have been led to believe. Isn't it funny or amazing how a lifeless (lifeless, from our way of innerstanding) object/clock can drain the life out of you? That happens when you become a slave of the external environment. A long period of time can be fleeting, and a minute can be hell. It is amazing what time can do to people, well, people do it to themselves by being slaves to time.

It is time to be creative, to work for yourself and not for corporations that don't respect your time. A salary is a bribe to forget your dreams. Asking for a raise is like begging for longer chains. Do not underestimate how powerful and creative you are. No matter how bad life may seem, you have the power to change things around.

Chapter 18

PAIN, PAIN, PAIN – WHEN IS USED AS A LESSON, YOU CAN ONLY GAIN

There is little that is more corrosive to our emotional state than chronic pain and suffering. When our experience involves great pain, we must work on understanding that everyone else shares a bit of that suffering in their own lives even though many of those that have interacted with us are not conscious of their actions or conscious of our actions. Some of us ignore what our or other people's actions cause to them or us. Some others hold on for a long time to what happened to them or others. Holding on to memories for a long time to the point of becoming a bitter person or holding grudge on people, it creates pain in different forms. To alleviate that pain, the one that is suffering will project their pain onto other which again I must repeat that solitude is the answer to pretty much everything. How can you know yourself if all you do is listen to other people's life (including their drama)?

But when you have spent a considerable time by yourself to the point that you have become a strong person mentally and emotionally, you will not be affected negatively by others. On the contrary, you will affect them in a positive way. While our personal pain can distract our objectivity and good sense, with effort, we can find an appropriate place to put our pain and suffering outside of inflicting our suffering on others. So many of us are experiencing physical and mental pain on a regular basis that it spills over into our daily discourse and perspectives; clouding our vision and our judgement. It is also very important to be aware of the suffering of others through empathy and understanding.

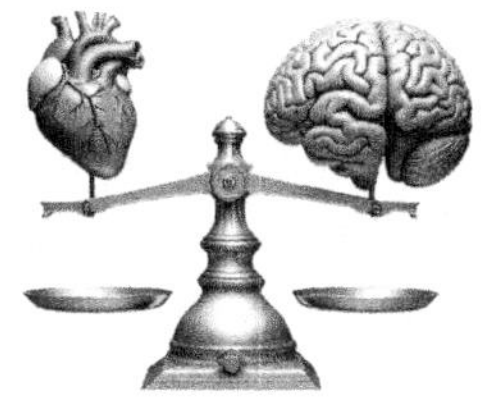

A balanced heart and mind that work in coherence will be able to handle any form of pain. Also, learn to be mindful not to let others' pain become yours. Real constant pain will make you avoid human contact. It desensitizes you from humanity in you, it suppresses empathy. Practice seeing things from an observant point of view so that you have a wider and broader idea of the darkness and light, pain and joy within you. Being constantly in pain suppresses the joy that is part of your original blueprint of existence. Pain is not there to keep you a hostage forever. Pain is there to teach you to be aware of the joy. Pain is a lesson and not a curse. Don't let pain become a drug/addiction.

Pain is all part of life, but a lesson, nonetheless. Pain is present manifestation based on memories of the past. Even if you got hurt physically and/or mentally/emotionally 5 hours ago, you're still suffering the pain of the past. The more distant the pain the heavier the burden in you is if you're still suffering that memory. Stop looking back in the rear-view mirror, because the longer you keep looking in back, you possibly might miss out on something really spectacular. Try (I do not recommend it) to look in the rea-view mirror of the car for 1 minute while driving, what do you think it will happen? No answer needed. The analogy is self-explanatory.

I hear people still complain or waste their time talking about the rain even when the Sun already came up. Or talk about their work problems with their spouses or children or their friends. After a long day of work, you are supposed to get rid of the work's toxicity by enjoying time with family and not spilling the poison on them. Don't bleed on people that didn't cut you. We can't move to the next chapter in our lives. Every time we are confused, anxious or scared or worried, we keep rereading the previous chapter, in this case a bad day at work.

Every day in life is like a chapter of the book. If you don't like a chapter of the book, move on to the next, don't ruin a beautiful read because of a bad chapter (*it may be bad because you deny information, don't understand the information or it could indeed be a bad chapter*). Remember that there's a lesson to be learned from each mistake we make, its all part of growing up. Life is an adventure, make sure you enjoy [IN-joy] the ride.

Pain is a result of many factors, some of them are:

- Trying to **control** your life or others trying controlling your life.

- Manipulative behaviour which derives from greed or low self esteem which causes us to fulfill the emptiness by destroying others and ourselves in the process.

- **Lying** has short legs. No matter how fast it runs it will get caught.

- **Gaslighting** is a very smart manipulative technique to hide the great pain. Being smart and being intelligent is not the same thing. You can be smart but not intelligent. If you are intelligent you are smart automatically. Being smart is like being a seedling. Intelligence is the whole tree including the fruit.

- **Bullying** is definitely a sign of weakness. Someone that bullies others has low self esteem and afraid of other people's strength without realizing that everyone can be strong without hurting others.

- **Fear/worry** has become the norm in our society. These stem as a result of bad memories of the past and uncertain bad things that could happen in the future. There is only NOW. When you live in the moment, fears and worries become non-existent.

- **Micro management** – One example of micro managing your pain is talking to friends and expecting them to say what you want to hear so that you feel better. This kind of micro-managing inner pain is simply a band aid that soon or later will rip off and could bleed more than before. Pain or anything that bothers you is like a seed. The more time passes the more it will grow. The bigger the problem the more effort it needs to be dealt with. The best way is to meditate so that you balance the brain waves, so that you learn to live in the moment and when your mind is clear you make better choices.

- Being **forced** to believe/support a lie. Technically, nobody forces you to believe or support anything. If you think that someone else forces you to believe something, then you gave your power away. You hold the power to believe and support anything you want. Nobody can take this power away from you unless you give it away. When we are weak and fragile we find excuses and blame others for our suffering. We blame the government, or our ex-spouse or the boss at the place we work at etc. Blaming anyone or anything will only postpone the healing that is required to become centered and grounded.

- Spoken to in a very **disrespectful** way in front of others. Even though respect is earned. But sure, there are people that are being disrespectful on purpose. They push your buttons. Those that know your weak points are the ones to push your buttons. When you are in a vulnerable state of mind and emotions you must heal in solitude and not in company, unless you have a very small circle of friends that you can truly trust who want the best for you. Otherwise, if you hang around with people just to socialize because you feel lonely by yourself, then when you are vulnerable, some of them will learn your weak spots and they will eventually use them against you whenever it benefits them. So, **be careful whom you share your consciousness** (*energy, thoughts and emotions*) **with.**

- Being **censored** when you want to speak your mind and be yourself.

These rob you of being present in the moment, they rob you of being healthy, strong, energetic, and joyful with high performance cognitive (critically thinking) function.

Those who purposefully cause you pain with their behaviour are all declining cognitively, mentally, emotionally, energetically and physically. They can make a comeback from anything by taking responsibility, and changing their behaviour and thinking. This requires courage and focused effort; this is a choice, and we all have the power of choice. The truth is what's REAL, and what's REAL creates our health, peace of mind, joy and quality of life experience adaptation. Denying the truth (reality) doesn't change the adaptation from the truth (reality). Your unique life experience is your unique responsibility; make your own choices, then put in the daily effort required to create the quality-of-life experience adaptation you want. Keep putting in the daily effort required, over time, until you get there. If you carry trauma you may feel more comfortable with rejection, with pain, with abuse, with the bare minimum than you

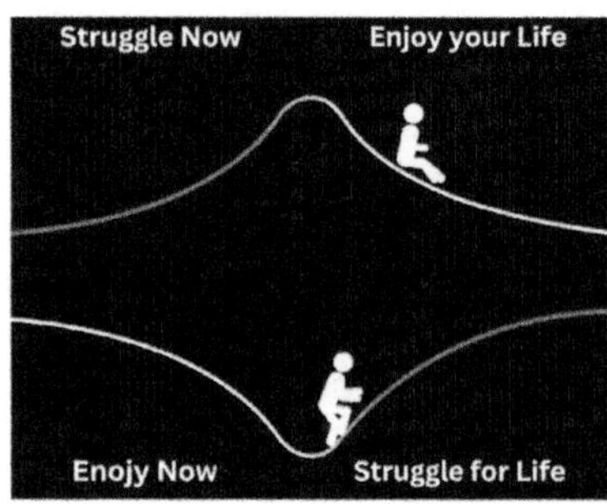

In both situations you will learn. It's your choice if you want to struggle temporary or for a long time.

are with peace, joy and with acceptance. This needs to change. When you heal, you're not healing to be able to handle more trauma. You're healing to be able to handle joy. Any disease has a mental and emotional cause before it manifests in the physical reality. One example is when a person you love or your pet passes away. There is a time that you process the grievance but don't let it pull you in the dark to the point you miss living in the light. Filling yourself up with gratitude, life force depletes if you waste it grieving, gossiping, bad foods/drinks, when you are lustful etc. The physical body is a 3D representation of what we feel, think and believe. When it is broken and in pain, we are broken and in pain on the inside too.

Change the way you think and the world around you will have to change since your newly realized/practiced energy will affect the circumstances. This means change your frequency/vibration and your physical will change. Lift your inner state to one where you feel humbled by gratitude and you will heal the physical body too. Every human has the ability to heal the body with their mind. When our mind is filled with worry, anger, or any low vibrating frequency about the illness and the things going on around us, we are sinking into sickness [*stagnant energy*]. When we flip the coin to the bright side and feel gratitude instead of worry or anger or grief or guilt, we heal the body, we let the energy freely flow without any obstacle [worries, fears, envy, feeling defeated, gossiping, anger etc.] Learn to be mindful when you are in pain so that you don't hurt others unintentionally.

The body is nothing more than the physical representation of frequency and vibration. Lift the vibration up to compassion, gratitude and love, and the body will reflect this change. Each one of us has full control over our frequency. We heal through gratitude, not worry, not anger, not boredom, not offence, not blame, not guilt, not any low vibrational emotion, but through grace and the emotion of grace is humble gratitude.

Pain happens because of disappointments, resentments over unfulfilled expectations in life. When you live in an unhealthy relationship pain is guaranteed. Money, job or sexuality issues are other forms of pain causes. Any trauma, shock, worries, fears and stress cause pain also. When you grieve for a long time without having let go of what has passed, pain will hold you a hostage. All these create trapped emotions and toxic thoughts that live in the mind. Pretty much all pain is self inflicted, with the exception of physical pain caused intentionally by others on us.

Realize your true power/talents. Appreciate the beauty of nature. Love people without conditions (without expecting anything in return such as, money, materialistic items, sex etc.). Going to the gym, eating organic food and taking supplements won't fix what is troubling your heart and your mind. The heaviest weight exist in your mind. Release thoughts and beliefs that don't serve you anymore and watch how pain will be a thing of the past. Pain was needed to build the path, now walk the path from the lessons. Walk **THE PATH TO GREATNESS...**

Take a minute of your time and review this book on Amazon if you found anything useful and empowering. ***THANK YOU***

<u>J.J & TAMO</u>

RESOURCES/BIBLIOGRAPHY

YOU ARE THE ONE by Pine G. Land

Essential Chakra Meditation by April Pfender

Body Mind Soul by Saimir Kercanaj

Eastern Body, Western Mind by Anodea Judith

Rebuild Yourself From Within by J.J. and TAMO

Think and Grow Rich – **https://amzn.to/3JEFhOH**

First Water: The Use OF Urine & Sexual Fluids As Medicine by Caraf Ayvnayt

GAIN WISDOM THROUGH PRACTICED KNOWLEDGE by Rimias K. Neo

I AM THE KEY THAT OPENS ALL DOORS by Saimir Kercanaj

Awakening The Ancient Power of Snake – **https://amzn.to/3W5N0wu**

The Perfect Matrimony – **https://amzn.to/4aE1JD7**

Not In His Image – **https://amzn.to/4d5HAYC**

The Semen Retention Manuscript – **https://amzn.to/44rPCqR**

The Coiled Serpent – **https://amzn.to/4aQwXHp**

Meeting the Shadow – **https://amzn.to/4dm7qHU**

The Multidimensional Human by Kurt Leland

The Shaman's Path To Freedom by Don Jose Ruiz

The Spiritual Awakening Guide: Kundalini, Psychic Abilities, and the Conditioned Layers of Reality – **https://amzn.to/3QfTBR7**

A Definitive Guide to Jungian Shadow Work: How to Integrate Your Dark Side **https://scottjeffrey.com/shadow-work/**

Purity is Power – **https://amzn.to/4aNGwqA**

The Aquarian Message by Samael Aun Weor

The Art of Seeing – **https://amzn.to/3xzHfwJ**

Third Eye Awakening – **https://amzn.to/3TXNgLu**

Human Race Get Off Your Knees – **https://amzn.to/3UmEsQM**
Bringers Of The Dawn by Barbara Marciniak

The **Fluoride** Deception by Christopher Bryson–**https://amzn.to/3VUvwmO**

Human Race Get Off Your Knees by David Icke –**https://amzn.to/4cUsRzl**

Understanding The Pineal Gland **https://lyndondavis.com/understanding-the-pineal-gland/**

How to Decalcify the Pineal Gland – **https://scottjeffrey.com/decalcify-your-pineal-gland/**

---

https://www.chakras.info

https://theserpentsway.com/recommended-books/

https://scottjeffrey.com/decalcify-your-pineal-gland/

https://buycbdhub.com/blogs/cbd-and-wellness/monoatomic-gold-the-ancient-elixir-or-modern-myth

https://www.anahana.com/en/wellbeing-blog/yoga/divine-feminine

https://www.themoonschool.org/divine-feminine/wounded-feminine-energy-signs/#google_vignette

A Fluoride-Free Pineal Gland is More Important than Ever –**https://wakeup-world.com/2012/09/10/a-fluoride-free-pineal-gland-is-more-important-than-ever/?expand_article=1#google_vignette**

Printed in Great Britain
by Amazon

62029317R00133